THRONE AND ALTAR

The Reviews and Essays
Bonald

West Martian Limited Company
1st Edition, October 2023

First printing 2023

The publisher can be contacted at westmartian.com

ISBN-13: 979-8-218-28574-6 Paperback

Contents

Introduction
Or: How I became a reactionary

When you think about it, my fellow reactionaries, it's really something of a miracle that there are any of us at all. Once upon a time, many people grew up traditionalist, but not any more. We all started out as Liberals of some sort. Like most of you, I started out as a classical Liberal, meaning belief in democracy, the social contract, sexual equality, and stuff like that. I was never brainwashed into being passionate about it; it's just that I was never made aware of the fact that there was any alternative to these ideas except outright despotism and slavery. One doesn't get passionate about the obvious. It is quite easy in today's world to go through life without questioning the basic premisses of Liberalism, or even imagining that they can be rationally doubted. It's very difficult to recognize and escape this mental prison. Here's how I did it.

Had someone asked me during high school, I would have expressed complete confidence in the following principles:

1. It's okay to do something as long as it doesn't hurt anyone.

2. We should always be suspicious of authority and see that it is properly checked and monitored.

Just about everyone agrees with these principles, but together they constitute the Leftist worldview that has desacralized the world, decimated the family, and eviscerated the Church.

Even though I agreed with these principles, I did have certain intuitions–hardly distinct enough to be thoughts–whose incompatibility with them I had begun to suspect. The first was my romantic view of the proper relations between the sexes. This probably came from the fact that, being physically unattractive and socially awkward, girls were unattainable to me. They never lost the aura of enchantment and mystery for me. I never became a cynic like so many of my peers whose sensibility to women was destroyed by easy conquest. I remember having a desperate, years-long crush on a girl in my class. It was utterly hopeless, of course. I became fascinated with stories about unrequited love. A proper ending always involved the hero's death. The idea of him moving on to another girl seemed obscene. *A Tale of Two Cities* was one of my favorite books at the time. Given my later interests, it's surprising that I ignored the stuff about the French Revolution and just concentrated on the love story. Sydney Carton sacrificing his life to save Lucy's husband–that was my idea of love. The essence of love, as I saw it, was throwing one's life away for one's beloved. For this reason, the only arrangement for lovers that seemed right to me (that didn't involve death) was the Catholic arrangement of indissolveable marriage. Through its irrevocability, it was able to capture this "thowing away", this complete donation of one's life. Catholic marriage is like death, and that recommended it to me. And if a couple decides that they (or at least one of them) would be happier splitting up? By principle #1 above, I should have to accept this, but I couldn't. The idea was revolting. It took a beautiful thing and made it meaningless. Add the possibility of divorce, and this sacred realm is profaned by the spirit of calculation. How could I resolve this clash between belief and intuition? For many years, by just not thinking about it.

The other issue on which my feelings clashed with liberalism was over the issue of fatherhood and filial piety. I remember once catching part of a television show on PBS about the spread of domestic abuse legislation. The show was very Liberal triumphalist: a hundred years ago, it implied, most fathers were brutal torturers, and they would be again except that the State now monitors them closely to protect poor, innocent wives and children. As I watched, I became more and more enraged, but not in the way I was supposed to be. I was supposed to be enraged by the brutality of fathers. But while I have always disapproved of child abuse, what upset me what the disrespectful attitude towards fathers. "They should not be talking about fathers this way. They're throwing dirt on something beautiful. If the State does have to intervene to stop child abuse, it should do so discretely, and not boast about it, because it is wrong for people to even think this way about fatherhood." I had the same sense, which I had before on the issue of divorce, that something sacred was being treated irreverently. This is, I later came to appreciate, the core conservative intuition.

For a long time, I've had a particular admiration for fatherhood. Filial piety comes easily to me. As a kid, whenever I'd watch movies about rebellious children clashing with their fathers, I always took the fathers' side, and I was angry when the movies themselves sided with the children. Why was this? It must have helped that my father himself is in every way an admirable man. As a provider, a teacher, and an example, my debt to him is incalculable. Equally important, though, was that, as the oldest child, I got to help babysit my younger siblings. I'm about 12 years older than the youngest, so watching and playing with her gave me a taste of the adult's role as caretaker and protecter for children. I had no trouble seeing that this is a sacred calling. Everywhere I looked, I saw parents living sacrificial lives for their children. Perhaps somewhere in my home town a child was being abused, but shall we let this blind us to the central fact of an institution that elicits self-donation at its finest?

The trouble, again, is that my attitude that we should not even *think* bad thoughts about fathers was in direct contradiction with principle #2. If fathers are authorities–and they surely are–then shouldn't their authority be checked? Shouldn't we be suspicious of them and guard against abuses of their authority? Again, I solved the contradiction by not thinking about it.

One day as an undergraduate I was wandering aimlessly through the university library, and my eyes spotted a book entitled *Aristotle for Everyone*, by Mortimer Adler. I remember thinking to myself that it might be nice to know a little philosophy, and since the book was quite short and looked like a very small investment of effort, I checked it out. Exposure to Aristotle, even in this popularized form, turned out to be a major event for me, because it showed me that one could make a credible ethical system out of something other than the "no-hurt" principle, and one could make a credible political theory out of something other than the "social contract" and suspicion of authority. From the reasonable idea that things have natures, Aristotle reasoned that they could have natural ends. Human nature finds its fulfillment in the polis; therefore, the state is not an artifice designed to further the wishes of the governed, but a natural means through which we find our natural fulfillment. "Consent of the governed" is never invoked, but the Aristotelian state is nevertheless both reasonable and humane. The social contract can be questioned, and once it could be questioned, I quickly found it repugnant—a replacement of noble patriotism with mercenary calculations of self-interest.

Soon afterward, I read Frederick Copleston's introduction to Thomas Aquinas, and I was surprised to find that classical theistic metaphysics actually has strong arguments in its favor, arguments that modern science has done nothing to discredit. In time, I would read some of the primary sources, the major works of Aristotle and St. Thomas themselves. Thomism gave me a richer mental framework, one that accommodated far more of my intuitions about human nature and morality than the utilitarianism we all pick up from the surrounding culture.

Still, there were lingering problems with my new philosophy. The emphasis on intrinsic teleology had the great advantage of giving morality and objective ground, but it had the disadvantage that morality still seems to be reduced to a higher form of self-interest. One easily gets the impression that morality, virtue, and even God Himself are reduced to means for fullfilling one's *telos*. I don't remember if this concern came to me from reading Kant; more likely it had been with me all along. There are answers to this criticism of course, e.g. that by making the apprehension and indwelling of God to be man's end, God is lifted from the realm of mere means. Then there is Aristotle's writings on friendship, and Thomas' on charity. Still, the emphasis in teleological morality seemed off.

One day, I came across a review of Dietrich von Hildebrand's *Man and Woman* on a Catholic weblog. It sounded good, and I managed to find it in the university library. (Like many great reactionary books, it's out of print, but I later found and ordered a used copy.) Von Hildebrand had the same problems with Aristotle that I did, so he formulated a different ethical theory based on value response. Reading this book, and later his *Christian Ethics*, I finally found an ethics that gave due centrality to the claims of reverence as I had intuited them. Values are not means to ends, but things recognized for their own sake. Von Hildebrand also had developed a rich philosophy of love that captured and exceeded my intuitions about self-donation. He also defended without apology the goodness of distinct gender roles. My only criticism of von Hildebrand's writings on marital love is that they give too little emphasis to parenthood, to the paternal and maternal roles, an oversight I try to correct in my *Defense of Patriarchy*.

The elements of a new worldview were now falling into place. There was only one piece missing: an understanding of the distinct essence of social authority. My thinking at this point was still overly individualistic; it was entirely focused on value responses by individuals and ignored the possibility of value responses by an organic community. About this time, I picked up an old copy of Fustel de Coulagnes' *The Ancient City* in a used bookstore. This book impressed me by showing how an entire civilization can be built up from an idea of the sacred. I think I was rather fonder of the pagan religion of the Greeks and Romans than was the author. About the same time, I read Voegelin's *The New Science of Politics* and Eliade's *The Sacred and the Profane*, which tried to show that all societies are built upon sacred symbols. From Abbot Vonier, I learned that understanding the signification of symbols is the key to understanding the sacraments. Just as Aristotle had taught me to see human fulfillment as an objective thing, Eliade and Vonier led me to see the meaning of symbols as objective and not merely conventional. Putting these together, a vision of society started to emerge–the social order is a sort of icon, a language of symbols, that helps us see God in the world.

With all the pieces available, I set out to put them together. This is what I've been doing on this weblog.

Book Reviews: History

A Study of History

By Arnold Toynbee, abridgement by D. C. Somervell, 1946

For Arnold Toynbee, history on the largest scale is the story of the rise and fall of civilizations. Spengler claimed to identify a distinct essence for each civilization he studied, but Toynbee attempts nothing of this sort. Two countries are identified as belonging to the same civilization by their degree of interconnectedness. Toynbee's interests are almost exclusively with dynamical questions, not what a society is, but how it is changing. In his schema, a society is presented with a "challenge" of some sort which either overwhelms it or inspires it to advance. The solution to one challenge leads to another challenge. When a society ceases to advance by solving challenges, Toynbee says the society has "broken down". In his scheme, the breakdown usually happens early in a civilization's life; a post-breakdown society can, and usually does, have long centuries of peace and prosperity with great technical and artistic advances. After the breakdown, the society goes through a "time of troubles", a "universal state" period, and a final disintegration.

The whole scheme—the identification of civilizations, challenges, breakdowns, etc. is incredibly ad hoc. Toynbee first developed his life cycle scheme by considering one event—the fall of the Roman Empire—and then he insisted on cramming the history of every other society into this pattern. For example, he is faced with the fact that both the Gupta and Mughal empires look like universal states for the Indian civilization. Could one civilization have two universal states? Impossible! Therefore, India has had two civilizations, which Toynbee calls the "Indic" and the "Hindu". They have the same race, same location, same language, same religions, but they are two civilizations— because the scheme demands it. Similarly, he divides the Chinese civilization into the "Sinic" and the "Far Eastern", and he claims the current Islamic civilization came into being after the fall of the Abbasid Caliphate. The Abbasid empire itself was the culmination of the Syriac civilization, a construct of Toynbee's imagination whose universal state period actually began with the Persian empire of Cyrus, but which was "interrupted" by a millennium-long incursion by Hellenistic civilization.

Then there is the question of what counts as a "challenge", and what is a "creative response". An aggressive state is swallowing its neighbors. Is the challenge to maintain political diversity, or to establish unity? A universal church is rent by doctrinal dissention. Is the challenge to live with plurality, or to eradicate heresy and reestablish consensus? To solve problems like this, there is Toynbee's unstated rule: the ideals of mid-twentieth century social democracy and liberal Protestantism are the ultimate standard of human perfection. So, for example, Assyria's conquests in the eighth century B.C. Syria were negative, but Piedmont's conquests in nineteenth century Italy were positive. Today's challenges are what any 1950 progressive would identify as such: to establish "social justice" and world unity. He is mildly troubled by some elements of the modern world. For example, he admits that mass education in a democratic age encourages rule by propaganda, but he thinks this danger has been averted by the BBC, which will educate the masses with the wisdom of their ruling elite. Thank God we've been saved from propaganda!

No discussion of Toynbee would be complete without mentioning his idea of "mimesis". Toynbee is relentlessly progressive. Civilizations only exist to advance. Any reverence for tradition is "idolatry". But creative change can only be accomplished by a creative minority with the mental gifts for it. The stupid masses are neither capable of creation nor of appreciating the higher forms of life into which they are being led. Ordinary men are, under a veneer of civilization, still superstitious, pagan primitives. They must be controlled by social drilling and made to accept the innovations of their creative betters. So far, so good. However, Toynbee also thinks that constant innovation is somehow the source of the creative minority's authority. He thinks that, when they stop being creative and become a mere "dominant minority", content to rule a society without improving it, they lose the aura of authority, and the people lose respect for them and plot rebellion. This obviously makes no sense. If the masses are as stupid as Toynbee thinks, they would never notice that the rulers are no longer creative, and if they are as conservative as he thinks, they would actually prefer that their rulers stop meddling. Toynbee seems to be making a mistake common among liberal historians—he attributes his own feelings to the silent masses.

The parts of the book, however, are much greater than the sum. One can spend many enjoyable and illuminating hours reading Toynbee's case studies of various societies. I particularly liked his discussion of "arrested societies": the Eskimos, the Spartans, and the Ottomans. Then there is a reoccurring theme in the book of the millennia-long war between settled-agricultural societies and the north-Eurasian nomads. This war was finally brought to an end when the Cossacks eradicated and replaced Nomad society in the seventeenth century, an event of world historical importance that I had never heard of till this book brought it to my attention. This book is full of little discoveries like that.

Christian Marriage: a historical study
Edited by Glenn Olsen, 2001

This book appears to be a collection of essays based on a conference held in 1994. All essays deal with the evolution of Christianity's understanding of marriage, with each essay covering a specific time period. There's a noticable Catholic slant; the last essay, on the twentieth century, focuses entirely on Catholic infighting. Nevertheless, all Christians will find a great deal of interest here. One of the biggest things readers will find is that the issues that exercised past generations of theologians were not the same as today's issues. For example, a major issue for the was whether it is the expression of consent or physical consummation that makes a marriage. Sacramental thinking leans towards the latter, but this was thought unacceptable, because then Mary and Joseph, and couples undertaking "spiritual marriages", wouldn't really be married. Some particular highlights:

1. From Francis Martin, I learn that the Stoics of the Imperial age produced a significant body of work on marriage and family life, with a "natural relationships" focus a bit reminiscent of Confucianism. I may have to read some of this when I get the chance.

2. Glenn Olsen has a nice discussion of Saint Augustine's writings on the ends (that is, the goods) of marriage.

3. Teresa Pierre shows that Hugh of St. Victor was a crucial figure in settling Christian marriage theology. Hugh taught that marriage is a sacrament in the rigorous sense: a sign of spiritual realities that confers grace. Both consent and consummation symbolize the union of Christ with the Church, but in different ways. Consent symbolizes the spiritual union of the soul with God. Consummation symbolizes the Incarnation, in which human and divine were corporeally joined.

4. In R.V. Young's essay on the Reformation, I came to appreciate what a potent force for evil John Milton (Mr. Divorce) has been. Milton claimed that Jesus' condemnations of divorce don't apply to the elect. For them, an unhappy marriage is no marriage at all.

5. John Haas defends the traditional understanding of marriage in terms of its ends from modern critics, who demand something more personally meaningful. As Haas points out, for essentialists like the scholastics, a thing's end is its meaning.

Conservatism in America

By Paul Gottfried, 2007

In the subtitle, Gottfried promises to help readers make sense of the American right. For him, the words "conservatism" and "the Right" are not synonymous. By "the Right", he means either any opposition to the revolutionary left in general, or—more often—defenders of the bourgeois social order in particular. By "conservatism", he means defenders of traditional, aristocratic societies, i.e. nineteenth-century counterrevolutionaries like Burke and Bonald. Gottfried believes that a political movement draws its character at least as much from the social class whose interests it defends as from its formal ideological commitments. The problem with the American Right, in his view, is that it represents no particular social class (or even any fixed social order). It is thus unanchored, and so its content tends to drift leftward with society at large. It claims to represent unchanging conservative principles (or "values" in Gottfried's paraphrases), but these principles have in fact been altered radically in the past half century.

American conservatives have no historical sense, Gottfried claims, and their understanding of their own past is particularly poor. In his telling, the American right has had three phases. First were the anti-New Deal Republicans of the 1930s-40s—classical liberals in ideology, primarily Protestant in belief, defenders of the bourgeois social order, and enemies of central government expansion. This right seems to be the one with which Gottfried most sympathizes. After the Cold War started, a new group of intellectuals, lead by Russell Kirk, reshaped the right's image of itself. They asserted (counterfactually, in Gottfried's view) that the American right was part of the European counterrevolutionary tradition. Ideologically conservative, strongly Catholic leaning, these friends of order and authority were much less hostile to the central government and rather saw it as a potential ally against the communist menace. Gottfried has some respect for conservatives like Kirk and Nisbet—although he questions their relevance to American politics. He does think that this first transition helped lead in the 1950s to a conservative movement defined totally by anti-communism. Gottfried has generally negative things to say about William Buckley's eventual leadership of the movement, which he says consisted mainly of expelling members of the Old Right. A mythology has grown up about these expulsions—that Buckley cast them off for being kooks or for being anti-Semites. Gottfried shows that neither charge is true; nor was it even made at the time. The offense of the Old Right was that they weren't committed to prosecuting the Cold War as aggressively as Buckley thought necessary—they were "isolationists". Eventually, the conservative right too would be displaced and expelled, this time by the neoconservatives. Gottfried hates, *hates, HATES* the neoconservatives. Primarily Jewish, admirers of the New Deal and the Civil Rights movement, and having an almost idolatrous devotion to American liberal democracy, the "neocons" transformed the American conservatism into a movement devoted to spreading democracy throughout the world. In other words, conservatism had transformed into what anyone a hundred years ago would have called Jacobinism. The expulsion of Southern Agrarians by Lincoln-worshipping neocons was fairly inevitable. Less so was praise for Trotsky and attacks on Joseph de Maistre in the pages of National Review itself. The displacement of the older conservatives generated a mythology of its own. The neoconservatives somehow managed to argue that the right had no intellectual seriousness before they came to champion it. This is obviously not true. In fact, older incarnations of the right had often addressed social, moral, and cultural issues with more depth and serious than is generally found on the right today.

This is a rambling book, and Gottfried is not entirely fair to his enemies. However, some of his criticisms of American conservatism are quite painfully true. There is no way an impartial observer could see the history of the American right as anything other than a capitulation to the Left. One doubts that the conservative movement has even slowed down America's march to the Left. However, I think the neoconservative takeover should be regarded as a symptom rather than the cause of this drift. The outside pressures from the liberal media and universities to move left proved simply overwhelming. Gottfried also compares the way the conservative movement controls its base's view of the world to the control the French communist party had over the thoughts of its members. Both bases were manipulated in degrading ways. Gottfried does point to a difference between the two cases, though. Unlike the contemporary American right, the communists did have a serious intellectual and historical consciousness. That point was quite painful to read, because of course it's true. Because there are no conservatives among artists and intellectuals, the conservative subculture is not illuminated by these things. However, I think the more appropriate response to such realizations is despair rather than anger. Even if there had been no Catholic traditionalists or Jewish neoconservatives, what high culture there is and what life of the mind there is would still certainly belong to the Left. They hold all the cards.

Conservatism from the French Revolution to the 1990s

By Pekka Suvanto, 1994

There aren't many histories of conservatism compared to, say, histories of liberalism or of socialism. This might seem odd given that conservatives are supposedly the ones most interested in their past. Really, though, we know the reason. It's that conservatism is just less important. Imagine trying to write a history of the 19th or 20th century without mentioning socialism. It's impossible. On the other hand, one could easily write a short history of either century without mentioning conservatives. After all, imagine that conservative writers and political parties had never existed—how would the world be different? We would have just gotten to our current point sooner. The Jacobins' wildest fantasies—and even things they couldn't have imagined—have become reality. Monarchy is gone, sex differences ignored, religion all but eradicated. The history of conservatism is a story of unmitigated failure.

This book doesn't quite see it that way. During the mid-1990s, when this book was published, it was still possible to see conservatism as having both wins and losses. Tories, Republicans, Gaullists, and Christian Democrats still won elections, but they had adopted largely liberal principles. Conservatives had surrendered to democracy and decided to make the best of it, they had surrendered to capitalism, and they were in the process of surrendering to secularism and abandoning their defense of Christianity. On the other hand, the thing conservatives hated most, the ideology of revolution, had been discredited by the fall of communism. Suvanto doesn't put it this way, but it sounded like conservatives were set to lose everything they held dear, but to lose it slowly rather than quickly.

This is a short but competent history of conservatism. The thing I most like about it is its range. It covers both intellectual and political movements, and it spends equal amounts of time covering England, France, Germany, and the United States. I am particularly grateful for the material on European continental conservatism; my main complaint about Russell Kirk's famous history of conservatism is that he excises the French and Germans from the story. The limitations of this book all stem from its brevity. The author often attempts to summarize the thought of an important intellectual in a few sentences, and the results are not good. As a history of ideas, the book is weak. It does do a good job, given its space requirements, in showing the link between intellectual and political movements. Like most political moderates, he praises conservatives most for their skillful capitulations. For example, he points out that conservatives immediately dropped their objections to democracy when it became clear that they (and the socialists) would fare better in elections than classical liberals. Suvanto is enough of a political philosopher to realize that American conservatism is thoroughly Lockean (i.e. it's actually a variant of liberalism), but, unlike me, he doesn't necessarily regard this as a bad thing.

The thing that struck me as I read this book was the futility of it all. When liberals win a victory, everyone regards it as permanent. When conservatives win a victory, it's only a temporary setback for liberalism. The liberals will try again, and they will succeed the second or the third time. Every historical contingency seems to work to the advantage of liberalism and the detriment of conservatism. Both world wars are said to have been disasters for conservatism, in both winning and losing countries, although it's hard to see what conservative belief was discredited by either war. The Dreyfus Affair is said to have been a disaster for conservatism. How can that be, when all of Stalin's show trials failed to make a dent in the fortunes of leftism? Why does conservatism seem so fragile that any misstep is ruinous for it? I wish the author would have discussed this point, but he seems to rather take it for granted. He often makes statements that imply that resistance to liberalism is unsustainable, that desire for liberal changes will just grow and grow until it becomes irresistible. Consider some examples: *"The main cause of the Bolshevik Revolution was that Russia had remained an autocratic state for too long."* How long can one viably be autocratic? How does human history lead us to believe that autocracy is unsustainable? *"[Jules Ferry] created free and secular compulsory schooling. The reform was inevitable since, in Germany, the first compulsory education law dated back to the eighteenth century..."* And if Germany jumped off a cliff, would France "inevitably" follow? Why was this attack on the Catholic school system (and homeschooling) necessary? Other countries like England and, yes, Germany continued to utilize religious schools. I agree with the author that liberal reforms have had a sense of inevitability about them for the last two centuries. The big question that needs to be answered to explain the history of conservatism—a history of defeat—is, "Why is this?" After all, non-liberal, traditionalist societies have endured for thousands of years. They can't be completely unstable.

Enemies of the Enlightenment

The French Counter-Enlightenment and the Making of Modernity, by Darrin McMahon, 2001

There's something that's always puzzled me in histories of eighteenth century thought. During the second half of the century, the Catholic Church was subjected to a campaign of vilification by a mob of hate-filled French pseudo-intellectuals calling themselves "*philosophes*". This whole time, the Church did nothing worth recording to defend Herself. Finally, the Revolution came, and the Church started being robbed and persecuted by self-declared disciples of the *philosophes*. It is only at this point that the great counter-revolutionary writers almost simultaneously appear: Burke, Chateaubriand, Bonald, and de Maistre. Why only then, and why all at once?

The standard explanation among conservatives, to the extent that there is one, is the genius of Edmund Burke. The *philosophes* were so brilliant, or the Catholics so stupid, that no defense of the Old Regime was possible until a Protestant genius developed entirely new arguments. This explanation has never seemed likely to me. First, it neglects how fundamentally different Bonald's thought was from Burke's. Second, the arguments of writers like Diderot, Helvetius, and Voltaire were so crude that even mediocre Catholic minds should have been able to counter them.

In this book, McMahon quotes extensively from pre-Revolutionary defenders of throne and altar to show that these writers did anticipate most of the characteristic arguments of the counter-Revolutionaries: the importance of religion to social order, the connection between the authority of God, fathers, and kings, the danger in reducing the state or family to a contract, the social value of prejudice and tradition, the inadequacies of abstract reason, and the idea of their enemies as a conspiracy of atheist anarchists. Most of the material in Burke *et al* was standard anti-*philosophe* stuff. Furthermore, they predicted, in gory detail, the persecutions of the Church and nobility, the massacres, and the wars that would come to pass if the *philosophes'* ideas were ever implemented. This last bit is the reason we only hear about anti-Enlightenment thinkers after the Revolution got underway. Before the Revolution, the idea that Voltaire's disciples would turn into bloodthirsty lunatics if they ever came to power sounded kooky; after the Terror, it sounded prescient. Needless to say, the counter-Revolutionaries weren't shy in pointing out these demonstrations of their prophetic powers.

McMahon himself seems to have a low opinion of what he calls "anti-*philosophe* discourse." He thinks it is an error to reify the "Enlightenment" as if it were an entirely unified thing. He also thinks it is wrong to say that the royalist Catholics successfully predicted that *philosophe* would cause the Terror because the precise sequence of events was "complicated". These qualms seem to have more to do with the nominalism of the author than any flaw in anti-Enlightenment thinking. He could make the same arguments against any attempt to classify thinkers or to assert historical causality. As McMahon acknowledges, the anti-philosophes were well aware (and liked to point out) that philosophe writers contradicted each other, and that some failed to realize the radical consequences of their ideas. Nevertheless, the Catholics identified, correctly I believe, a common commitment and way of viewing the world that distinguished Enlightenment thinkers. It can be summed up in the word "impiety." Catholics realized that impiety has a logic of its own, and that its adherents will tend to be dragged further and further along it, regardless of their initial intentions. The impiety of philosophe must eventually destroy religion and monarchy, promote sexual immorality, and attack parental authority. That is its nature. Who can deny that, for two and a half centuries, it has done just that?

Fascism: Comparison and Definition

By Stanley Payne, 1980

88 years since the March on Rome, and historians still can't agree even on a definition of fascism. As Stanley Payne shows in this book, one reason must be the fundamental differences between the regimes asserted to be fascist. Even the two "classic" fascisms— in Italy and Germany—differed profoundly. Nazi ideology was founded on race, fascist ideology on the nation as a political-cultural entity. Nazism established a nearly totalitarian state, while Mussolini mostly just talked about being totalitarian. The Nazi party was a powerful body in Germany; the Fascist party was largely absorbed in the Italian state. Until the late thirties, the Fascists ridiculed Nazi anti-Semitism. (I sometimes wonder if Mussolini would have been remembered as a good leader if only he had kept out of WWII.)

Confusion also comes from the tendency of some historians to label as "fascist" certain ideas or practices that were shared by fascists and others. For example, having party militias and militant youth groups was common practice in the thirties, having been pioneered by the radical Left.   The most important example would be the economic doctrine of corporatism, which was embraced but not invented by many Fascist groups. Payne helpfully notes that the corporatism of Catholic traditionalists was different in intention from that of the Fascists. The former wanted to limit the state by making it recognize other authoritative bodies; the latter wanted to bring these bodies under direct government control. To clarify matters, Payne distinguishes between three classes of authoritarian nationalism: the conservative Right (think Franco, Salazar, or Dollfuss), the radical Right (not clearly defined to my satisfaction— examples include the Austrian Heimwehren, the Mexican Cristeros, and the Spanish Carlists), and the Fascists (such as the Spanish Falange, the Croatian Ustasa, the Romanian Iron Guard, Mussolini, and Hitler). Only the latter had all the main fascist characteristics.

And what would those be? Here is Payne's list of the characteristic Fascist ideology and goals:

1.   Creation of a new (nontraditional) nationalist authoritarian state

2.   Organization of a regulated, integrated national economy (corporatist or syndicalist)

3.   The desire to radically change the nation's relationship with other powers

4.   Espousal of an idealist, vitalist creed (anti-materialism)

This is a very suggestive list, but Payne himself admits that it doesn't add up to identifying a unitary fascist essence, as does Nolte's definition of fascism as the rejection of theoretical and practical transcendence. Payne doesn't think that such an ahistorical definition exists. He thinks of "fascism" as a vaguer term to describe the historical reaction of some countries to very particular circumstances in the interwar period. These countries were in the middle of a transition to urban industrialism, with traditional norms broken and liberal democratic norms not yet solidified. They were radically dissatisfied with their international status (e.g. because of losing WWI). They were threatened by Marxism. They were immersed in a culture enthralled by idealism, vitalism, and social Darwinism. Under these conditions, an anti-communist, anti-traditional nationalist authoritarian movement can naturally arise. Payne thinks that fascism has now definitely passed from the scene and cannot return unless this particular set of circumstances should recur. Assuming they do not, he thinks it unhelpful to call any contemporary movement "fascist" just because it shares some particular fascist characteristic. No one fascist characteristic is enough to make a movement meaningfully fascist.

Liberty: the God that Failed

By Christopher Ferrara, 2012

A better title might have been "Liberty: the demon that succeeded". After all, the story Ferrara tells is of an ideological/Constitutional machine set up by John Locke and the American Founders that has, from 1787 to the present, has been successfully cleansing America from all taint of our classical-Christian heritage. And Liberty is certainly demonic, in that its only consistent content is opposition to God's sovereignty. Nor is its outworking unintended; Ferrara easily shows that the major Founders were Deist *philosophes* (often freemasons to boot) committed to marginalizing a Christian religion they despised. And they manufactured their revolution against Britain–a distant government so mild and benevolent that they could only incite the people by initiating unprovoked mob violence and stoking insane paranoid fears about popish plots–with conscious intent to overthrow the ancient order of throne and altar. Since that time, America has had its share of controversies–Federalist vs. Anti-Federalist, Union vs. Confederate–but reactionaries have had no dog in any of those fights, because each side was as Lockean as the other. The only American movement Ferrara does pause to praise is the National Reform Association, a group of nineteenth-century (mostly) Presbyterian intellectuals wishing to amend the Constitution to recognize Christ and His sovereignty. As we know, America has instead followed the path of a "separation of Church and State", meaning in practice the subordination of Christians to a State operating according to its own aggressively secular religion of Liberty. As Justice Scalia decreed in *Employment Division v. Smith*:

> *To make an individual's obligation to obey such a law contingent upon the law's coincidence with his religious beliefs, except where the State's interest is 'compelling'...contradicts constitutional tradition and common sense'....The right of free exercise does not relieve an individual of the obligation to comply with a 'valid and neutral law of general applicability on the ground that the law proscribes (or prescribes) conduct that his religion prescribes (or proscribes)'*

Note well, a State recognizing no restrictions of natural (let alone divine) law claims that it can order you to act against your conscience (not just preventing you from doing good, but commanding you to do evil) without even bothering to claim a compelling need. We were promised that disestablishment would give us religious freedom, but it has secured us nothing.

My main criticism is that Ferrara harps too much on the hypocrisy of the Founders in crushing rebellions against their new republic when others decided to play by the same Lockean script. As I see it, since the social contract/right of rebellion theory is nonsensical, the fact that the Founders didn't bind themselves to it speaks in their favor. I actually came away with a higher opinion of Washington, Adams, and Jefferson after reading about how they crushed threats to their own authority.

Liberty: the God that Failed is the only full-length American history book I know of written from a reactionary perspective. Given such a radically unique perspective, it's amusing that the conclusions Ferrara argues are mostly conventional wisdom for everyone but conservative Republicans. The Founders were guided by John Locke. The South seceded over slavery, an institution it practiced in a grossly unethical manner. And so forth. To understand his odd insistence on commonplace observations, one must remember that Ferrara is primarily arguing against American conservatives letting their imaginations run wild looking for an American lineage for their movement. Hence their implausible claims of a "moderate" Enlightenment meaningfully distinct from its radical variety, a conservative War of Independence (a revolution not made but averted, don't you know?), an outpost of Christian feudalism in the South, and so forth.

It is also a challenge to my own writings on American conservatism. In my essay *Can there be an American Conservatism?*, I consider the dilemma of being a traditionalist in a country that has been liberal from its inception. What tradition am I trying to conserve? I answered by distinguishing America's official ideology from the claims of authority and loyalty that ideology is used to justify. Americans claim to base everything on freedom, equality, and social contract, but our social order belies this in many taken-for-granted practices. Conservatives want to preserve our citizens' implicit sense of legitimacy and group solidarity, but I claimed we must be cautious in weaning our fellow citizens from their false mythology of Liberty lest we destroy their patriotism altogether. Ferrara obviously thinks that it's better to just give people the whole truth. And in fact, the truth, when presented whole–as opposed to being snuck in piece by piece–is a compelling thing. So I guess I was wrong; the time for circumspection is over. Things have come to a point now that Christians are better off being fortified in the knowledge that the government that oppresses them was rotten from the beginning.

Progress and Religion

By Christopher Dawson, 1929

Arnold Toynbee is generally regarded as the English-speaking world's answer to Oswald Spengler, the great interpreter of the rise and fall of cultures, but Christopher Dawson deserves this regard far more. Like Spengler and Voegelin, his work combines disciplines from theology to literature to history; indeed, he is unique among the great meta-historians in that he seriously engages the results of sociology and anthropology regarding primitive peoples. He also has the virtue of conciseness: this book is under two hundred pages, with the latter half of it giving the best short history of mankind that I've yet encountered.

Meta-historians like Spengler and Dawson concern themselves mainly with two questions. First, what quality or qualities sets one culture apart from another? Second, what drives the evolution of a culture: its growth, decline, etc? To the first question, Dawson answers that a culture is a combination of two elements. The first is the material base: how do people extract their livelihood from nature? This is informed by geography and technology, and it includes the basic social structures (e.g. family, property) associated with this extraction. Dawson here bases himself on the work of Frederic Le Play. The maintenance of this basis is crucial for a culture's spiritual vitality, because it is that culture's direct contact with nature. So, for example, he claims that the Hellenic culture was based on a wide class of free-holding farmers, and this culture was ruined by over-urbanization and slave-driven commercial agriculture. The second element defining a culture is religion. Religion is not a mere epiphenomenal superstructure determined by the base; it is based—even among the most primitive peoples—on a profound metaphysical intuition of pure being. Anticipating Voegelin, Dawson claims that the progress of human thought has been in the clarification of this intuition. A culture is a unique combination of these two elements: change either one and you will have a different (or dead) culture. The two are united in a way analogous to body and soul; like body and soul they interpenetrate to form one substance. Religion can act on the material base, while this base provides the contact between people and nature on which the religious sense depends.

Change can be driven by an alteration of either element, but for Dawson religion is by far the more dynamic of the two. He regards most human progress to be driven by advances in religion. First, there was the transformation from shamanism to organized priesthood; this drove the development of the first archaic civilizations (Sumer, Egypt, etc). These were city theocracies, based on the idea of a sacred order immanent in the universe which governs both the motion of the heavens and the behavior of men. These civilizations were disrupted by a series of barbarian invasions, after which it became difficult to identify the current society with the sacred order. So this order was reconceived—its moral element became paramount, and it came to be seen as transcendent rather than immanent. This was the Axial Age, later to be described more famously but with less insight by Jaspers, and it included the great spiritual movements of Confucianism, the Upanishads, Taoism, Buddhism, and Greek philosophy. The new movements tended to deflect attention away from the physical world and towards contemplation of the Absolute. The exception was the Hebrews, for whom salvation was tied up to historical events and to the fate of a particular people. Christianity, through the idea of the Incarnation, carried forward this idea of divine manifestation through the physical and the particular. Western Christendom was distinct from other cultures in that the religion didn't grow up with the other elements of the culture's social structure, but came to them as an outside transforming source. It was a civilization held together by the Church, rather than by a political structure. This worked largely because secular culture and authorities were too weak to assert their independence. When they became stronger, they did so, and the Renaissance and the Reformation were the forms of southern and northern cultural self-assertion, respectively. The loss of religious unity led to Christianity being replaced by the liberal/humanitarian religion of progress. This religion is now undergoing a crisis, mostly because it based its claims on the authority of science, which was supposed to answer men's age-old religious questions and provide a justification for faith in future progress. The trouble is, science can do neither of these things if it is to remain true to itself. Nor does history, which records both rises and falls, provide justification for the progressive faith.

According to Dawson, the current situation cannot be maintained, because culture lacks a unifying religious vision, which all stable cultures must have. He thinks that Europe's future depends on a return to the historical Christian faith, which preserves (and, indeed, is the ultimate source of) the attractive features of the progressive faith, while providing the metaphysical and historical foundations that progressivism lacks.

It should be taken as a tribute to this book that my main complaint is that it wasn't longer. Many interesting statements call for further explanation or defense. I regret that Islam is hardly mentioned, and Dawson shows here little of the appreciation for the achievements of Byzantine culture which he was later to acquire. Then there is my feeling that belief in "progress" is too silly a faith to serve as the starting point of a book this serious. Dawson thinks that progressivism is the faith that drives peoples' quasi-religious devotion to liberal humanitarianism and socialism. Whether or not this is true, I'm glad that Dawson didn't confine himself to this issue, but went on to engage the great spiritual movements that have driven the human race.

The Ancient City

By Fuestel de Coulanges, 1864

The Marxists believe that economics is the key to history, and, indeed, the fundamental social reality. Religion, morals, and culture are merely rationalizations used to justify the distribution of economic power. Fustel de Coulanges takes the opposite approach —he takes religious beliefs t o be the fundamental reality in a civilization, and then he tries to show how all the other aspects of that civilization follow from its religion. In *The Ancient City*, this method is applied to the classical civilization of Greece and Rome, and it produces fascinating results. The difficulty with the method is that the religious beliefs under which the Hellenistic civilization was constructed are not the beliefs of the educated elite of later times whose writings have come down to us. Most of classical history available to us is the history of the dissolution of the civilization's original structure, and even classical writers themselves in the age of, say, Cicero, often did not really understand the meaning of their ancient practices. Therefore, Coulanges must try to infer the original belief system using those bits of ancient rituals and popular folk beliefs which happen to have been recorded, and by looking for clues in the ancient laws and languages. His occasional recourse to the Laws of Manu, on the assumption that all Aryan peoples must have had the same original culture, seems to me to be somewhat risky, but few of his conclusions rely on this. The final result is inevitably somewhat speculative, but I strongly suspect that Coulanges has correctly captured the essential truth about the earliest Greeks and Romans.

According to Coulanges, the belief on which Hellenistic civilization was originally built was ancestor worship. The family's primary duty was to provide worship and material sustenance for its divinized ancestors. The spirits of the dead fathers are associated with their bodies (buried on the family's property) and also with the sacred fire which must be kept burning in the household at all times. Each family was an exclusive cult, with its own gods and rituals, and its own high priest (the *paterfamilias*). To participate in the worship of an ancestor-god was a privilege allowed only to family members. When she is married, the bride is alienated from her own ancestor-gods and initiated into the cult of those of her husband. Coulanges' analysis of wedding rites is most interesting. From this description of these ceremonies, the transfer of cults is clearly what is being accomplished, although its contemporary observers might not realize this. For example, the bride must appear to be forced by her husband into the house of his ancestors, since she does not yet have the right to enter of her own will. Even in our own day, the groom carries the bride across the threshold, although we have forgotten the meaning of this custom. Originally, the extended family, the gens, was quite powerful. The city was a union of families, not of individuals. The city itself was a religious body (for the ancients had no other form of organization), with its own gods, its own cult exclusive to citizens, and its own high priest (the king).

The second half of the book describes the dissolution of this society. As men's religious ideas evolved, the ancient customs became harder to justify. More importantly, the old organization excluded a large fraction of the populace, who therefore had an interest in its downfall. These were the plebs, the people without recognized ancestral gods who did not belong to families participating in the civic cult. Coulanges doesn't really explain why it should be that some families should have their ancestors recognized as gods, and some don't. It would seem like anybody who knew who his father was and knew how to make a fire could participate in this religion, but apparently that wasn't the case. Anyway, the old order collapsed through a series of revolutions. Monarchy was replaced by aristocracy, the gens were broken up, aristocracy was replaced by plutocracy and finally by democracy. At this point, the old order had been completely destroyed and replaced by the secular individualist state. Finally, the populace converted to Christianity, a religion which satisfies their desire for the sacred without making the unreasonable demands of their old faith.

Coulanges doesn't seem to be much of a fan of the religion he describes, but it seems admirable to me in many ways. It powerfully affirmed the dignity and independence of the family. It promoted chastity and filial piety. It gave each member (except maybe the clients and slaves) an honored place with his or her own rights and duties, so that the family could associate these duties with its ultimate beliefs about the nature of the cosmos. Sure, Christianity is better, but not because it's easier.

The Crisis of the Modern World

By Rene Guenon, 1946

Of denunciations of the modern world, I can never get my fill. Guenon claims that the West has abandoned tradition, contemplation, and metaphysics (all more or less synonymous for him), and created the world's first anti-metaphysical (materialist and individualist) civilization. The Eastern civilizations have preserved the wisdom that the West has abandoned, but today the West is working aggressively to spread its poison abroad. The West itself is so far gone that it will most likely require expert help from the East to resuscitate our spiritual traditions.

This is not a great book, but it does make some original points. A couple of things I found interesting:

1. Guenon sensibly identifies the Catholic Church as the main repository of the West's traditional spiritual wisdom. She must be the starting point of any future revitalization of the West. To play this glorious role, Guenon insists that the Church wouldn't need to sacrifice any of her dogmas; in fact, she would get to stop watering down her faith to accomodate modernity. I'm not sure if I trust Guenon here. He seems to think that all traditional religions transmit the same essential truths. Catholicism, however, carries historical as well as metaphysical truth claims. Guenon doesn't attack these claims, but they don't seem to interest him either.

2. The most fascinating part of the book for me was the defense of non/pre-modern science. For the ancients (and contemporary Easterners), the main point of science is not to quantitatively model and predict natural phenomena, but to use natural phenomena as mental aids, stepping-stones, to the contemplation of eternal, incorporeal truths. (Remember all the images of the Trinity that medievals liked to find in the natural and psychological world?) For this goal, Guenon pronounces contemporary science inferior to what it replaced. He even goes so far as to say that our contempt for astrology and alchemy is based on misunderstandings.

The Cristero Rebellion

The Mexican People between Church and State 1926-1929, by Jean Meyer, 1976

How is one to understand the Cristero rebellion, the great peasant uprising of 1926-1929 in central Mexico against the revolutionary government, and what is one to make of the anticlerical persecutions that precipitated and followed it? One story, put out by the government, and accepted through most of the world, goes like this: The peasants were stupid and superstitious dupes of the clergy, and the clergy pushed them to rebel. The clergy in turn were tools of the wealthy classes, who were threatened by the government's selfless quest for social justice. As Jean Meyer shows in this book, every part of this story is a lie. There is another story, put out by the Church, of priests heroically facing martyrdom at the hands of socialist revolutionaries. Meyer shows this story to also be absurdly unrepresentative. Both accounts ignore the experience of the movement's protagonists, the peasants themselves. This is what Meyer captures for the first time through an impressive study of the primary material, including new surveys and interviews of former Cristeros.

Let's correct the inaccuracies in the common beliefs one by one. It was not true that the Church represented the interests of the upper classes; the Church had led movements for social reform before the state ever thought of getting involved. She had started and encouraged the Mexican trade union movement, and so far from being an instrument of wealthy landowners, the Church and her massive federation of unions were feared by the revolutionaries as competitors for the allegiance of the workers. For that matter, the Church got along perfectly well with the more radical movement of Zapata. Meyer shows that the Cristeros were drawn entirely from the lower classes, while the wealthy classes all supported the socialist government. Nor were the peasants incited to rebellion by the clergy, who followed a craven policy of appeasement before, during, and after the revolt. In fact, it was the women who proved to be the most enthusiastic rebels. The bishops were mostly hostile to the uprising, and they ordered their priests to abandon the rebellious countryside for the government-controlled cities. About one hundred priests refused to abandon their parishes, and many of these were martyred by the federal troops. For each martyred priest, a hundred peasants gave their lives for Christ, on the battlefield, before firing squads, or under the hideous tortures unleashed by the army against Catholic peasants. Finally, Meyer's interviews and his review of the preceding history of evangelization refute the myth that rural Mexico was pagan with only a veneer of Christianity. Meyer finds evidence of a profound and orthodox faith.

What then was the Cristiada? It was a reaction of a society against the aggression of a centralizing state. The ambitions of the Mexican revolutionaries were openly totalitarian: to destroy every authority outside the state, to uproot the village and family, to control the minds of the young. The Catholic Church was their largest and best-organized obstacle. Not only was the Church the center of religious life, it was the center of the social life of the countryside, and the attack on the Church was here an attack on communal life itself. The revolutionaries were all men from the Protestant-anticlerical north, men who hated the religion and traditions of central and southern Mexico. Their policies harassing the clergy and restricting worship eventually triggered the rebellion, much to the surprise of the bishops. The three year war was extremely asymmetrical. The Federal troops had much more money and arms, and they had the support of the United States. The Cristeros had only the ammunition they could steal from their enemies. But they had strong support in the countryside among those whose religion, traditions, and community they were defending. This support was only strengthened by the behavior of the Federal Army, who decided the way to pacify the countryside was to forcibly relocate villages, desecrate churches, torture men who refused to apostasize, rape women, and loudly proclaim their allegiance to Satan. The government set up in Cristero-controlled regions was the Catholic equivalent of a puritan democracy: very little social hierarchy, strong enforcement of public morality. Neither side could decisively defeat the other, so a compromise was inevitable. In 1929, the government and the Church cut a deal—without consulting the rebels—which allowed the resumption of public worship. No sooner had the Cristeros, on the order of their bishops, dispersed, than the government tracked down and murdered 5000 of their leaders. The government then resumed its policy of persecuting the Church, which, because of the stupid naivety of bishops who traded an army for a worthless promise, was now defenseless.

This book has lots of interesting details about the experiences of the rebels and the Federal troops. Apparently, trash-talking your enemy during battle was a common practice. Here is one recorded exchange:

"If you don't surrender, we will bring our women to bugger you good and proper.

"If you let them that means you are not men, and long live Christ the King, son of a whore!"

"Death to Christ and to his mother the great whore, long live Satan, long live the great Devil!"

"Long live Christ the King, you son of a whore!" I like that. I may have to put it on my banner.

The Culture of Critique

The far right is sharply divided on Kevin MacDonald; some think he's brillant, others that he's an obsessive nut. I've just finished reading *The Culture of Critique*, and I lean toward the position that he's brilliant (with a touch of obsessiveness). He's the only author I've encountered who more-or-less shares my principles of thinking about Christian-Jewish beliefs, namely:

1. Jews and Christians are separate groups and sometimes have incompatible interests. This, rather than some inherent evil in Christianity, is the reason why they sometimes fight.

2. Jews are in widespread agreement about what their interests are (massive immigration, the sexual revolution, marginalization of Christianity), and they are very aggressive in using their considerable influence to promote these interests.

Today, most everyone accepts the double standard–group identity for Jews, individualism for white gentiles–so that it seems like the most natural thing in the world. Jews can be proud of their heritage, but Christians should be ashamed of their past; Jews demand that gentile countries, but not Israel, open their borders; they promote and preserve their own ethnicity while accusing whites of "racism" for doing the same. And, of course, they congratulate themselves on their great moral courage when they tell their ethnic enemies to commit suicide.

MacDonald's main argument in *The Culture of Critique* is that this double standard is the result of Jewish intellectuals, like Boas, Freud, Adorno, and Horkheimer, who consciously saw their theories as weapons to discourage gentile group solidarity and prevent antisemitism. The chapters are of uneven quality, so I will focus on what I think are MacDonald's strongest examples: psychoanalysis and the Frankfurt School's study of "authoritarianism". Although posing as science, neither meets scientific standards of clarity and empirical falsifiability. Both operated from the beginning more like cults than open-minded investigations, with predetermined ethno-political prejudices determining how the "data" was to be manipulated.

MacDonald's critique of *The Authoritarian Personality* is absolutely devastating, worth the price of the book in itself. Not only did the double standards abound–group cohesion is a sign of a warped psyche when gentiles and right-wingers do it, but not Jews or communists–but in crucial places the book asserts the exact opposite of what its evidence shows! The authors claim to have proven that filial piety and in-group identification ("ethnocentrism") are the products of psyches wounded by authoritarian parenting.   Not surprisingly, their interviews seem to indicate otherwise, the "ethnocentric" subjects, having stern but loving parents, tended to be happier and more successful by any measure.   But in the upside-down world of psychoanalysis, everything is the opposite of what it seems.   Expressions of affection and gratitude toward parents mean that the subject is consumed by hidden fear and resentment. Stories of neglect, abuse, and estrangement are a sign of a fundamentally healthy parent-child relationship, because the subject is confident enough to be honest. And so on.   MacDonald quotes perhaps a dozen jaw-dropping examples of this sort of reasoning.   Overall, it would seem one could more easily cite this data as evidence that low enthnocentrism is an artifact of teenage rebellion resulting from bad parenting. Except that the American Jewish Committee wouldn't have sponsored a study with that conclusion.

MacDonald's background in evolutionary sociobiology gives him an interesting perspective here. He claims that psychoanalysis and the sexual revolution both have the effect of discouraging adaptive behavior that would help gentiles in their competition with Jews for resources.   In particular, sexual libertarianism undermines monogomy and high-investment parenting by gentiles, leaving them a mess of broken families and poorly-raised children. Of course, Jews too will be affected this way, but MacDonald speculates that their higher IQ means they don't need as much social pressure/support to avoid self or child-destructive behavior. Note MacDonald doesn't say that Jewish intellectuals deliberately set out to destroy gentile families. Their behavior has been guided by normal out-group negative stereotyping of majorities. (Indeed, MacDonald quotes a number of prominent Jewish intellectuals on the genetic and ethical superiority of Judaism which are so outrageously prejudiced against gentiles that they are inadvertently comic.)

In the conclusion, MacDonald speculates on the long-term consequences of high-IQ ethnic minorities (Jews and East Asians) for Western civilization. Jews comprise some 20% of the American elite, and control a corresponding fraction of the economy, but they donate several times as much money to ethnic-related activism than gentiles, meaning that Jewish support is the dominant influence on issues of high Jewish interest, such as immigration and abortion. In a meritocratic, individualistic society, the ambitious and intelligent Jews and Asians will rise to the top; white gentiles will form a powerless lower class, riven by family breakdown, ruled over by an ethnically alien elite that despises them. MacDonald does not think that white gentiles will embrace this fate willingly, so he predicts an ugly ethnic balkanization of Western countries.

The book is not without flaws. MacDonald is given to the sort of reductionism common among evolutionary psychologists.   He sometimes seems to think that because Leftist radicalism has served Jewish interests, it is essentially nothing but Jewish self-seeking. In fact, I think things like multiculturalism and Freudo-Marxism, whatever their origins, have by now taken on a life of their own. Also, MacDonald seems to accept in his discussions of Boasian cultural relativism and American immigration reform that loyalty to an ethnic group requires one to believe in significant phenotype differences between races. In fact, this is no more true for an ethnicity than it is for a family. MacDonald himself seems to have some attachment to Western caucasians, even though we are, by his admission, genetically inferior to the Jews in just about every way that matters. Critics of MacDonald say that he tends to reduce everything he doesn't like to Jewish machinations. There may be something to that, but it isn't a problem here, when he's writing a book about Jewish intellectual activism.

To sum up: Christians should not resent Jews for being loyal to their own kind and pursuing what they see as their interests. This is what we should expect them to do. We should, however, start showing some concern for our own interests.

The Decline of the West

By Oswald Spengler, 1918

What is it that sets one civilization apart from another? We all sense that an Englishman and a German share something with each other that they don't share with an Indian or a Japanese. What is that exactly? And do these civilizations, whatever they are, have fixed life cycles? Is the West destined to go the way of Egypt and Rome? Professional historians tend to be suspicious of these "metahistorical" questions, but they're too interesting to ignore. I'm a sucker for books about the natures of civilizations, and Oswald Spengler's masterpiece *The Decline of the West* is my favorite. It's original, profound, and daring to the point of recklessness.

For Spengler, a culture is the embodiment of a vision of the world. This vision expresses itself in all the works of a culture, so that each culture has its own distinctive art, religion, ethics, science, and mathematics. Each society has a creative stage, which Spengler calls "culture", during which it works to express its vision more perfectly in all areas. When a culture has exhausted its possibilities, it stagnates, becoming what Spengler calls a "civilization". Civilizations are "soulless" societies, marked by materialism, irreligion, civic disengagement, and demographic implosion. Spengler presents a memorably glum picture of a civilization's decline. Culturally distinct towns evolve into monstrous cosmopolitan "megalopolises". Concentrated wealth rules under the pretext of democracy. In the West's civilizational phase, the people's very thoughts are controlled by the press. Eventually, plutocratic sham-democracy gives way to naked tyranny, and the new Caesars reign over the long centuries of a civilization's "winter", until a new culture arises with a new vision, and the cycle repeats. Spengler claims that the West began entering its civilization phase around 1800. The process is inevitable—to resist it would be pointless. Instead, Spengler suggests that Germany assume the role of Caesar, defeating the forces of (English) money, and preside over the decline of the West.

Spengler considers three cultures in detail: the "Apollinian" culture of classical Greece and Rome, the "Magian" culture of the Middle East, and the "Faustian" culture of Western Europe from around 1000AD to the present. The basis of each culture is its conceptualization of depth. (Bet you didn't see that coming.) As Kant pointed out in his Transcendental Aesthetic, we don't directly experience 3D space. Each eye provides a 2D image, and our slight experience of depth is much different from that of length and height. We make sense of these images by imagining that the objects we see are embedded in space, which we picture as an infinitely extending 3D Cartesian grid.

According to Kant, this idea of space comes from the mind; space is neither directly observed, nor strictly deduced from observation. The mind imposes this idea on the sense data, which would otherwise be a meaningless jumble of colors. According to Spengler, what Kant is describing is only the a priori idea of space for Western "Faustian" man. Apollinian man conceptualized space on the model of solid bodies; Magian man based his picture of space on the idea of space enclosed in a cavern. Spenglerr predicts a future Russian civilization which will use the image of the plain, for which depth is analogous to length. Spengler produces a bit of evidence for these astounding claims, particularly the Apollinian and Faustian cultures which are his main focus, but I think most readers will remain skeptical. Connected to the depth experience is an understanding of mathematics, of science, of artistic expression, of ethics, and of God. Classical math was based on rational numbers, Magian math on variables, Western math on functions. (Of course, a mathematical proof is valid in any culture, but the culture determines what mathematical problems it seems sensible to study.) Classical science was statics studying forms, Magian science was chemistry (alchemy, actually) studying substances, and Western science is dynamics (physics) studying forces. Classical man's characteristic form of art was sculpture, while for Faustian man it is instrumental music and impressionistic painting. Magian ethics was an invitation to grace, while Faustian ethics is categorical imperatives. Apollinian culture was polytheistic, thinking of separate gods like solid bodies, while Magian and Faustian cultures are monotheistic, believing one God to be everywhere (like Cartesian space). If the connections between the above ideas are not obvious to you (e.g. what Newtonian physics, instrumental music, and monotheism have to do with each other), you're not alone. Some of Spengler's arguments are more convincing than others. However, I think that to look too hard for rigorous proofs in this book is to miss the point. The idea that all these things are connected through an overall vision was so new and so interesting that further studies, making related but perhaps more modest claims, should have been undertaken by others.

This never really happened, though, because nobody took Spengler's analysis of cultural unity seriously. The Decline of the West is usually seen as a cultural artifact, a book was temporarily popular because it captured the widespread post-WWI sense of gloom. No doubt Spengler's picture of "Civilization" isn't pretty. However, it's not as depressing as it could be. The really depressing thought would be that the progressive "optimists" are actually right, and that one of their inhuman ideals like atheistic socialism is about to engulf mankind forever. If Spengler is right, a new culture will eventually arise after the long centuries of civilizational winter have passed. Then great-souled men will live again.

The Desolate City

By Ann Roche Muggeridge

The worldwide implosion of the Roman Catholic Church during the years 1960-1980 is, in my opinion, one of history's greatest mysteries. How could a millennia-old institution so large, vigorous, and self-disciplined collapse essentially overnight? I've read several books on this topic, and *The Desolate City* is, by far, the best. Muggeridge claims that the Church has suffered a revolution, and so she proceeds to study the crucial post-conciliar years by analogies with revolutions in the secular/political sphere.

Her template for a revolution begins with a vigorous but disgruntled class—usually the class next to the top rather than one of the lower orders—that feels that it is not being given the power its merits deserve. The disgruntled class uses its authority within the system to undermine the system by criticizing and ridiculing the ruling order in front of the lower classes. These "rituals of revolution" prepare the public psychologically for the overthrow of the old order. The government tries in various ways to appease the revolutionaries, which they take to be a sign of weakness. Finally, the revolutionaries move into open defiance. When the government fails to suppress them, people start defecting to the new revolutionary power center en masse. The revolution solidifies its control of all public institutions, and the old government is effectively overthrown.

This, Muggeridge claims, is what's happened to the Catholic Church. Here, the government is the Magisterium: the Pope and loyal bishops. The disgruntled class is the clerical intelligentsia: the teaching religious orders, the bureaucrats in the national episcopal conferences, and (especially) the theologians. The revolution, as Muggeridge calls it, has succeeded in establishing control over the Church at all levels except the very top. How did the revolutionary intelligentsia gain so much power? It came through a dreadful miscalculation on the part of the bishops. The latter had hoped at Vatican II to secure more freedom from curial (i.e. papal) interference, and to this end they allied themselves with the radicals (who at the time were pretending to be mostly orthodox). Once the radicals had established their control over the conciliar implementation commissions and the bishops' bureaucracies, the masks were discarded and the bishops found they could no longer control their own diocese.

One of the strengths of this book is that it quotes copiously from revolutionaries like Edward Schillebeeckx and Rosemary Ruether to show just how radical their denial of the Catholic faith is. They reject core doctrines like the existence of God the Father and the sacrificial nature of the Eucharist, and they reject key Catholic moral teachings like those regarding contraception, abortion, and communism. Catholic feminist nuns have gone particularly far: they reject the entirety of Catholic doctrine and morality, and they engage in bizarre neo-pagan self-worship rituals, some of which are described in this book. The revolutionaries have been very aggressive in promoting their views. One organ for spreading the revolution was the RENEW program, which went from parish to parish telling lay Catholics that the New Testament is a bunch of lies—all with the approval of local bishops! The two main fronts of the revolutionary assault have been in the areas of liturgy and sexual morality. Muggeridge does a good job of emphasizing how crucial these two areas are, how they embody and symbolize the Catholic sacramental worldview, and how quickly this worldview disappears when they are tampered with. The whole purpose of the changes to the Mass (as she proves by quoting the revolutionaries themselves) was to change Catholic belief. The transcendental/sacrificial/sacramental aspects of the Mass were deliberately obscured, so what was left was just a communal gathering. By facing east, the priest led the people in prayer to God. By facing the people, the priest becomes a performer and the congregation his audience.

The revolution's attacks might not have been so successful without the help of a sympathetic secular press. Muggeridge shows how the rebels manipulated the press and used their journalist allies to apply pressure to the Vatican and to delegitimize its authority in the eyes of ordinary Catholics. The importance of media partisanship during the Council and the rebellion against Humanae Vitae cannot be overestimated.

Muggeridge tells a number of "Catholic horror" stories about clergy attacking Catholic doctrine or engaging in sacrilegious acts. It should be pointed out that these are not accusations she's making about things that allegedly happened in secret. These are things publicly done, publicly recorded, and publicly boasted about by the perpetrators. It's simply no good to pretend that what she's talking about isn't real or isn't widespread. Anyone who's spent much time in Catholic churches has his own clerical blasphemy stories, myself included.

Muggeridge ends the book on a somewhat hopeful note. John Paul II has recently been elected Pope, and she sees this as a sign that the Church will now stop appeasing her enemies, start working with her friends, and launch a counter-revolution. A quarter-century later, though, the revolution seems as powerful and Catholic orthodoxy as marginalized as ever. I admit I found the optimistic parts of the book more depressing than the pessimistic parts.

Does this book solve the mystery of how the Church fell? It certainly does a better job than most, but some things are still unexplained. Most importantly, why did the theologians turn to heresy in the first place? If power was what they wanted, the Church would have been much likelier to accommodate them if they had remained orthodox. Why weren't orthodox Catholics able to counter the influence of a biased secular press with their own journalistic organs? There still seems to have been an almost preternatural competence of the revolutionaries and incompetence of the orthodox that I still don't understand.

The Myth of Religious Violence

By William Cavanaugh

The reason I would like to see more conservatives in academia is so they can write books like this. In this important study, William Cavanaugh deconstructs one of liberalism's primary legitimating myths–that religion is unusually violence-prone, and their secular rule is necessary to keep us Catholics, Protestants, and Muslims from killing each other. The story–and I know you've heard it a thousand times, as have I–is that religion and politics used to be illigitimately "mixed", but that led to the wars of religion in the sixteenth and seventeenth centuries when Catholic and Protestants tried to impose their creeds by force, and the slaughter was only ended when the secular state stepped in, regulated religion to its proper (private, socially irrelevant) role, and established peace, reason, and tolerance. Today that happy settlement is threatened by crazy Muslims who haven't yet privatized their religion, but we're going to cure them of their craziness by bombing, invading, and shooting them into rationality–for their own good, of course.

There are just three things wrong with this great myth of liberalism: 1) It's wrong; 2) It's incoherent; 3) It's self-serving propaganda for the secular warfare state.

1) It's wrong

No historian of early modern times accepts the mythical view of the wars of religion. The thirty years war was primarily a war between the Catholic Holy Roman Empire and Catholic France. Both this war and the French "wars of religion" were as much about the consolidation of power in the emerging nation-states (and resistance to that consolidation by German princes and French nobles) as anything else. Both the Huguenots and the Catholic League were mowed down as obstacles to French state centralization. Confessionalization, the establishment of sharp confessional boundaries and imposition of religious uniformity in a realm, was part of this process of consolidation. So the rise of the nation-state was more a cause of the "wars of religion" than their solution. What's more, it's simply wrong that these nation-states separated politics from religion. In both Catholic and Protestant lands, the state siezed control of the Church and appropriated its of aura of sacrality for itself. Liberalism didn't come for more than a century later, when the sacredness of the nation-state was so firmly established that Christianity could be discarded.

2) It's incoherent

Cavanaugh spends a significant fraction of the book reviews the vast literature on the allegedly violence-prone nature of religion. He shows that each of these studies is hopelessly muddled with contradictions; none of them even succeed in defining "religion" in a way that would exclude secular causes like nationalism or Marxism. Religion is supposed to be dangerous because it divides the world into "us" vs. "them", because it presents utopia to the imagination, because it makes absolute claims about right and wrong and the proper ordering of the cosmos, etc. In each case, ostensibly secular, modern political/economic systems do the same things, so why single out Christianity, Islam, etc? Why not just study how belief systems in general, or communities in general, can become violent? But that would defeat the purpose of these studies, which is to show that something called "religion" is uniquely violence-prone in a way liberalism, nationalism, and the like are not, or at least that its type of violence is worse somehow. Bizzarely, many of the studies Cavanaugh reviews cite secular violence–nonreligious murderers like Timothy McVeigh or Joseph Stalin, assaults against Jehovah's Witnesses for refusing to salute the American flag, G. W. Bush's "Axis of Evil", tribal violence worldwide–as evidence that religion is particularly violence-prone! The idea is that these secular things or people must have been contaminated by religion. Here religion is defined as violent and secularism as peaceful, making the claim "religion is violent" tautological. One writer asserts that Christian just war theory is a concession to secular concerns which had nothing to do with the teachings of Christ, and in the next breath he cites just war theory as evidence of religion's inherent violence! The only conclusion I can draw from all this (and there's more silliness I haven't mentioned) is that liberal academics are simply incapable of thinking logically when it comes to the issue of religion in society.

3) It's self-serving propaganda

The secular state is our deliverer from religous kookery! It tells us so itself. Sure, sure, secular causes like nationalism, liberalism, and socialism have been known to engage in a bit of violence themselves, but that's totally different. The state's violence is rational–regrettable but often necessary. Religious violence is irrational. A man who'll kill for his religion is a fanatic; a man who'll kill for his country is a patriot. This self-serving, question-begging nonsense doesn't just muddle people's thinking; it serves two definite political purposes. First, in domestic political debates, it unfairly marginalizes views that are labeled as "religious", so that they are automatically dismissed as irrational. (Think of the times you've heard someone say that belief in global warming or opposition to embryonic stem cell research is "religious". They didn't mean "deserving of special consideration and respect".) Cavanaugh relates how this has affected U.S.

Supreme Court decisions. Each time the Court bans some public display of religion, it makes some utterly implausible claim about the dangers of sectarianism to national unity, backed up by invoking what we all "know" about the wars of religion. Second, in the area of foreign policy, it leads us to dismiss the concerns and interests of Muslim peoples as "irrational". So, for example, to understand Muslim hostility to American policies in the Middle East, we feel entitled to ignore the secular grievances that they themselves give as their motives, because we all know that that's just a mask for religious craziness. Cavanaugh cites some amusing examples of this thinking, which give the impression that Western atheists are often more focused on religion than Arab or Persian Muslims. Worse, since Muslims are irrational, while we are by definition reasonable, we are entitled to impose our reasonable way on them by force. New Atheists like Sam Harris and Christopher Hitchens take this line of thinking to hair-raising extremes to justify outright murder–for Harris, genocidal mass murder of the Muslim population, including possible nuclear first strikes! This is an extreme, but hardly isolated, instance of a rule that obsessive focus on one kind of violence ("religious") ends up blinding us to the danger of other types.

My only quarrel with this book is that Cavanaugh borrows from nominalism and postmodernism a seeming hostility toward "essentialism" and an intent to find political manipulation behind every narrative. Perhaps this was included to put his presumably majority-liberal readers off their guard. Certainly it serves his purposes, but, then, postmodernism can be used to discredit anything, which makes it useless. Not all labels are arbitrary, and not all stories are masks of the will to power, but these particular labels are arbitrary and this particular story does exist to mask the liberal *libido dominandi*, as Cavanaugh proves. Cavanaugh thinks the word "religion" is meaningless, but I think that goes too far. Both essentialist definitions (based on a phenomenology of the sacred, a path I follow) and functionalist (Durkeimian) definitions are reasonable and useful. The problem is just that the authors Cavanaugh critiques keep switching back and forth between the two arbitrarily in order to reach their predetermined conclusion. Even if "religion" were not well-defined, I certainly think "Christianity" and "Islam" are, and investigations into their essential natures is a reasonable task.

All my readers should buy and read this book so they'll be ready for the next time someone tells them that religion is the cause of most of history's violence. Also, you'll be aware that calling for the secularization of the Muslim world makes one a dupe for atheism and tyranny.

The Origin and Goal of History

By Karl Jaspers, 1949

This is the book that popularized the phrase "Axial Age" to describe the period of cross-civilizational cultural creativity from 800-200BC–the age of Confucius, Buddha, the Upanishads, Zarathustra, the Hebrew prophets, Homer, and the Greek philosophers. Jaspers regards the Axial Age as the most important time of human history so far, and that since then, mankind has mostly just been living off our Axial capital. This may be about to change, however, as mankind is entering a new era of creativity which promises to give us—wait for it—socialism and world government.

Honestly, I'm baffled that Karl Jaspers is widely regarded as an intelligent person. This book shows all of the marks of an unserious mind. Jaspers simply regurgitates all of the catch-phrases and prejudices of postwar European liberalism. He makes dubious statements without argument, and he seems oblivious to the tensions between his statements. He claims his unity of history is "empirical", when he means simply that it's not tied to Christian revelation. (As Hume pointed out, even the unity of a human mind is not empirical.) He claims to admire the Axial Age whose main thrust was towards relating man to the totality of being through philosophy and religion, while at the same time rejecting this quest by claiming that philosophy and religion are more or less nonsense because only science gives real knowledge. Of course, he doesn't have the clarity of mind to say it this simply. No, Jaspers encourages us to have faith, just not in anything in particular—that would be dogmatic. Religious truths are only "true for us", never objectively true. To think your beliefs are "objectively" or "absolutely" true (i.e. to actually believe them) is to be a fanatic and to betray the true spirit of religion.

If Jaspers could think outside his liberal clichés for an instant, he might realize that he has confused different things. Since the confusions are so common, I'll elaborate. All truth claims are objective truth claims—even truth claims about one's beliefs or feelings. The claim "absolute truth claims are bad" is self-contradictory, because it is itself an absolute truth claim. If a statement P is meaningful, then the law of contradiction applies: if P is true, not-P is false, and vice versa. You can't think P is true without thinking that those who believe not-P are in error. If this is intolerant, than thinking itself is intolerant. Most of the confusion hinges on the word "absolute". It's not clear how "P is true" and "P is absolutely true" differ, so that the latter should be particularly objectionable. I might understand if it meant "exceptionless general statements are bad" (although even this is self-refuting), but the charge of dogmatism is usually leveled against people for holding beliefs in particulars like "Jesus rose from the dead" and "there is a God". Jaspers' point seems to hinge on the partiality and cultural embedding of each revelation, but these are not obstacles to objective truth. A statement may be true—absolutely and objectively—without being the complete and whole truth. (e.g. I may know the mass of a rock but not its composition. I don't know the whole truth about the rock, but what I know is absolutely, objectively true.) A statement may be, and of course always is, expressed using a particular language and cultural imagery. But although not everyone will be equipped to understand the statement, it may still be objectively true—true "for everyone". Any functional language has this property, that it references pre-linguistic realities. All of this is, or should be, obvious. Karl Jaspers has obviously lost his faith. He thinks Jesus' body was eaten by worms and maggots. Fine. But he shouldn't assault the rules of logic in order to hide his apostasy from himself.

The Southern Tradition

By Eugene Genovese, 1994

How is it that Marxist historian Eugene Genovese has written a fairly positive book on the agrarian conservatives of the American south? One big reason is the author's disenchantment with communism, which was growing while he was writing this book. In fact, the state of being a "recovering" Marxist gives Genovese a unique and valuable perspective on his subject. Both Marxists and southern agrarians have pointed out the atomizing and alienating effects of industrial capitalism, but both have lived to see it triumph over their preferred forms of social organization. (Finding oneself on the wrong side of history tends to deepen a man's sympathies and strengthen his character, in my experience.) Furthermore, the southern and communist causes are not only defeated but discredited—no one wants to bring back either slavery or the Soviet Union now, no matter how bad capitalism gets. However, this doesn't mean that the critiques of Marxists or southern conservatives were without value, and in fact Genovese has painfully to realize that it was the conservative arguments that were the better of the two. The southerners appreciated the limits of our fallen nature, and they appreciated the value of local community, local self-government, religion, and tradition. In other words, they saw the folly of both capitalism and socialism. The author's Marxist training also leads him to appreciate the fact that the southern conservatives realized that a traditionalist/organic society can only exist under suitable (non-capitalist) economic and social arrangements. This he compares favorably to the standard conservatives of his own day, who (he claims) think they can defend traditional values without attacking a tradition-destroying consumerist free-enterprise economy. Unfortunately, the alternate economic base recommended by antebellum southern critics was slavery. The real difference, they thought, between northern wage labor and southern slavery was that southern slaveholders had paternal responsibilities toward their slaves, while northern employers could exploit their workers as far as the market would allow. Interestingly enough, Genovese shows that it was this reason, and not any idea of racial superiority, that was used to justify slavery. He even mentions that some southern intellectuals recommended that slavery be extended to whites. Now, if slavery is the only alternative to capitalism, maybe we'd better make our peace with capitalism. However, there is another element in the agrarian conservative tradition that fit uneasily with the defense of slavery. This was the Jeffersonian ideal of a republic of independent small farm owners. A much more attractive vision of country life than the slave model, no doubt, but it too has proven unable to withstand the pressures of large-scale commercial agriculture. Finally, there are the ideals of state's rights and local government. Genovese sees great value in these and thinks it a mere historical accident that they have been associated with slavery and segregation.

I am, of course, sympathetic to some of the ideas Genovese describes, and I'm glad that he used this book (and the series of lectures on which it is based) to bring them to the attention of the academic world, which tends to be a leftist bubble. On the other hand, the book is not particularly well organized; it seems to drift from one topic to another and then back again. I would have appreciated a more systematic approach. Still, if you're one who thinks that the only two poles of the American mind are Puritanism and liberalism, and you think "southern" is a synonym for "stupid", this book will make you realize how one-sided your education was.

Three Faces of Fascism

By Ernest Nolte, 1963

What is fascism really? Sometimes one hears that fascism is organized hatred or irrationality, but saying this is to insult rather than to try to understand. We also hear that fascism is one form of totalitarianism. Perhaps, but if "totalitarian" is the genus, what is fascism's specific difference? I'm also suspicious of definitions like "fascism is an extreme form of X", where X is nationalism, anti-communism, or some other such thing. These would deny fascism any essence at all, and make it a mere matter of intensity. I don't buy this. Is it credible, for example, that fascists are more anti-communist than Catholics or more patriotic than ancient Romans?

Historian-philosopher Ernst Nolte has written a book trying to figure out what fascism really is. His technique is to look at what he regards as three definitely fascist movements—Action Francaise, Italian Fascism, and German National Socialism—and study their history and the writings of their leaders. This seems to me to be the way to go. Unfortunately, important figures like Mussolini failed to expound a definitive and self-consistent doctrine. Therefore, the student of fascism must do some systematizing for them, and this raises the danger of constructing something different from what real fascists actually believed.

Nolte first characterizes fascism as revolutionary anti-communism, i.e. an anti-communist movement whose practices are in some ways modeled on the movement they're opposing. However, from the writings of Maurras and Hitler, he decides that this definition doesn't capture the heart of the phenomenon. Fascism, Nolte comes to believe, is a response to man's possibility of transcendence. By "transcendence", Nolte means a man's ability to mentally see past his own particular time, place, and community. Transcendence can be either "theoretical" or "practical". Theoretical transcendence means fixing one's mind on the absolute or the totality of things, i.e. metaphysics and religion. Practical transcendence means breaking free of the obligations of particular communities and traditions, usually to embrace a universal/transcendental moral code such as Kant's categorical imperative. Bourgeois industrialism, liberalism, and socialism are forces for practical transcendence in the modern world. However, this world movement has not gone without resistance. Practical transcendence presents a danger to actually existing societies; it erodes their legitimacy by comparing them unfavorably with its own universal ideals. Those who wish to defend their societies from such criticism have two options. They can affirm theoretical transcendence but deny the practical kind. These people are conservatives

—they say that man is indeed ordered to God, but his moral duties are necessarily mediated by particular communities and traditions. The more radical alternative is to deny both theoretical and practical transcendence. This is the position of fascism. Those who take this route regard transcendence as the hobby of sick and resentful minds; it is sowing hatred for the good things that actually exist in favor of illusions. So, for example, Maurras saw his political thought as an outgrowth of his atheism, and he saw the revolutionaries' zeal to destroy the actual France in the name of their abstractions as forms of "monotheism". Similarly, Mussolini and Hitler insisted that the state must be completely independent, i.e. outside the judgment of, any other body, from within or without.

I myself found the distinction between theoretical and practical transcendence to be the most intriguing part of the book. How much does it really have to do with historical fascism, though? Nolte provides sufficient evidence to prove that the above philosophy was a part of the thought of the fascist leaders. I'm worried that he hasn't demonstrated that it held as central a position in their minds as it does in his. Perhaps Nolte would say that this doesn't matter, since fascism has its own inner logic independent of how well its expositors understand it. This is true, but I'm always wary of systemizations of bodies of thought produced by their enemies. My other reservation is in regarding Action Francaise as a fascist, rather than a conservative monarchist, organization. Nolte is probably right that Maurras himself was, at the deepest level, a proto-fascist. However, the movement as a whole had, before the Vatican's condemnation of 1926, a large number of Catholics who certainly had no problems with "theoretical transcendence". Perhaps we should see Action Francaise as a mixture of two anti-liberal groups which were separated in 1926, with one group evolving towards fascism and the other toward Christian Democracy.

The Legend of the Wandering Jew

By George Anderson, 1965

As Christ was carrying His cross to Golgotha, He stopped for a moment to rest outside the house of a shoemaker named Ahasuerus. When Ahasuerus saw this, he jeered the Savior, asking Him why He was dallying. Christ then looked at Ahasuerus and pronounced the curse: "I will stand here and rest, but you must wander the Earth until I return." And so it was the Ahasuerus became the Wandering Jew—a man cursed to live for century after century, never knowing the release of death until Judgment Day. He has no home on this Earth and no rest from his wandering. Some say he seeks death but can't find it, and some say he still rebels against Christ and the One who sent Him, but most say that he has repented and hopes for God's mercy on the Last Day. He spends his centuries of waiting in prayer and good deeds. So, at least, goes the legend whose lifetime is now nearly half that attributed to its subject. In this book, Anderson spends 400 pages cataloging and describing all the variations in the story in both folk tale and literature from its appearance in the 13th century to the 1960s. I ended the book somewhat disappointed, because the Legend seems to have such great dramatic potential that it's just waiting to be turned into a literary masterpiece, but like Ahasuerus, it's been waiting a long time. Many famous writers have tried their hands at it—including Goethe, Shelley, Hans Anderson, and Dumas, but their efforts didn't really pay off. In fact, the best treatments have usually been by lesser-known authors. Anderson spends more than half of the book describing bad fiction. This gets rather tedious for both reader and author (again, bizarrely appropriate for the subject), but the author's frustrations can sometimes be amusing, such as when he describes reading David Hoffman's 1700 page chronicle as a "penitential achievement", or in his appropriate disgust with the quasi-pornographic retelling by Viereck and Eldridge ("partners in literary crime"), in which a Wandering Jew and a Wandering Jewess spend their millennia in the pursuit of sexual gratification. More seriously, Anderson points out a fundamental weakness in the legend—that once the Jew commences his wandering, there aren't any dramatic incidents left until Doomsday. This is why many versions of the story devolve into disguised history and geography lessons. To have a compelling story, an author needs to add things.

The story has endless variations. Sometimes Ahasuerus is an old man; sometimes he remains forever young; sometimes he ages and then returns to youth. In the English poetic drama *The Immortal Jew* by S.R. Lysaght, he lives, dies, and is reincarnated over and over again, but unlike the reincarnations the rest of us are imagined to go through, Ahasuerus is condemned to remember all his past lives. When the Wandering Jew is the main character, his redemption is usually the main issue. Very often, Ahasuerus is a secondary character in fiction, a sort of *dues ex machina* who comes out of nowhere and does good deeds: reuniting separated lovers, and the like.

It seems that Anderson's favorite dramatic adaptation of the legend is the 1833 French work *Ahasverus* by Edgar Quinet. This version has several things going for it. First, it works hard to capture a sense of vast stretches of time unfolding. (The story goes from the creation of the world to mankind's old age, to Judgment Day, and then to a time after the death of God Himself.) Second, it introduces the character of Rachel, an angel expelled from heaven for her pity towards Ahasuerus. They meet on Earth and fall in love, and she follows him through his eons of wandering. According to Anderson, their love is portrayed quite well. (Not having read the play, I can't comment.) Anderson gets to Quinet about half-way through the book. Unless you're a serious enthusiast about the legend, you might consider stopping after this point, because the masterpiece you're waiting to hear about hasn't been written yet, and the last hundred years of work on the legend hasn't been too impressive.

Book Reviews: Philosophy

Against the Current

By Isaiah Berlin, 1979

There's a lot to like about Isaiah Berlin. As one of the best historians of ideas, he covers not only the best-known figures, but also draws our attention to unjustly neglected thinkers and overlooked general trends. Most importantly, he does make a serious effort to understand the positions of those on the losing side—the critics of modernity, the dissenters from the established liberal views, people like Herder, de Maistre, or Sorel. Although a moderate liberal himself, Berlin seems to have a fascination with critics of the Enlightenment. That said, Berlin's conclusions always seem a bit off to me. This is because, whoever he discusses, he always seems to read them through the lens of his two big ideas:

1. It is possible that there is more than one valid conception of the good life, more than one set of virtues, and that these sets of virtues may conflict. It may be that an individual or society can only have one virtue at the expense of another, and that there's no unitary natural law to tell us which virtues to favor. Berlin doesn't explicitly affirm that this really is the case, but he treats it as one of the big interesting ideas. In this collection of essays, he attributes this idea in some form to Machiavelli, Vico, and Montesquieu, which, in my opinion, makes these thinkers seem more interesting than they really were. Although each of them may have described incommensurable systems, it's not hard at all to tell which system each favored, and none of them seemed very concerned about losing the virtues of the other systems.

2. Berlin divides European thinkers in a unique way. First, there is the Enlightenment view, which is basically that there is a single best way of doing things, and we can discover it through reason. This "Enlightenment" view includes not only the philosophes, but also the Greeks, Romans, and medievals. Then there is the romantic view, which can be summarized as saying "it's better for you to do your own thing, because what matters is not being right, but being authentic." The "you" in the previous sentence might be an individual, or it might be a group. Several essays in this collection concern romantic nationalism and its concern for the authentic expression of national cultures. In Berlin's scheme, the Enlightenment was actually defeated in the nineteenth century, and the twentieth century has been largely shaped by romantic impulses. While I find this organization of thinkers interesting, it is ultimately unconvincing. Take three famous thinkers:

Aquinas, Voltaire, and de Maistre. In Berlin's scheme, the first two would be classed closer to each other than either is to the third. Doesn't that seem odd? In fact, what strikes me about most of the rationalist and romantic thinkers of the eighteenth and nineteenth centuries is that, even though they had very different reasoning styles, they always seemed to reach the same conclusions: republicanism, sexual permissiveness, hatred for the Roman pope and the Russian tsar. Beneath the differences was a common core: the emancipation of human will at the expense of conceptions of a meaningful universe. Some preferred to say they were bringing the world under rational management, others that they were freeing human creativity. In either case, the goal was to free the human will from the restrictions of religion and tradition. Given this fundamental convergence, the differences between rationalists and romantics seem almost a matter of rhetoric.

Three philosophers on freedom: Anselm, Pico, Sarte

Man's free will has been a preoccupation of Western philosophers since Saint Augustine. All of them think it to be a central (usually the central) aspect of the human condition, but their understanding of freedom has evolved dramatically over the past millenium. In this essay, I propose to chart this evolution by looking at four short essays–each of them a classic of Western thought: Anselm of Canterbury's *On Free Will and On the Fall of the Devil* (1080), Giovanni Pico della Mirandola's *Oration on the Dignity of Man* (1486), and Jean-Paul Sartre's *Existentialism is a Humanism* (1945). Together, they come to less than one hundred pages and are well worth the time.

Anselm starts by considering the definition, popular in his time, that free will means the ability to sin or not to sin. This doesn't seem right, because it makes a good thing (freedom) dependent on a bad thing (the possibility of sinning). What's worse, it would seem to imply that God Himself and the blessed souls in heaven are not free, because their wills are indefectably turned to the good. Instead, Anselm proposes the following definition of freedom: the ability to maintain righteousness for its own sake. That is, what makes us free is that we can will the good, not out of instinct or even rational desire for our own happiness, but for its own sake. This freedom of the will is an awesome thing; although the body can be overpowered, the will can only be bested with its own collusion. Strictly speaking, temptation cannot overwhelm the will, for sin requires a choice. Such a strong affirmation of free will would seem to eliminate the need for divine grace, but Anslem is anxious to show that this is not the case. While humans are able to preserve a just will, it remains a gift of God, and they cannot recover it without divine assistance if they freely cast it off through mortal sin. This claim is asserted rather than proved in *On Free Will,* but *On the Fall of the Devil* introduces some new ideas that make it seem less arbitrary. Here Anselm introduces the issue of motivation. Men and angels have two wills–it would be better here to say "two desires"–one for happiness and one for justice. The former comes from nature (angelic or human); the latter (if I understand Anselm properly) supernatural. Both are ultimate, in that they are willed for their own sake rather than as means. Both are metaphysically good, and both are part of God's plan–since only a being that cared both for its own good and for justice could both enjoy beatitude and deserve it. Satan and the reprobate angels cast away righteousness by putting their own wills before God's in some way unknown to us but presumably based on the happiness motivation. As punishment, they lost both the justice that they themselves cast off and the happiness they had hoped to advance. Anselm points out that we can't make ourselves will something for its own sake when we don't already; therefore, we can't recover the will to justice on our own. Left with only his will to happiness, the sinner is a slave to sin, although he remains free because he could maintain righteousness if it were given back to him. Here seems to be the most questionable part of Anslem's construction. Why should we think that there is no natural desire for righteousness? Does sin really alter our mental states so much? Later theology built on Anselm but qualified some of these claims, distinguishing natural benevolence from supernatural charity, for example.

Fast forward five centuries, from Anselm the Catholic bishop to Pico the Renaissance humanist. God, the great architect of the cosmos, made creatures at every level in the hierarchy of being: the vital world of plants, the sensible world of animals, the intellectual world of angels, and the simplicity and charity of God Himself. Every slot was filled, but God's greatest creation was man, the creature with no fixed nature, no fixed place on the scale, one who could pick his place through his own free choices. Man may descend into sensuality or lift himself up to the angelic and divine realms. Since God has given us so great a gift, our efforts should be to use it well. Philosophy is crucial to this enterprise of human self-improvement, by which Pico means the accumulated wisdom of mankind in its entirety, from natural philosophy to the religious writings of every people. Pico is positively enthusiastic about studying the wisdom of other cultures, an enthusiasm grounded in his confidence that every religion's sacred writings will corroborate the Catholic faith.

We see that Pico has essentially embraced the definition of freedom that Anselm rejected–the ability to choose good or bad. Both think of freedom in terms of man responding to some external order. For Anselm, the order is primarily moral; for Pico, it is primarily ontological (the great chain of being). We see difference and continuity.

Fast forward five more centuries, from Pico the Catholic humanist to Sartre the atheist communist. Like Pico, Sartre thinks that, for humans to be free, they must not be tied down to any distinct nature, but must rather fashion themselves–"existence preceeds essence", as he puts it–but Sartre takes this farther. For Pico, freedom is only significant because there is an objective hierarchy of being and value on which humans place themselves. For Sartre, man is free because there are no objective values, no normative human nature, no God. There is nothing outside of us that can decide for us how we should live; the responsibility for making this decision is all on us. Each of us must be a legislator of values, although the responsibility that comes with this freedom is more likely to inspire anguish than jubilation. Existentialism doesn't ask us to rejoice or lament in this freedom, only to acknowledge it manfully and honestly. Sartre thinks that appeals to natural law, categorical imperative, or authority are really forms of self-deception. A man pretends his will is bound, when in fact the law or authority in question only binds him because he himself chose it. It's a way of making a decision, and then telling oneself dishonestly "I had no choice." But, one might object, if there is no "correct" answer to question of what to do with one's freedom, isn't the choice arbitrary and ultimately unimporant? Sartre recognizes this objection and tries to diffuse it by pointing out cases where a person is caught between two conflicting duties. There may be no unambiguously right choice, but the decision is not thereby unimportant. However, in such cases, the seriousness of the situation would seem to come from the objective importance of both of the conflicting duties, so such cases aren't necessarily evidence for Sartre's position.

A surprising thing about each of these three theories of free will is that they all depend more on the nature of the world in general than on the nature of the human mind. Whether or not human behavior is deterministic is not the central concern. For Anselm, the key is an objective moral order whose claims a rational creature is able to heed. For Pico, it is the hierarchy of being in which man is able to choose his place. For Sartre, freedom is the situation of a man who has realized that there is no moral or metaphysical order outside himself, but rather that he must create an order from himself. Each vision of freedom is compelling in its own way. Today's intellectual elite are mostly won over to Sartre's autonomism; average people probably think more along the lines of Pico's humanist vision. Those who worry about reconciling freedom and virtue might gain from giving Anselm a second look. Whichever vision we choose, debating free will seems to be a primary way for Westerners to meditate on the human condition.

Beauty

By Roger Scruton, 2009

In this short and elegant book, English philosopher Roger Scruton invites the reader to consider the main questions of aesthetics: What does it mean for something to be beautiful? How can one word describe such different things as landscapes, music, human beings, and stories? Can beauty ever conflict with truth or morality? Are there objective standards of beauty? Can art be erotic without being pornographic? Is there a connection between art and religion? Can one extract "the message" from a work of art? Although a work of philosophy, there is little in the way of rigorous argumentation in this book—and nor could there be. Scruton rather proceeds by evocative descriptions, examples, and gestures towards the reasons his claims are true. At each step, we are invited to see what he sees and have the insight for ourselves. If it is true, as Scruton claims and I believe, that the meaning or message of a work of art is inseparable from its mode of presentation, then he could not have proceeded in any other way. In a sense, this book is itself a work of art.

The book would be difficult to summarize, since it is itself a synopsis of Scruton's lifelong work in aesthetics. Instead, I'll just mention a few things that struck me.

1. Scruton makes good use of the Kantian idea that a key aspect of the appreciation of beauty is that it is disinterested. This means that we experience a beautiful object not just as a means to our pleasure, but as something that deserves our attention for its own sake. In this way, aesthetic judgment is like practical reason (morality), except that it is ordered to contemplation rather than dutiful action. Scruton points out that this aspect of objective value also connects art to our experiences of other people and of the sacred. Because it regards the object as an end in itself, appreciation for a beautiful object is always appreciation for that object as an individual, rather than as a member of a class. Another object can overshadow our desire for a beautiful object (or person), but it could never satisfy it.

2. The distinctive beauty of a human body comes not just from its physical shape and proportions but from its being the embodiment of a person. When I look at your body, what I see is not your body, but *you*. If I kiss your body, I kiss *you*. We are particularly struck by those parts of the body—such as the eyes and the mouth—that we regard as windows to the soul. When a piece of art shows us the body apart from the person, we have obscenity.

3.   Scruton draws a sharp contrast between imagination and fantasy. The former maintains a certain intellectual distance from the object it contemplates. In the latter, one imagines oneself in the action. True art excites imagination; pornography and special effects invite us to fantasize, to vicariously fulfill forbidden desires.

4.   Art satisfies our desire for order, our desire for there to be a reason for things, or at least to find them "fitting". This can be seen even in the humble acts of "everyday beauty" such as when we arrange a garden or set the dinner table. It is also found in art's highest forms, and especially in the way they provide a sort of redemption to suffering and loss. They do this by taking away the sense of chance and arbitrariness that accompanies suffering in the real world, and they present it as somehow meaningful. The doom of characters in a tragedy has a logic to it, even if it's only a dramatic logic. As Scruton says, *"Beauty reaches to the underlying truth of a human experience, by showing it under the aspect of necessity."* I think Scruton has scratched the surface of a great and mysterious truth here.

There's a lot more in this book that I haven't touched on. Roger Scruton certainly makes me wish I were a more cultivated man.

God, Philosophy, Universities

Alasdair MacIntyre has produced an introduction to the Catholic philosophical tradition, based on a class he has taught to beginning graduate students at Notre Dame University. MacIntyre has two preoccupations. The first is to identify the characteristic beliefs that unite those in the Catholic intellectual tradition, particularly regarding the relationships between theology, philosophy, and science. The second is to consider the social embodiment of Catholic intellectual effort. What structures are needed or have been used to carry it out? How must people be trained if they are to participate in it?

MacIntrye himself is, obviously, a moral philosopher of some note. I had been a bit worried that his idiosyncratic communitarianism might color his narrative too much, as it certainly did in *Whose Justice? Which Rationality?*, in which he presents his image of society as a sort of moral philosophy debating club (an image that could only appeal to a moral philosopher), with morals being the rules that keep the club on track, and taking this to be somehow a Thomist position. Fortunately, that doesn't happen. The book is very well balanced. Metaphysics and ethics are both covered. Augustine, Aquinas, and Newman receive the most attention–which is certainly defensible–but Boethius, Anselm, Scotus, Ockham, Descartes, and Pascal are given some not entirely negative attention. He even mentions some more contemporary Catholic non-Thomists such as Edith Stein and Elizabeth Anscombe.

The chapter on Augustine is quite good. In it MacIntyre introduces his first point about how philosophy and theology should relate. Faith purifies the intellect. Only in relation to God to we see ourselves truly. Otherwise, our self-knowldedge is bound to be obscured by pride, defensiveness, and prejudice. As MacIntyre puts it, the *Confessions* had to be written as a prayer. In discussing Ibn Sina and Aquinas, MacIntyre presents the cosmological argument. He makes an excellent point that theists and atheists see their differences differently. The atheist thinks that he and the theist agree on everything in the universe, except that the theist believes (unjustifiably) in one more thing. According to the theist, he and the atheist disagree on everything, because they disagree on the intelligibility of finite things. God provides an ultimate explanation, an ultimate ground of intelligibility, for finite beings. The atheist doesn't agree that finite beings have that sort of intelligibility. MacIntyre also gives the clearest explanation I've read on the Thomist position of the body-soul relationship. According to Aquinas, the soul performs immaterial acts (making it more than a material form), but it is individuated by the body it informs (making it less than a separate substance).

My main criticism–which will be entirely unfair–is that MacIntryre usually feels the need to discuss his subjects' more unfortunately famous thoughts. I almost wonder if it's a conspiracy among secular philosophers to make sure that every major Catholic philosopher is remembered only for his dumbest thought. So, for example, Anselm is mainly remembered for his ontological argument, Aquinas is mainly remembered for the Five Ways, and Pascal is remembered for his wager. MacIntyre defends his subjects a little, presenting Anselm's *Reply to Guanilo* (which makes much better points than the original *Proslogion*) and arguing that maybe Pascal wasn't speaking in his own voice in the *Pensee* concerning the wager. I would have rather MacIntyre had ignored these issues and focused on the more impressive, but less discussed, contributions of these thinkers.

So, what defines the Catholic philosophical tradition? MacIntyre is grateful to Pope Leo XIII for rebooting Thomism, but he disagrees that the Catholic philosophical tradition is simply identical to Thomism. Refreshingly, he even acknowleges that there are some problems, like the problem of individuation, that Thomas failed to solve and are unsolved still. Joining this tradition means being inducted into some live debates, and allowing oneself to be informed by the history of those debates. True, the debates take place in a context of consensus on key issues, and MacIntyre, in a surprising but welcome move, supports the right of the Magisterium to intervene in philosophical debates to maintain this consensus and keep the intellectual project on track. One crucial feature of an authentic Catholic intellectual culture is the felt need to bring all the separate intellectual disciplines into some overall conceptual unity. This is the job of philosophy and (since it is ultimately God that is the source and summit of this unity) theology. Therefore, MacIntyre doesn't like the way the modern research university is organized, because each discipline goes its own way, with philosophy being just another specialty. We must reject secular models and organize ourselves appropriately for the great task ahead. And what task is that? Nothing less than the reunification of human knowledge and the confution of the Church's enemies.

This sounds great, and I'd even like to chip in on this project of Catholic intellectual unification (and hopefully I do, in my very small way, through this blog) as long as I get to keep doing my specialized work too. As MacIntyre recognized, we need both.

Groundwork of the Metaphysics of Morals

+ Critique of Practical Reason, by Immanual Kant, 1797

Earlier thinkers—such as Aristotle, Cicero, and Augustine—had considered ethical matters, but almost always as part of a general discussion of what behavior best accords with reason, where "because it's your duty", "because it's good for you", and "because it'll make you happy" are all valid considerations. Immanuel Kant was, to my knowledge, the first to consider only the first consideration, duty, to the explicit exclusion of the other two. Arguably this makes him the founder of the modern discipline of ethics, and it so revolutionized the way we categorize arguments that we are often surprised when we read an earlier thinker, like Cicero or Aquinas, appealing to both duty and self-interest in the same writing. Surely these pre-Kantian thinkers were confusing hypothetical and categorical imperatives? No, they just weren't doing ethics in the specialized sense that we now take it.

Kant's goal is to understand duty. The first thing he notices is that you can't understand duty through incentives, i.e. "do X so that you can have Y". This is a hypothetical imperative. Suppose I say "well, I don't want Y". Then the command "do X" loses all its force. Duty can't be like this; it must be rooted in a categorical imperative, i.e. something of the form "always do Z". "Always do Z" can have no motivation outside itself. Kant thinks it must be utterly independent of any consequences that follow from Z, e.g. it mustn't be that we do Z because it promotes H. Why is this? After all, Aristotle also saw the need for moral reasoning to rest on an axiomatic first principle, but he concluded from it that there must be something that is good in itself which it is always right to pursue for no other purpose than itself. Why not say "Z is to be done because it promotes the supreme good, H"? Kant won't allow this for two reasons, both of which are fundamental to his whole philosophical enterprise. First, for Kant, everything in the human consciousness is either imposed by the mind itself, or is experiential data. There is no third thing. Furthermore, we can tell what comes from where, because these two components of our experience have different characters. That which comes from the ordering functions of the mind, "reason", has the character of necessity. That which comes from outside is contingent. From this follows Kant's refusal to believe—as the scholastics and phenomenologists claim—that we can apprehend essences. If these were anything other than organizing principles in the mind, they would have to be something like sense perceptions, meaning they could be wrong. Furthermore, they could only refer to the essence I perceive right now, so they could never be universal, as essences are supposed to be. I have not found an explicit argument for this belief; it seems to be a sort of intuition on which the philosophy rests. Anyway, Kant also thinks the apprehension of value or goodness is also like this. I may think H is the supreme good, but because it's something outside myself, I can't be sure of it (e.g. how do you know the beatific vision is so great?), so a morality based on H is ultimately uncertain. The second reason Kant rejects the idea of basing ethics on a good to be pursued is that it would mean that the will would be fixed by something outside itself. He calls this "heteronomy", and he thinks it a degrading condition. The will should not be constrained, even by human nature. The moral law must come from reason itself, uncontaminated by external motivations. Only thus will the will be autonomous, i.e. self-determining and free. Absolute devotion to duty is Kant's ideal of freedom.

From the above, we can imagine how the true categorical imperative is to be found: we must simply subtract off everything that has to do with my (or anyone else's) external incentives, and see what's left. What's left will be something universal and impartial, and it's fair to say that Kant's categorical imperative consists of nothing but universality and impartiality. His main statement of it is to only do what you could will to be universal law. That is, if you wouldn't want everyone to do it, don't do it yourself, because you're no exception. Another version of the imperative (Kant thinks they're all equivalent, but I'm not sure how to see this) is to always treat every person as an end, not just a means. This is, I think, a profound statement, one that arguably is the basis of all morality. It certainly has the ability to clarify a number of moral problems, and one can see from it why consequentialism is immoral. On the other hand, the command is rather too abstract as it stands. How are we to treat other people as ends if we don't have a fixed (non-empirical) idea of what is good for them? Kant has abolished Aristotle's moral teleology, and in doing so arguably burned the bridge between his imperative and its application. One way out is liberalism: treating people as ends means promoting each person's preferences without favoritism between people or negative judgment of anyone. Another way out, the Thomist route, is to re-admit teleology, but one that includes the imperative intrinsically. Another way is that of the value ethicists, to postulate objective values which it's good for people to appreciate and share. Finally, there's the Hegelian solution, that abstract morality only becomes concrete in a rational social context.

Kant thinks that certain ideas are presumed by ethical reasoning. Most obviously, ethical deliberation presumes free will. I wouldn't be thinking about what I should do if I didn't have the idea that I have the power to decide. Thus, free will is a "truth" of practical reason. We can't in any way prove from this that the will really is free. If it isn't, then our moral reasoning doesn't make sense, but so what? Maybe our moral reasoning doesn't ultimately make sense. Whether it does or not, we can't avoid moral deliberation, so we can't escape its logical presuppositions. Therefore, Kant suggests, it's reasonable to go ahead and believe them. He also thinks that we can derive the existence of God and the immortality of the soul that way. If these things aren't true, our day-to-day moral reasoning doesn't make sense. Nevertheless, they might not be true, but that's not a useful thing to consider. The argument given from morality to God is pretty weak, but I think good arguments could be made for this claim.

Kant was the greatest philosopher since Aristotle, and his ethical writings are deservedly regarded as masterpieces. In my opinion, his ethical doctrines are correct as far as they go, but incomplete.

Man and Woman

By Dietrich von Hildebrand, 1966

I read this beautiful little book about conjugal love years ago, and on re-reading it and comparing with my own *Defense of Patriarchy*, I see that it has had a larger effect on my thought than I had realized. For example, von Hildebrand makes the point, as I was to do later, that amorality in sex is worse than immorality. One who sins out of weakness may still be conscious of the beauty and majesty of conjugal relations, and he has the opportunity for repentance, while the amoral, "scientific" man who "doesn't see what the big deal is" about chastity is cut off from an important dimension of human reality. Von Hildebrand also emphasizes the importance of reverence in sexual ethics, in particular of not making sex an object of manipulation through contraception. I've this same point, but I'd forgotten where I'd first heard it.

Von Hildebrand emphasizes that we should not see love as an appetite, as an extension of self-love, or as a means to happiness. Rather, he understands love to be the supreme response to the objective value of another person. Unlike other value responses, such as admiration, love responds to the overall beauty of the beloved, to her value as a unique person, rather than to one of the beloved's isolated qualities. Love is not a delusion, but sees the beloved's true self. One of the book's most interesting suggestions is that a person can only be truly, objectively known through love.

> *"In the case of someone whom we do not love, qualitative values and disvalues* [i.e. good and bad character traits] *are accorded the same rank, so to speak. But where there is genuine love in response to the other person's beauty taken as a whole, in is to be expected that his negative traits will not be considered typical. Instead they take on the quality of being out of character with his true nature...Where there is love, our perception of other's faults is more objective...We come to better grips with reality when we see another's failings in the light of his whole personality..."*

The love between a man and a woman has the special quality that it aims at an irrevocable gift of self. The bond formed by this mutual self-donation is made possible by the complementary nature of man and woman. The differences between the sexes are not only physical, but also spiritual:

> *"we find in women a unity of personality by the fact that heart, intellect, and temperament are much more interwoven, whereas in man there is a specific capacity to emancipate himself with his intellect from the affective sphere...In a woman, the personality itself is more in the foreground than objective accomplishments; whereas man...is more called than she is to objective accomplishments."*

These spiritual differences mean that a man can know a woman better than another woman could know her, and a woman can know a man better than another man could know him.

The sex act is uniquely suited to express the gift of self at the heart of marriage.

> *"In a certain sense, sex is the secret of the individual. Every disclosure of sex is the revelation of something intimate and personal; it is a glimpse into our secret...[It's] real attraction is indissolubly linked to this intimate and secret character. As soon as one no longer feels shame in projecting this sphere into the public realm, as soon as one deals with it as if it were merely a biological problem that can be discussed publicly like a medical problem, one inevitably kills the real charm and the mysterious character which sex possesses."*

If only those sex educationists always wanting to "demystify", to "get it out in the open" would read this!

Spousal union is the meaning of sex, but procreation is its superabundant end. That God has joined these two goods is a great and beautiful mystery; attempts to sunder it are therefore profoundly irreverent. I admit that it would have been better if von Hildebrand had elaborated on why this is the case. Here is the one weakness of the book: it does not sufficiently appreciate the extent to which procreation gives sex and gender differences their meaning.

The final chapter considers non-marital relations between men and women. Von Hildebrand condemns the tendency to see men and women as rival interest groups.

When men and women forget their mission to and need for each other, men lose their masculinity and women lose their femininity, and the world is a much poorer place. Von Hildebrand insists that men and women should not avoid each other for fear of sexual temptations, but he also thinks it would be better if they did not associate at work, because this can dull people to the mystery of the opposite sex.

This book is only one hundred pages, but it contains an enormous amount of wisdom. I strongly recommend it.

Persons: The Difference between 'Someone' and 'Something'

By Robert Spaemann

"Person" is a funny category. In its contemporary sense, the world managed to do without it before 300AD. The category "human" fit our fellow intelligent creatures, and the word "person" originally meant "role". It was elevated to a philosophical concept by theologians in order to explain what it was that is multiple in the Trinity and one in Christ. Unlike "human", which refers to a nature, "person" is defined in contrast to nature, that which is one in God and two in Christ. The settled definition of a person, given by Boethius, is "the individual substance/subsistence of a rational nature". The emphasis, then, is on being a particular existent, as being the existing subject that holds a nature (or, in the case of Jesus, holds two). As Robert Spaemann, the author of this intriguing book, explains, "person" refers not to a particular nature but to the particular way intelligent beings relate to their nature. This personal mode of existence is alluded to in saying that a person "has a nature", implying non-identity with that nature and a degree of freedom in engaging with it.

The key quality of personal existence is transcendence. Like all animals, we have drives, and we naturally regard other beings according to how they relate to those drives' satisfaction. But we are not stuck regarding the world this way. Even to realize that this is a limited perspective is to step beyond it. Even to, like Descartes, wonder if all one's perceptions might be false is to maintain the personal attitude of transcendence, because one retains the knowledge that there is an outer world, an outside perspective, in addition to one's inner world. That we can try to respond to things according to their objective truth or goodness (the "view from nowhere" rather than my self-interested view) is the mark of our dignity. Thus, a dying man would prefer to hear a distressing truth to comforting lies even when he is beyond the point where the truth can practically affect him. As free beings we can choose illusion, retreat into immanence, relinquish our specifically personal dignity, but even this is a distinctively personal act.

The other side of transcendence of oneself is recognition of others. Acknowledging "the world outside" means acknowledging other people, other inner worlds, like one's own. Spaemann says persons relate to each other as members of a community rather than instances of a type. Only a Triune God, a God with "otherness" on the "inside", could be personal, self-sufficient, and infinite all at once.

The ability to, in a sense, transcend oneself and open up to others in recognition, justice, and love is also the special mark of personal freedom. Spaemann points out that this is also a distinctively Christian discovery, going back to Saint Paul and the Christian concept of conversion. Note, then, that although it is common nowadays to treat autonomy–meaning, roughly, having one's acts informed by one's "inside" rather than "outside"–as a synonym for freedom, the two ideas are in fact nearly opposite. Acting according to one's own immanent drives is the mark of a subpersonal animal; giving others their objective due is a personal virtue.

It is equally important to realize what a person isn't, that a person is *not* just an ego, not a consciousness or even a self-consciousness. With the inner-outer distinction, one recognizes that, from the outside, one is a physical being with a nature, and this realization is itself an important part of personal existence. Spaemann insists that personal identity in a human must rest on his's continuity as a physical organism. He criticizes Locke's theory that a person can only be identified with himself at an earlier time by memory, arguing that this in fact reduces the person back to instantaneous immanence and fails to really establish identity over time at all.

We intelligent beings are unique in another way, one that hardly feels like a blessing: our knowledge of our own mortality. The certainty of my own eventual death prompts a particular kind of self-transcendence. It radically relativizes the egocentric viewpoint of my own interests, because I and my interests will someday cease to exist, as will those of every particular other particular person alive. If meaning only came from my and other peoples' interests, we would be tempted to nihilism. Why sacrifice for another person when we're both just going to die anyway, and it will be as if it never happened? However, we can take a wider perspective outside of time, what Spaemann calls the perspective of the future perfect tense. Of noble and beautiful acts, one can say that it forever will have been good that they were done, even when the "payoff" is gone.

I was struck by this book's wisdom when I first read it a couple of years ago, and I can see it's influence on all my subsequent natural law writings and much else besides. If nothing else, it demonstrates the fruitfulness of engaging scholastic and early modern philosophy together, holding them in respectful dialog rather than holding up one as a punching bag for the other. Spaemann has thought deeply over the writings of both schools, and he allows Aristotle, Boethius, Richard of Saint Victor, Thomas Aquinas, Descartes, Locke, Kant, and Hegel all to voice important insights. Occasionally, the book will disappoint by making what seem to me easily-counterable arguments–if Spaemann announces ahead of time that he's going to provide six arguments for something, don't expect most of them to be strong–but the depth of insight is never missing, and that's what's most important in a work of philosophy.

Book Reviews: Politics

Authority and its Enemies

By Thomas Molnar, 1976

For three centuries, authority has been under attack by liberals. Conservatives can respond in two ways. Most try to defend some besieged institution (the family, the church, the army, etc) by downplaying its authoritarian character, implicitly conceding that authority itself is bad and that freedom should always be maximized. This line of defense never works—from liberal premises follow liberal conclusions. The other form of apologetic, followed by a line of conservative thinkers from Louis de Bonald to myself, is to defend authority itself as a positive good. This is what Thomas Molnar attempts in this book.

Authority, argues Molnar, is the only rational and reliable way to organize a community. Authority makes complex, coordinated actions possible. Authority, by symbolizing man's integration into society, also allows society to be seen as rational. It mediates the moral law and orders society towards rational goods. People need authority; it should not be thought of as a necessary evil. In fact, Molnar suggests that people with especially strong public spirit and willingness to sacrifice—traits we would regard as admirable—have a special need for authority to perfect and channel their self-discipline. Of course, Molnar also presses the argument that authority is needed because of human malice and weakness. People should not be left free to "authentically" follow their spontaneous impulses, because most of these impulses would be wicked. Authority is necessary for moral (as well as any other) education.

Next, Molnar considers attacks on authority in specific areas: in the family, in the schools, in the church, in the law courts, in the army, and in the state. Horrible as things are in 2009, some of the incidents he relates from the 1970's still seem shocking: communist propaganda in the military, judges who refuse to punish established criminals, widespread sympathy for left-wing terrorist groups, etc. According to Molnar, the real reason authority is weakening is because it is not exercised. Those who hold authority are no longer confident of its legitimacy and are afraid to exercise it. A breakdown of authority in one sphere of life cascades to others. The author thinks the only hope for restoration is in a new Augustus, someone assuming power with the will to use it to shore up society's authority structures. The alternative—long-term anarchy being unbearable—would be a despotism in which the power of the state is used to destroy all other authorities and to rule by fear.

I agree with the arguments in this book, but I do have some issues with the exposition. It would have been better if separate arguments were more clearly distinguished.

Arguments should be laid out at length in one place, rather than given briefly and then reworded several times later in the text, as Molnar does a few times. I also wish he would have been clearer in his treatment of the sort of authority that enemies of authority (e.g. communist governments) wield, what he regards as a sort of "pseudo-authority". Molnar thinks pseudo-authority is not real authority because it is not rational and generally operates by fear. But communists do have reasons for holding power—there is a "good" they're pursuing with it—and legitimate authority sometimes must use fear. I think Molnar is right to draw this distinction; anti-authoritarians themselves never regard their powers as forms of authority. However, from what he's written here, Molnar is vulnerable to the charge that he is using "authority" to mean "authority I like" and "pseudo-authority" to mean "authority I don't like."

Beyond the Global Culture War

By Adam Webb

he name of this book is unfortunate. Usually when someone says they want us to get "beyond" the culture wars, he really means he wants conservatives to surrender to liberalism. That's not what the author, Adam Webb, means. He wants to fight the culture war more aggressively and win. His key idea is that we antiliberals need to expand our horizons and realize that we are part of a global struggle; people are fighting the same fight in the Muslim, Hindu, Far Eastern, and Latin American worlds. Our best, perhaps only, hope of victory is a trans-civilizational alliance of communitarians and traditionalists of various sorts.

This is a very important point. Unfortunately, while conservatives in the West resist (albeit ineffectively) liberalism at home, we tend to uncritically accept the liberal perspective on the rest of the planet. So we cheer for secular democracy in the Muslim world, for the Indian Congress Party, and for Chinese capitalism, not realizing that we're promoting liberal hegemony and our own isolation. Liberalism, secularism, and feminism are–we imagine–right about the rest of the world, but wrong about us. This is a difficult position to defend; it grants far too much to our enemies. If the rest of the world's traditions were ignorance and oppression, it would be hard to believe ours are any different.

Webb retells the culture war of the last century from a global perspective. In his telling, each society has four different ways, which he calls "ethoses", of understanding itself, and the culture war is a battle between the adherents of each ethos. *Demoticism* is the egalitarian communitarianism of the village peasant: community is the supreme value, roles and duties are clear, but distinctions other than age and gender are frowned upon. *Perfectionism* is the individualistic ethic of self-cultivation found in aristocrats and mystics. Society is the arena in which virtue is developed and exercised, but most important is the society-transcending ideal of virtue or holiness to which individuals try to conform themselves. Demots value embeddedness in a community at the expense of having a transcendent horizon, while perfectionists keep society-transcending standards at the cost of spiritually separating themselves–to some extent–from their communities. *Virtuocracy* tries to combine the two: there is a transcendent standard of goodness, but it can be embodied in the life of the community through the ministrations of a clerical class, such as the Catholic clergy, the Muslim ulama, the Hindu Bramins, and the Chinese mandarins. Finally, there are is *atomism*, which combines the demot's dislike of hierarchy and transcendent standards with the perfectionist's dislike of community. Historically, atomists like the Greek sophists and the Chinese legalists have rarely held power, but in the last century they have launched a worldwide coup, achieving global hegemony and marginalizing the other three ethoses.

The West succumbed early, but in most places the atomist insurgency really only got going a century ago, when atomist intellectuals started criticizing native traditions for holding their countries back and slowing down modernization. In midcentury, the atomists made a sort of pact with demotic sensibilities; virtuocratic elites were attacked, marginalized, and largely destroyed, as enemies of the common folk. By 1980, atomists were powerful enough to revoke this pact and turn their hostility on the common people, who were now denounced as bigots and fanatics who need to be controled by their enlightened (atomist) betters. Antiliberal activism since then has been largely demotic (populist/fundamentalist) and has suffered from demots' limited horizons and weak sense of group agency. In only one case did a virtuocratic elite sieze power–in the Islamic Republic of Iran. While Iran is certainly a most promising center of antiliberal resistance, it is compromised–according to Webb–by being limited to one nation-state.

According to Webb, the world's cultural capital is being eroded quickly by atomist attacks. In another few decades, the damage could be irreversible, and history really will end. Therefore, he believes the whole world order must be overthrown and reconstituted before that time. The rebellion should represent the other three ethoses but be led by the natural leaders, the virtuocrats. Unfortunately, he's not able to be more specific than that. Many of the virtuocrats he mentions, like neo-Confucian intellectuals, are just a few isolated academics who probably aren't going to be overthrowing anything. One can't help but think that Islam is going to have to provide most of the manpower if this fantasy is actually going to come true.

Webb would like to see the antiliberal crusade commit itself to righting what he sees as the great injustice of capitalism, namely that the global South is so much poorer than the global North. He thinks that, since we're not so attached to economic freedom as the liberals, we will be able to offer the world a much more drastic wealth redistribution. I think this is probably backwards. Historically, atomists gave us socialism, after all, while in places like Iran the clerical faction has been more careful to guard property rights (considered an Islamic principle, as it is considered a Christian one) against atomist social engineering. It is also not clear to me that justice demands nations' wealths be equalized, or that it would be good for the global South to start essentially living on the dole. Nonliberals might arrange an uptick in foreign aid, but I wouldn't expect more of us than that.

Webb's diagnosis is excellent, and I hope for that reason that conservatives will read this book and take it to heart. While overthrowing the world order would be nice, I would like to start thinking about a more basic step. How can we Christian conservatives make contact with our Muslim, Hindu, and Confucian counterparts? How can we learn about them? What sort of collaborations might be immediately fruitful? What sort of structures might we put in place to foster regular contact and collaboration?

Essay on Catholicism, Liberalism, and Socialism

The nineteenth-century Spanish reactionary Juan Donoso Cortes occupies an intriguing place in the history of Reaction. His critique of liberalism is distinctly theological; he grounds all his social principles in Christian doctrine: the nature of the Trinity, its manifestations in creation, mankind's collective Fall, and its collective redemption. In some ways, he anticipates the Christian communitarians and Radical Orthodoxy schools of our own time. Unlike them, he was tied to an actual, living traditional society, and he defends kings, hereditary aristocracies, Catholic establishment, and many other things that would cause today's communitarians to faint from fear.

Throne & Altar reader William McEnaney has kindly sent me a copy of Dononso's main work, his *Essay on Catholicism, Liberalism, and Socialism*. Bill works with Preserving Christian Publications[1], a small business that sells out-of-print pre-conciliar Catholic books. I would be pleased for such ventures to flourish and so am happy to offer this bit of free advertising. What follows will be an exploration of one key theme in *Catholicism, Liberalism, and Socialism*.

Writing in 1851, Donoso saw the great issue of his age as an ultimately theological battle between Catholicism and socialism. Catholicism had dignified both authority and obedience by locating the former's source in God. Even the legitimate authority of fathers (as opposed to their mere primacy of age and power) is explicable primarily through the Trinitarian relation it reflects. Alongside the family and state, Catholicism fosters a vast network of associations, each embodying it its own way the fundamental law of unity-in-diversity rooted in the Trinitarian heart of Being. Socialism would destroy all of this, reducing the order of mankind to a vast and unitary yet illegitimate statist tyranny.

In the twentieth century, all of this would be explained in terms of the supposed Catholic principles of solidarity and subsidiarity. As you've often heard the story, the Left basically owns solidarity, and Catholics criticize Leftists only for neglecting the second principle of subsidiarity, a vague council to—all other things being equal—favor small and local agency. This is inadequate for a number of reasons. Donoso gets to the real heart of the matter. What's wrong with socialism is not that it is solidarity unchecked; socialism is solidarity denied, misunderstood, reduced to a shadow of its true self. The socialist believes in solidarity too little, rather than too much.

---

[1] https://www.pcpbooks.net/prestashop/

This is because the socialist denies original sin. Donoso of course agrees with the standard conservative complaint that socialists error in ignoring innate human depravity. However, the important point is not that socialists won't recognize the effects of original sin in man. The important point is that they won't recognize that it could be just and proper for God to punish all of us for the sin of Adam. They will not admit that we bear responsibility for our ancestors, and *yet this simply is the heart of solidarity*. Shared responsibility is the essence and core experience of all social unity. Donoso even carries this to the level of each individual, saying we would have no sense of ourselves as unitary beings persisting through time without the sense of responsibility for our past acts.

From inherited responsibility comes the family, aristocratic lines, particular nations, and the unity of mankind in Adam–each social unity passing on its stock of glory and guilt. Long before the ascendancy of international communism, Dononso was warning that socialism would end up making war on the existence of distinct nations. The socialists foolishly reject the principle of solidarity at its most obvious and direct level (the family, associations, ethnicities), while claiming to retain it at the level of mankind as a whole. Donoso thinks they mangle the principle even there, as they must because the socialist does not recognize free will, sin, or individual responsibility. They therefore must see the social organism itself as the sole bearer of responsibility.

It is interesting that Donoso rejects this organic, corporate notion of responsibility, since such ideas have long been part of anti-liberal thought. Corporate responsibility is how I naturally understand collective responsibility. Donoso himself recognizes the corporate character of families, arguing that it is families rather than individuals that can fittingly own land. However, he thinks corporate responsibility reduces individuals to components of the social organism without their own moral agency. Responsibility is collective in that I inherit it from past generations (Adam's fall along with the particular glories and shames of my own family, nation, profession, etc) and in that my own acts echo through all future generations. Such, he believes, is the true unity of mankind and the awesome agency of each individual. And yet he insists that this collective responsibility inheres in each of us as individuals. (That is, not "humanity, of which I am a part, bears Adam's guilt" but "I bear Adam's guilt".)

Men have always had some idea of collective responsibility, as the very existence of their institutions attests. We also see it, according to Donoso, in the widespread practice of animal and human sacrifice. In these practices he sees mankind responding to a valid intuition about collective guilt and atonement, but human sacrifice he thinks comes from forgetting the aspirational, symbolic aspect of pre-Christian offerings, the acknowledgement that man's own sacrifices fail to achieve this atonement but only point toward that time when God Himself would provide the perfect victim to accomplish our redemption.

Like other great works of the counter-revolutionary era, Donoso's work is primarily valuable for laying out counter-Enlightenment principles for which conservatives fight rather than in convincingly arguing for their truth. As a practitioner of "conservative dogmatics" I find this a valuable service. However, the arguments in places certainly do need work. For example, much of his argument for the transmission of original sin (a key point of his, as we've seen) seems to rest on a pseudo-Lamarckian belief in the inheritance of acquired characteristics, which even if it were still scientifically credible would not obviously apply to the spiritual level of original grace and sin. Again, the idea—found in many Western Christian writers and also here—of human nature being originally contained in Adam and corrupted for all of us is arresting but difficult to understand. What do we mean by "human nature"? If it is an abstract essence or a Platonic Form, then Adam would be as distinct from it as any of us, and it could in no way suffer the vicissitudes of time and corruption. And yet when I speak of "mankind" I do mean something more concrete than an essence and yet more unitary than a statistical statement about aggregates of individuals. "Mankind lives on Earth" is true even if there are beings identical to us on another planet, because mankind is not just a kind but a distinct lineage.

Understanding original sin is, of course, a task for Christianity as a whole and not just the philosophers of Reaction, but it is a fact that political philosophers when they confront their most fundamental issues must grapple with theological questions. This is, in fact, the observation with which Donoso begins his book.

Italian Fascisms

I've recently finished reading *Italian Fascisms: From Pareto to Gentile*, an anthology edited by Adrian Lyttelton that was recommended to me by Drieu a long time ago. After a few half-hearted efforts to understand fascism as a distinctive ideology, things are finally starting to click for me. The quality of the collections is uneven–as was the actual quality of fascist writers: lots of vitalist idiots, but four contributors that were really first rate: Vilfredo Pareto, Alfredo Rocco, Giovanni Gentile, and Benito Mussolini. Pareto was a sociologist who emphasized the importance of elites; what are presented as revolutions of the masses are always just the replacement of one elite by the another (usually of the class immediately behind the ruling one). The Marxists would agree, except that Pareto is more consistent, applying the rule to socialist takeovers as well. Rocco does a good job of explaining fascist corporatism and presenting the fascist view of history from the fall of Rome to the present as the story of the State asserting itself against rival forces and, by subjugating them, putting an end to those awful Middle Ages. Mostly, though, I would like to focus on Mussolini and Gentile, who try to directly present the key fascist doctrines.

First, it's important to understand what the fascists mean when they call their doctrine "totalitarian" (and they do call it that). It does mean that no power, no organization, no social force of any kind is to exist outside of the state. Now, when we hear that, we imagine the State just doing the minimalist sorts of things a liberal state does, and everything else wiped out–a social wasteland. The fascist would say that this is a complete misunderstanding. None of the peoples' collective activities–their arts, commerce, festivities, scholarship, and religion–is to be lost. The state is to make itself the guardian of them all, only directing them to the common good. *"The Fascist State... takes over all the forms of the moral and intellectual life of man."* The fascist state does this not by obliterating lower levels of organization (as it accuses the socialist of doing), but by incorporating them into itself, providing a context where they can truly come into their own. For example, private ownership of factories is to continue, but they are to be subordinated to the state via corporations, governing bodies where both owners and workers are represented. One might well ask what good private ownership is without private control. The fascist would probably reply by pointing to the high degree of subsidiary control: most decisions would be made at the lowest levels by the owner/manager/worker organizations.

The fascist understanding of the state is the key to their system. As Mussolini put it

> *The State, as conceived by Fascism and as it acts, is a spiritual and moral fact because it makes concrete the political, juridicial, economic organization of the nation and such an organization is, in its origin and in its development, a manifestation of the spirit. The State is the guarantor of internal and external security, but it is also the guardian and the transmitter of the spirit of the people as it has been elaborated through the centuries in language, custom, faith. The State is not only present, it is also past, and above all future. It is the State which, transcending the brief limit of individual lives, represents the immanent conscience of the nation. The forms in which States express themselves change, but the necessity of the State remains. It is the State which educates citizens for civic virtue, makes them conscience of their mission, calls them to unity; harmonizes their interest in justice; hands on the achievements of thought in the sciences, the arts, in law, in human solidarity; it carries men from the elementary life of the tribe to the highest human expression of power which is Empire; it entrusts to the ages the names of those who died for its integrity or in obedience to its laws; it puts forward as an example and recommends to the generations that are to come the leaders who increased its territory and the men of genius who gave it glory. When the sense of the State declines and the disintegrating and centrifugal tendencies of individuals and groups prevail, national societies move to their decline.*

Given the State's charge to the people's "spirit", it is obvious how fascism will reject the liberalism for its individualism and socialism for its materialism. What is more interesting is the fascist reason for rejecting conservatism in its religious, nationalist, and traditionalist forms. This is because of fascism's other key doctrine: immanentism. The State is prior to individuals and groups, but nothing is prior to the State. It has no goal outside of itself; it can be judged by nothing outside itself. How could it, since the State is supposed to already embody the people's highest spiritual ideals? The reactionaries, nationalists, and theocrats (as the fascists characterize them) disagree, seeing the state as ordered to some good–God, dynasty, nation, tradition, race–that is conceived as existing prior to the State. Gentile is particularly clear on this. Regarding the nationalists:

> *The nationalists' "nation" is, in a word, something which exists not by virtue of the spirit but as a given fact of nature, either because the elements that give it being, such as the land or the race, depend on nature itself or else because they must be considered as human creations: language, religion, history. Because even these human elements contribute to the formation of the national entity, inasmuch as they are already in being and the individual finds himself face to face with them, since they pre-exist him, from the moment he begins to act as a moral being; they are therefore on the same plane as the land and the race...This naturalistic attitude is a weakness...This naturalism was particularly and obviously visible in the loyal support shown by the nationalists for the monarchy....*

So basically, fascists are as devoted to autonomy as liberals, but autonomy for the collective spirit known as the State rather than for individuals. Note that racialism is incompatible with fascism. Strictly speaking, Hitler was not a fascist. Regarding the Church:

> *The Italian Fascist state, desirous...of forming one single unit with the mass of the Italians, must be either religious or else Catholic. It cannot fail to be religious because the absolute nature which it attributes to its own value and authority cannot be conceived except in relation to a Divine Absolute. there is only one religion based on and indeed rooted in the mass of the Italian people and meaningful for them, on which they can graft this religious feeling of the absolute nature of the will of the country...So the Fascist state must recognize the religious authority of the Church...*

> *This, too, is a difficult problem since the transcendental conception on which the Catholic Church is based contradicts the immanent political conception of Fascism; and Fascism, I must reiterate, far from being a negation of liberalism and democracy, as people say– and as its leaders, for political reasons, are often justified in repeating–is, in fact, or strives to be, the most perfect form of*

> *liberalism and democracy, as defined by Mazzini, to whose doctrine it has reverted.*

So, Fascism in its Italian incarnation must preserve the Catholic Church, because it gives the people an imaginative apparatus for experiencing awe for the State. However, Catholicism has the drawback that it is ordered to something outside and above the State and the national community. That is a dilemma, and Gentile doesn't really point the way out.

The contradiction between fascism and conservatism is quite instructive. Is the nation a completely immanent being, ordered to nothing outside itself, or is it the collective response of a particular people to the order of being around it? The goal of fascism is to take the nation's spiritual resources and give them an entirely immanent frame, but can that be done without doing violence to them? What would it even mean to have a religion without a "transcendental conception"? That's practically the defining feature of a religion! I would say the same thing about arts and sciences; they are essentially ordered to apprehending a cosmos that transcends us, and only accidentally express the genius of a people. Perhaps if fascism had lasted longer, we would have seen how its best thinkers–represented in this book–would have dealt with this.

On Divorce

By Louis de Bonald, 1802

Edmund Burke, Joseph de Maistre, and Louis de Bonald are generally regarded as the "big three" founders of political conservatism. Of the three, only Burke is accorded any respect by most historians of thought, and him only because of what are regarded as his judicious concessions to liberalism. Maistre and Bonald are regarded as too extreme to be taken seriously. I, on the other hand, think that Bonald is the most important of the three, and if you want to get a clear idea of what motivates conservatives, you're better off reading *On Divorce* than *Reflections on the Revolution in France.*

In this book, Bonald explicitly rejects two of the main beliefs embraced by Enlightenment thinkers: the idea that society is based on consent via a social contract, and the idea that the only purpose of government (and other social organs) is to help men be happy by promoting their individual interests. On the contrary, says Bonald, the most important elements in society are not autonomous individuals, but certain relations between people, and the main purpose of social policy should be to defend those relationships. Nor are those relations to be defended as means to the end of personal fulfillment; they are to be defended because they are willed by God Himself, and it is in fulfilling the duties associated with our relational roles that we submit ourselves to Him. Of course, Bonald doesn't intend to found society on just any sort of relationships—he believes that the foundational ones all share the same logical structure. They have three components: the power (i.e. the focus of authority), the subject (whose good is the purpose of the association), and the minister (who mediates between the power and the subject). So God created the world through the Logos; so the father rules his children through his wife; so kings or laws (both formulations work) rule the people through ministers, and God rules the people through governments. Both the family and society are based on this idea of mediated authority; an attack on one will tend to spill over to an attack on the other. In modern times, authority has been replaced by consent, leading to democracy in government and divorce in marriage. Divorce is an abomination because, by allowing the minister (wife) to leave her husband, it destroys the authority of the power and the security of the subjects. Bonald is convinced that the monarchy will not be safe while divorce is legal. Of course, some people would be made unhappy if they cannot divorce, but then others would be happier without this possibility hanging over their heads. In any case, Bonald says that we must protect public morality rather than the happiness of individuals. And public morality is synonymous with the strength of these authoritative relationships and the understandings that legitimate them. Here we see, as far as I can tell for the first time, the conservative program spelled out explicitly. We also see (as one could not from reading Burke or Maistre) why gender, sexuality, and kinship issues must always be central areas of concern to conservatives.

Bonald also relates a view of history embraced by many subsequent conservative thinkers. Both liberals and conservatives have their distinct historical myths. For liberals, history consists of an age of primitive simplicity followed by an oppressive "dark ages", which are only now subsiding, followed by a future of enlightenment and freedom. So the sequence is pretty good followed by horrible followed by wonderful. For conservatives, there was a pagan era of healthy immaturity followed by the mature perfection of Christian civilization followed by democratic, impious decadence. So the sequence is pretty good followed by really good followed by awful. Of course, Bonald associates each phase with a particular type of government, a particular family type, and (underlying them both) a particular understanding of authority. Despotism is connected to polygamy, monarchy to indissoluble monogamy, democracy to sexual license. As society advances and decays, the relation between public and family authority also evolves. Unfortunately, Bonald doesn't present nearly enough evidence to justify these sweeping claims. They are intriguing ideas, though, and they were later taken up more carefully by scholars such as Frederic Le Play and Carle Zimmerman.

I hope the above will convince you of Bonald's importance in the history of political thought. The book itself does have a number of weaknesses. The writing is adequate but not exceptional; it is repetitive at times and never achieves the eloquence that Burke and de Maistre could summon. There are a number of weak arguments which are likely to distract from the book's strengths, and some good arguments are not spelled out sufficiently. What the book does do is bequeath an original vision of governance as relationships-maintenance.

The Person and the Common Good

By Jacques Maritain, 1946

Do individuals exist for the community, or does the community exist for its individuals? The former possibility seems totalitarian, so most of us in the liberal West were brought up to think the latter possibility must be true. However, in this wise and elegant book, French Thomist Jacques Maritain argues that this formula is also wrong; it eliminates consideration of the distinctively common good, and it even impoverishes our understanding of the individual himself. Maritain argues that the citizen is both above and below his collective; he does this by distinguishing the citizen considered as an "individual" from the citizen considered as a "person". As an "individual", the citizen has his own needs and wants that distinguish him from his fellows. As a "person", he can reach out of himself through knowledge and will, he can make a gift of himself through love, and he stands personally before God and His laws by his free will and moral sense. The easiest way to get to this distinction would have been to use Kant's distinction of the "empirical" and "transcendental" ego, but Maritain doesn't like Kant, so he builds this up from hylamorphic dualism. The common good trumps the individual, but not the person. Maritain gives a nice example for a mathematician: the state may if necessary demand that he teach students math (even though, as an individual, he might want to spend his time otherwise), but it may not demand that he teach rubbish he doesn't believe, like "Aryan math", because, as a person, he apprehends the eternal order of mathematical truth.

In fact, Maritain maintains that a conflict between the person and the common good is impossible, if we understand both terms properly. One can easily see that, since "personality" has been defined mainly in terms of morality and love, that demanding a man sacrifice himself for his country does not, in itself, disregard this man's quest for personal development. Self-sacrifice is the supremely "personal" act. On the other hand, the common good, if correctly understood, can never disregard persons. Maritain's understanding of the "common good" is the key to the book. What does "common good" mean? First, it must be truly common; the common good is not the sum of individual goods. Examples would include a local environment, a cherished tradition or historical memory, or a cultural masterpiece. Each of these things is numerically one, and each belongs to all members of the community and no one in particular. The supreme common good is God's Divine Nature, which each of the three Persons possesses in its fullness. We mere mortals never achieve such a degree of commonality, but that's just because we're so low on the scale of being—matter gives us "individuality" (see above). Second, the common good, or at least the most important part, is distinctly moral. (Maritain isn't too interested in the material common good.) Its purpose is to promote personal morality. (This may seem to set the person definitely on top over the community, but remember that communal love is a big part of "personality", and that morality is itself a means to participate in the community of the Holy Trinity.) Third, the common good must be personally appropriated by the members of the community. It is not sufficient for the members to all benefit from a good, as when all the bees benefit from the organization of the hive. Maritain points out that there can be no truly public good except among persons. So, for example, Shakespeare's plays are a common good because most of us have read and appreciated some of them.

In the last chapter, the errors of modern times are identified. Liberal individualists ignore the common good and concern themselves solely with private goods. In so doing, persons are degraded to individuals, to mere bearers of private interests. Fascists and communists recognize the common good, but mistake its relationship to persons. The fascists treat the common good as an end, and people as mere means, and in so doing they forget that a truly common good must be personally appropriated. The communists deny the common good's moral nature, going so far as to deny man's transcendental end (his orientation to God) altogether. This degrades man by denying his highest goal, and it degrades the common good by reducing it to an economic order.

I like this book very much; it aptly expresses the Catholic communitarian point of view. One could certainly make one criticism—that the reconciliation of the "person" and the "common good" has only been achieved by moralizing both terms beyond their commonly understood meanings. The difficulties will come when one starts the work of balancing "individual" goods, which certainly will conflict. However, given that the liberal West has grown accustomed to thinking of politics only in terms of such balancing, it is important that we allow books like this to remind us that community has a distinctly moral aspect which must be protected.

Politics

By Aristotle

Not only is Aristotle's *Politics* one of the greatest works of political philosophy ever written, one seriously wonders whether Aristotle left anything for his successors to do but repeat him. His refutation of communism has never been bettered; indeed, it's astounding to think that anyone has subsequently been able to take the idea seriously. Before Cicero, he pointed out that the key feature of feature of the state is that it is founded on an idea of justice. Before Montesquieu, he divided the functions of government into legislative, executive, and judicial. He even propounds Montesquieu's central idea—that different regime types call for different virtues in their citizens. (In fact, one could say that *The Spirit of the Laws* is just the *Politics* with updated examples.) Before Maritain, he pointed out that man's ability to communicate and share moral ideals makes him more social than the bees. The list goes on.

Man, says Aristotle, is a political animal, meaning he attains his natural perfection only as a citizen in a state. Life in society not only allows man to receive help from his fellows in satisfying his basic needs, it also allows him to fulfill his social nature. Society is divided into three layers: the family (which satisfies man's daily needs), the village, and the state (the largest level, and the one which is entirely self-sufficient). Attempts to secure complete unity by stamping out private property and the family are wrong and monstrous, because personal relations are more meaningful than collective ones: *"How much better it is to be the real cousin of somebody than to be a son after Plato's fashion!"* Aristotle is strongly republican in the old sense of the term: he defines citizenship as the ability to participate in the responsibilities of government. The form of government is the constitution. Constitutions are good—whether they are monarchical, aristocratic, or democratic—if the common welfare is their aim. The state exists to promote the good life. In a good constitution, the virtues that promote the polis will be the same virtues that make one moral—the good man will be a good citizen. In perverted forms of government, this may not be true. A major concern for Aristotle is how power is distributed among economic classes, because the relative strength of the classes determines, or at least constrains, the type of constitution. Ideally, the middle class should hold the most power.

Aristotle considers the question "who should rule" both from a practical standpoint—given the strengths of the various classes, what best ensures stability and responsible rule?—and from a moral viewpoint—who deserves to rule? He believes that it is the last question which divides the partisans of different types of governments. Everybody, he thinks, agrees that equals should be treated equally, and those who are better should be treated better. But what differences are relevant? Is quality based on freedom, on numbers, on wealth, or on virtue? Each has their partisans. Aristotle concludes that the quality which determines worth is the capacity to serve the state, so wealth, virtue, and the rest all figure in to some degree.

Here is the place where Aristotle starts really sounding strange. After all, nobody obeys public officials because we think their private virtue gives them a title to our obedience. It's not a question of justice to that individual; it's a question of obedience to legitimate authority. Here we come to the one thing Aristotle didn't think about, the thing that was invisible to him, and that is authority. Where does authority come from? What sort of moral constraints can it place on me? With the coming of Christianity and Islam, these would become the central issues of political philosophy. Followers of the great monotheistic faiths were confronted with two sovereigns: the state and God. How were they to be reconciled? The only viable solution is the one proposed by St. Paul: all authority belongs to God, but he has delegated it to the state (as well as to the Church and to heads of families). But how is this delegation accomplished? Is authority given first to specific individuals, to the mass of the people, to the state considered corporately, or what? What authority has the state been given, and what has been withheld? Since the coming of Christianity, political thought has been divided in its concerns. Some have continued to consider Aristotle's question of the best organization, *The Spirit of the Laws* and *The Federalist Papers* being examples of great works in this genre. Others have focused on the origin of authority: Aquinas would be a classic example, but so too would Locke's *Treatise on Government.*

Aristotle exudes so much common sense and common decency that even prepared readers are apt to be shocked by his defense of infanticide, the enslavement of "natural slaves", and his restriction of "the good life" to a small minority of mankind. To allow oneself to be distracted by these things would mean a tremendous loss, though. In all of political science, this is the one indispensible book.

Selected Writings of Edmund Burke

Edited by Walter Bate, 1960

Edmund Burke is generally regarded as the founder of political conservatism, and it's true that he is one of conservatism's earliest, most profound, and most eloquent spokesmen. However, historians of ideas who trace conservatism back to Burke often make two erroneous reductions. The first is to reduce conservatism to only what Burke wrote about. This is certainly a mistake, since Burke barely discussed some issues, such as family structure and sexual morality, that are of central concern to conservatives but weren't live issues in England in 1800. The second error is to reduce Burke's criticism of the French Revolution to an argument for caution and gradual change. One often reads the following as a summary of the "Burkean" philosophy: Society is a complex organism, with each part affecting the others in subtle and poorly-understood ways. It is reckless to try to overhaul the entire system based on some abstract dogma about the "rights of man" or whatever, a dogma that can't possibly capture these complexities. Our inherited traditions, on the other hand, are a store of the wisdom accumulated from past ages. If there's a problem with the system, it's better to make slow and piecemeal changes so that you can safely "work out the bugs" while not jeopardizing the whole structure. Now, Burke certainly does make this argument, but to reduce his thought to prudence and caution is to trivialize it. After all, what political philosopher is in favor of recklessness?

No, the key to Edmund Burke's conservatism is his defense of prejudice and sentiment. He was the first political philosopher to emphasize how much a society depends on the sentiments it fosters in its members. So, for example, he defends the monarchy and other traditions for their ability to elicit the affection of citizens for their country. Casting these aside, the revolutionaries can secure obedience only through force:

> *"On the scheme of this barbarous philosophy…laws are to be supported only by their own terrors…Nothing is left which engages the affections on the part of the commonwealth. On the principles of this mechanic philosophy, our institutions can never be embodied, if I may use the expression, in persons; so as to create in us love, veneration, admiration, or attachment. But that sort of reason which banishes the affections is incapable of filling their place…There ought to be a system of manners in every nation, which a well-formed mind would be*

> *disposed to relish. To make us love our country, our country ought to be lovely.”*

Well-formed moral prejudices are a surer guide to the distressed mind than naked reason:

> *“Many of our men of speculation, instead of exploding general prejudices, employ their sagacity to discover the latent wisdom which prevails in them. If they find what they seek, and they seldom fail, they think it more wise to continue the prejudice, with the reason involved, than to cast away the coat of prejudice, and to leave nothing but the naked reason; because prejudice, with its reason, has a motive to give action to that reason, and an affection which will give it permanence. Prejudice is of ready application in the emergency... [it] renders a man's virtue his habit...”*

The dignity given to social life by these sentiments will not survive their banishment:

> *“All the pleasing illusions which made power gentle and obedience liberal, which harmonized the different shades of life, and... incorporated into politics the sentiments which beautify and soften private society, are to be dissolved by this new conquering empire of light and reason. All the superadded ideas...which the heart owns, and the understanding ratifies, as necessary to cover the defects of our naked, shivering nature, and to raise it to dignity in our estimation, are to be exploded as a ridiculous, absurd, and antiquated fashion.”*

The sentiment of reverence for past generations, in particular, is needed as a spur to virtue in the present generation. Burke actually suggests that, if the French really felt the need to make their constitution more democratic, they should have, like the English in 1688, presented the change as a defense and reinstatement of ancient freedoms, even if they had to look far back in the past to find a suitable heritage! The important thing is to see one's freedom as a sacred trust, to be gratefully received, judiciously used, and faithfully passed on. Instead, by seeing themselves as the pitiable victims of tyranny, with no heritage worth mentioning, the French preemptively excused themselves for all the crimes and debaucheries they were about to commit.

Suggestions like these may tempt one to understand Burke in a way that is, I believe, incorrect. One might think that he agrees that the moral sentiments and traditions of mankind are just illusions (we have, after all, seen him actually use this word). They are falsehoods, but they must be maintained because of their function in supporting a tolerable social life. To put it another way, when the "men of speculation" find the reason for a prejudice, what they do is not to provide an articulation of the same intuition which produced the prejudice, but rather they find a positive function for an emotional reaction that is, in itself, irrational. I am quite sure that Burke didn't intend to be read in this way. He claimed that our sentiments are natural and that they are supported by religion. He affirmed that the political order of Christendom was a reflection of the order of the cosmos. Although it is true that he bases his argument more on the usefulness of our moral sentiments than on their intrinsic validity, we may be confident that he affirmed the latter as well.

One advantage to this collection is that it has some of Burke's later writings on France, including his *Thoughts on French Affairs* and excerpts from *Letters on a Regicide Peace*. These will dispel from the minds of readers the myth that Burke was more moderate in his opposition to the French Revolution and its principles than were the French counter-revolutionaries. In fact, Burke believed, as much as de Maistre did, that the Revolution was a Satanic assault on the divine and natural order, that it was atheistic to its wicked core, that no peace was possible between it and legitimate authority, and that the war between the two must be carried on to the extermination of one party or the other.

The American Republic

By Orestes Brownson

Orestes Brownson was arguably the greatest American conservative intellectual of the nineteenth century. Most narrowly, this book could be read as the conservative "take" on the just-concluded American Civil War. Brownson insists that the Union victory was not a victory for freedom as liberals understand it, but a victory for legitimate authority. More broadly, this book is a reflection on the nature and destiny of the United States. Brownson follows de Maistre in believing that each nation has an unwritten constitution given to it by God through history; in fact, he develops this idea more precisely than did de Maistre himself. The question is, what is America's providential constitution? To put it another way, where is authority ultimately vested in the American system?

By 1865, it had become common to say that America is a democracy, and authority comes "from the people", but Brownson distinguishes three types of democracy based on their idea of authority. The first he calls "personal democracy", the idea that authority belongs to people as individuals. This was the basis of tribal and feudal systems, which were based on personal loyalty. It is also the idea behind social contract theories, in which authority belongs to the people as individuals, while the state only rules by the consent of the people and only as a means to promote individual interests. Most Americans of Brownson's time believed some such theory, but he identifies it as a return to barbarism. It has led to Americans foolishly sympathizing with rebels and traitors against rightful authority throughout the globe. Now, with southern secession, Americans have gotten a taste of their own medicine. If the Union is a contract based on consent, why shouldn't the Confederate states have been allowed to break off? In fact, under a personal democracy, there is really no authority at all.

With the Greek and, especially, the Roman peoples, a new kind of state came into being: the territorial or public state. Here authority is invested in the people, not as a mass of individuals, but as an organic and corporate unity tied to a particular piece of land. The state is sovereign over a particular territory, rather than, as in a tribal state, over a certain bloodline. For example, the nation of England is a corporate entity distinct from all Englishmen, and Parliament rules as representative of this nation, not from any personal authority of the legislators, and not even as representatives of the mass of voters. In fact, the franchise itself is a delegation of the nation's governing authority to the voters, not a right they possess on their own. One might say that the difference between personal and territorial democracy is the difference between power to the people and power to the community. What makes a people an organic unity? Brownson insists on two points. First, they are attached to a particular territory. Second, they have an unwritten constitution, an organization and way of doing things that has evolved from a common history. The ultimate source of all authority is God, our Creator, but God's authority is mediated; it is delegated to the organic people through the natural law and the unwritten ("providential") constitution. According to Brownson, only the territorial state is civilized in the strict sense of the word.

The emerging threat to the public, civilized state is what Brownson calls "humanitarian democracy" or "socialism", the idea of authority belonging to mankind as a whole. The humanitarians have no respect for national boundaries, and their passion for equality will soon lead them to attack gender roles and private property. Brownson's description of this cosmopolitan, egalitarian menace leaves no doubt that he had in mind more or less what we today call liberals. He believes that territorial democracy decisively defeated personal democracy in the Civil War but is galled that those who he regarded as socialists and humanitarians were claiming the victory as their own.

Brownson believed that America has a particularly excellent providential constitution. Ultimate authority lies neither with the individual states or the federal government, but in the "United States", the states as members of a union. Broken off from the Union, a state ceases to exist—it only exists as a member of the United States. On the other hand, the states couldn't be dissolved without destroying the nation, because the national government only exists as a union of states. The states acting together are completely sovereign, but in practice they have divided their power between the federal government and the state governments. This is not, Brownson insists, an attempt to balance antagonistic powers: federal and state governments operate in different spheres, and they derive their authority from a common source.

Brownson is quite optimistic about America's future; he looks forward confidently to the day the USA annexes Mexico and Canada. He thinks America will solve the European problem of the relationship between Church and State. In Europe, the Church is everywhere either controlled or harassed by the state. This is because the organizations of these states conflict with Christianity. On the other hand, the USA, we are told, is thoroughly Catholic in its principles, although its citizens don't realize it. As a territorial state, it recognizes God's sovereignty and its mediation; as a unique combination of general and state power, it is analogous to the personal subsistent relations of the Trinity. Therefore, America and the Catholic Church should get along just fine. Without restricting religious freedom, but just by maintaining its own (implicitly Catholic) principles, society will be pulled in a Catholic direction.

There's clearly a lot of wishful thinking going on here. But I think the discussion in the first part of the book on the nature of authority is quite solid, and the analysis of the seat of authority in the USA is quite compelling but not inarguable. I wonder if it may have been true in the nineteenth century but not today. The book admits that unwritten constitutions can change slowly with time. I wonder if, in the minds of both people and jurists today, the federal government has become the ultimate authority. If so, we have lost our uniqueness.

The Concept of the Political

In this book, Nazi political philosopher Carl Schmitt sets out to identify what distinguishes politics from other human concerns like ethics and economics. He claims that political thinking has its own distinct criteria of evaluation. Just as ethics distinguishes good from evil and economics distinguishes profitable from unprofitable, politics distinguishes friend from enemy. The identification of a friend or enemy is, Schmitt insists, entirely independent of other evaluative criteria. The enemy needn't be identified as immoral, ugly, or unprofitable as a trade partner. I will follow Schmitt in concentrating mostly on the category of "enemy". Political consciousness is at its highest in identifying an enemy. What does this mean? A few key points.

- Enmity is a relation between two rival groups of people. It is distinct from one's personal adversaries. Schmitt claims that the Gospel imperative to love one's enemies refers only to the latter group.

- The enemy is a threat to one's group's way of life.

- Between oneself and one's enemy, there is no higher authority recognized by both sides to resolve disputes.

- Political discourse can be recognized from the fact that its key concepts are purely polemical, i.e. are vacuous aside from the context in which they are being used to attack some other group. Schmitt mentions words like "society", "dictatorship", and "constitutional state". If he were alive today, he'd probably add "racist".

- Identification of an enemy–and, hence, politics itself–requires the possibility of armed conflict. An enemy isn't just a group of people you profoundly disagree with. The prospect of physical killing must be there.

- The political entity is defined as the one competent to decide for war. The substance of this entity–whether it is motivated fundamentally by religious, economic, or other considerations–may vary, but from the moment a Church / labor union / whatever acquires the power to make friend / enemy decisions, it becomes most fundamentally a political entity, a sort of state.

This definition will sound odd to Americans, since political enmity as Schmitt describes it sounds more like a description of the relation between rival nations like France and Germany than like what we call the political contest between Republicans and

Democrats. The latter would only be "political" in his sense if the parties were organized such that civil war was possible.

According to Schmitt, liberalism is intrinsically hostile to the concept of the political. Its philosophy recognizes only moral and economic categories. As a form of individualism, it can't justify the sacrifices demanded by war. (Schmitt, by the way, argues that pluralist doctrines are ultimately individualist, because the individual ultimately gets to pick which association's authority to recognize.) Most of all, liberalism puts faith in neutral procedures, while the ascription of friend and enemy, the absence or presence of an exceptional threat, is inescapably a decision. In being presented with this decision, a people is forced to take responsibility for preserving its way of life.

Is it not a good thing, though, for liberals to attempt to squeeze out the political–the realm of violence and repression–in favor of profit and humanitarian morality? Schmitt denies it. First, it is hypocritical. So long as there are multiple states, the logic of the political cannot be avoided. Economic and moral doctrines that become sufficiently powerful simply become political themselves, at which point they act like any other political forces. Economic exploitation of less developed states is defined as peaceful; resistance is defined as violent, while the retaliation of the economic powers (including, as Schmitt quotes from a League of Nations resolution, cutting off the food supply of the civilian population) is defined as peaceful. France may loot a defeated Germany, but since these are "reparations", it's supposedly an act of disinterested justice. Wars fought in the name of "humanity" implicitly place the enemy outside of humanity, as enemies of the human race. By moralizing the conflict, the enemy is no longer just a threat that must be neutralized but an evil that must be exterminated. Humanitarian wars are thus particularly inhumane.

The book's argument is most compelling where it comes closest to self-contradiction. The picture of humanitarian hypocrisy is indeed outrageous, but my outrage is, of course, a moral response. Because Schmitt wants to argue the independence of the political, he must avoid falling into moral categories. The most he can say is that liberalism fails to overcome the logic of the political and that its self-understanding is therefore false. However, this will only seem important to the reader because of the moral critique he suggests but doesn't make. One wonders if Schmitt is using words like "morals" and "ethics" ironically to refer to a liberal conception of ethics that he doesn't share, and whose inadequacy he is in fact demonstrating. Mustn't the political trade in morality, at least in some extended sense, if it is to invoke a duty to sacrifice one's life for one's country? Whether or not they are justified on "humanitarian" grounds, duties are intrinsically moral phenomena. It is clear that Schmitt really believes that the political decision itself, the identification of the enemy which is made by the ruler, transcends claims of moral duty and economic calculation. He explicitly rejects the idea of a just war, for instance.

What are we to make of this? As a picture of the essence of politics, it is surely too narrow. I would not wish to define contests over the order of the polis around the prospect of physical warfare. However, that there is a qualitative novelty in one's relation to an enemy is an important insight. I disagree at least to some extent with everybody, but there is a threshold beyond which my difference with another person is in our loyalties rather than our understandings, in the ends we seek rather than the means we recommend. Debates with people on my side are part of a common effort to get at the truth; debates with people on the other side are about neutralizing an ideological threat. Another important point is the importance of appreciating the contingency of a social order. In moments of peril, we cannot evade our responsibility by blind appeal to procedures.

The French Right

The French Right: from de Maistre to Maurras, edited and introduced by J.S. McClelland

Critics of the Enlightenment: readings in the French counter-revolutionary tradition, edited and translated by Christopher Olaf Blum

These are two good anthologies of writings by leaders of the French counter-revolutionary movement. They compliment each other very well; the editors of each volume had very different ideas about the significance of the French Right. *Critics of the Enlightenment* (hereafter CotE) has a forward by Philippe Beneton, who takes the standard line that the French Right were immoderate and inferior copies of Burke. He misrepresents the French reactionaries' beliefs, saying they rejected reason and based themselves solely on French tradition, and then proceeds to critique those beliefs. I seriously wonder if he even read the book he was forwarding, because *none* of the authors therein make such an argument, and Le Play at least claimed to derive his conclusions from systematic observation. Blum in his introduction makes it clear that he sees the French Right's critique of individualism as culminating in Catholic social teaching, and it is a fact that Pope Leo XIII was strongly influenced by them. The writers Blum chose are all Catholics (although Le Play spend much of his adult like outside of the Church before returning to the faith) and they are very focused on economic issues, culminating in la Tour du Pin's vision of a Catholic Corporate State.

McClelland is uninterested in Catholicism, and he seems to regard conservatism as a defunct ideology, interesting only because it was one of the currents of thought that coalesced into fascism. The entire importance of the French Right, for him, as a cause of Vichy France. Thus, his introduction to every speaker seems to end with "...which had strong echos in Vichy". (Incidentally, if the French Right is only interesting as a cause of Vichy, then it must be much less interesting than the German army.) Like Beneton, he thinks the French Right rejected universal reason, and again this can be disproved by the very writings he's collected. Maurras says quite clearly that he rejects the *philosophes* not just because they used abstract principles and ignored French particularities, but that the abstract principles they used are wrong even on the abstract level. *The French Right* (hereafter TFR) and CotE only overlap with one writer: de Maistre. Characteristically, Blum includes passages from *On the Pope*, and McClelland takes his musings on war from the *Saint Petersburg Dialogues*. The writers in TFR are overwhelmingly nonCatholic. It would seem that these books show two distinct counter-revolutionary traditions; let us call them the "Catholic" wing and the "positivist" wing of the counterrevolution, and let us recall that, before the Vatican's foolish condemnation of *Action Francaise*, they were allied.

Several reoccuring themes in CotE deserver note. First, there is much effort on the Catholic side to construct a useable past, a good core of the *Ancien Regime* underneath the abuses that deserves to be preserved or resurrected. I don't mean that they falsify history, any more than the imposition of a single narrative on a nation's history must be a falsification; I mean that they felt a need to counter the Enlightenment narrative of a past of nothing but ignorance and oppression brought to an end by the glorious rule of revolutionaries. Authors identify what they see as key aspects of the ancient French constitution. For Maistre, it is theocracy, and was even before the French became Christian. For Bonald, it is familism: the state regards families rather than individuals. A familiy itself holds a title of nobility, and such titles are (or rather should have been) tied to duties. Le Play also points to the family, but to its independence. The norm is that each family has a separate house. (He congratulates the West on not falling into the shame of rental apartment buildings.) He also credits the West with hitting the sweet spot in family inheritance with the so-called "stem family", in which family patrimonies are preserved by inheritance going to one brother, while other brothers make their own way, giving them a spur to innovation while leaving a family support mechanism they can come back to. For Keller and la Tour du Pin, it is the medieval corporate structure, in which every way of life had a publicly and ecclesiastically sanctioned organization to give it voice and order, that should inspire us.

Eugene Genovese credited American Southern conservatives with giving due consideration to the kind of economic base they would need to support the traditional society they wanted. In this, he says they were unlike modern conservatives. The French Right certainly also deserves credit for its attention to such basic issues. For Bonald and Le Play, the attention was on preserving France's agrarian way of life, and primogeniture as part of that life. By the time of Keller and la Tour du Pin, this was apparently a lost cause, and they decided that the pressing task was to rescue the urban prolitariate. Their proposed associations/corporations would be more like medieval guilds than modern labor unions in that they would be mandatory across a trade, they would set quality and training standards, they would have social and mutual-help functions, and they would have a part in the government.

Most of the space in TFR is given over to Barres and Maurras. Of all the writers included, Barres comes closest, in his writings on the Dreyfus Affair, to the anti-universalism that supposedly drives the French Right. He does think that the intellectuals' commitment to Kantian universalism leads them to ignore the need to protect the French nation's interests and character. I expect he was right that very few

Dreyfusards gave a fig whether Dreyfus was innocent or guilty; they just saw in the case an opportunity to humiliate the nation, eviscerate the army, and persecute the Church. Barres makes it clear that he himself doesn't care. He would rather Dreyfus had never been tried, or that the case had never been revisited; either would be better than letting the nation tear itself up about it.

The exerpts from Maurras in TFR are worth whatever you pay for the book in itself. Especially good is "Dictator and King", his royalist manifesto. A healthy constitution, Maurras says, should have authority at the top and freedom at the bottom, but the Third Republic had reversed this, with a centralized bureaucratic despotism controling every aspect of a citizen's life, while at the highest level of government is a parliamentary anarchy where no one thinks past the next election. In his ideal order, citizens would govern most of their own affairs through local associations, while a strong king would revitalize the army, suppress usury, and look to the common good.

The selections are not of uniformly high quality. In CotE, Chateaubriand's contribution and half of Bonalds', are rather forgettable. In TFR, we have Drumont's rant against the Jews, which combines some reasonable criticisms that Rightest still make against this people with bizarre claims, such as that Jew's have a particular stink. Georges Sorel is included, even though he was a far-Left wacko, presumably because his writings on violence and the social myth sounded fascist to the editor.

The counter-revolutionaries made some solid points, but they seem to have overstated their case. Nearly to a man, they predicted that liberal rule would bring the French nation, and the other nations of the West, to total ruin. France would be prey to foreign powers. The middle class would disappear and the working class be immiserated to the point of destitution. This obviously hasn't happened (although Keller's prediction that low-paid Chinese would become the world's workforce has come disturbingly close). Liberalism is obviously not as suicidal as the counter-revolution imagined. It did prove able to counter foreign threats–indeed, rival Leftist powers, the USA and USSR, were able to divide the world between them in 1945–and it proved able to check capitalism's worst excesses, partly by adopting some of the measures recommended in CotE. Today, many reactionaries are still predicting liberalism's imminant self-destruction. We should learn a lesson from past generations and avoid predictions that will someday make us look foolish.

Every conservative should read these books. It is important for us to reclaim our past, a past that the mainstream has forgotten and the Burkeans have deliberately sidelined. Conservatives should know that it is not true that we have failed to critique liberal economic systems or to pose our alternatives. We perhaps cannot adopt corporatism wholesale–economic policy must be reevaluated each generation because of changing circumstances–but we do have examples of how conservatives have reasoned about these issues in the past. Conservatives should know how untrue is the picture painted by hostile historians (including Catholic ones) of Charles Maurras, who was neither an irrationalist, nor a lunatic, nor an aspiring tyrant. One will not find here a complete exposition of the conservative philosophy, for the reason that no one (including Burke) has yet produced such a thing. As I've said before, the Right has yet to produce its equivalent to John Rawls. That can't happen, though, until all the materials that must go into such a system have been gathered up, and the input of the French Right will be indispensible.

The meaning of conservatism

By Roger Scruton, 1980

One of the snares for a conservative movement—and one into which they have repeatedly fallen—is to forget what conservatism actually is and to embrace some kind of liberalism (e.g. "small government" or "free market") in its stead. It's quite depressing. One never sees a liberal party embrace conservatism in a fit of confusion. I suppose this is because real conservatism is so unpopular: there are a hundred idiots determined to advance "freedom", "equality", and "democracy" for every man willing to defend the things that make actual life decent. Regardless of the cause, by the late 1970's, the English Conservative Party had definitely drifted into liberalism. In response, the philosopher Roger Scruton wrote this book to recall English conservatives to their true principles. He failed as far as the official Tory line goes—it's as asinine as ever—but he succeeded in establishing contemporary conservative political philosophy.

Scruton gets to the heart of the matter. Conservatism is not about freedom, but about authority; its main preoccupation is not the freedom of individuals but the health of the social organism. The state is not a means to the end of social justice or maximum freedom or anything else; as the representation of the community to itself, the state is an end in itself. In some of the best parts of the book, Scruton considers a whole range of institutions that have this character: they are not means to external ends; rather, their purposes are internal. Examples he gives include the family, schools, and organized sports.

The most important insight of this book is the appraisal of social "surfaces", by which Scruton means roughly what Marxists mean by "ideology"—the way an institution appears from the inside to those who are part of it. Marxists use the idea of ideology disparagingly. For example, the ideology of authority is said to be a "mask" which hides the reality of raw power. Marxists regard the surface as a lie, as something one must see through to deal with the true (economic) realities. Rather than deny the Marxist distinction between "surface" and "depth", Scruton accepts it but switches the focus. Conservatism, he says, is concerned with the "lived surface" of social life. That is, it is concerned with how things appear to those living in society. Does power seem legitimate to them? Does its exercise seem rational? Can each see himself as having a meaningful place in the social order? The Marxist would, of course, be exasperated by this—surely what matters is not how things *seem*, but how things *are*? By making such an insistence, the Marxist would betray his limitations as a materialist. The way people see things is a real fact about the social order, too; often it's a more important one than some purely material facts. A person's sense of his place in the community may have more to do with living a good life than the ultimate truth (if there is such a thing) about the nexus of economic power.

This "affirmation of the surface" was a huge advance in the intellectual articulation of conservatism. It has had a profound effect on my own political thought. Unfortunately, Scruton's subsequent thought has taken what I regard as a dangerous turn. It appears in the appendix added to later editions of this book. Here, Scruton introduces what he thinks of as an anthropologist's viewpoint for evaluating social surfaces. For example, a primitive tribe performs a ritual dance to appease the fire god. The observing anthropologist regards the idea of a fire god as silly, but he realizes that the real purpose of the dance is to increase group cohesion in the tribe. However, this is a truth that must remain hidden from the tribesmen, or the ritual won't work—it depends for its effectiveness on the false understanding. Realizing this, the anthropologist would be careful not to disillusion those he observes. Scruton proceeds to identify the conservative view with that of the sympathetic anthropologist. He claims that the liberal is the one who can't adopt this "third-person" viewpoint but demands that society justify itself in ways that are impossible for it. Now it is the conservative who is fixated on the "depths", though now sociological rather than economic. I think this line of thought, which has grown in importance in Scruton's later works, has unfortunate consequences. It implies that our conscious motivations for engaging in traditional practices are not only poorly expressed, but actually false. They would be forms of manipulation. This would effectively reduce surface consciousness to a means, which is just the fate Scruton had originally intended to defend it against.

The New Science of Politics

By Eric Voegelin, 1952

This short book, originally called *Truth and Representation*, is, in my opinion, the greatest work of political philosophy produced in the twentieth century, and it has had a profound influence on me. Voegelin examines societies by exploring the symbols they use to understand themselves. The very self-consciousness of a people as a distinct group (of which the state is one expression) is one such symbol, the symbol of "existential representation." Whatever else they express, the public institutions of a society (e.g. the state) express the people's existence as an organized group. Of course, most societies see deeper meanings in their organizations than mere existence. Ancient societies see themselves as part of a cosmic order, like the laws of nature or the motions of the stars. This is the symbol of "cosmological representation". The ancient empires saw themselves as representatives of divine truth, and their expansion was thought to spread God's order through the world. It should be pointed out that Voegelin does not regard these symbols as illusions; still less does he see them as tools for the cynical manipulation of the populace. These symbols really do represent the truth about man's place in the world. The order of being which he senses and tries to express through cosmological symbolism is real. However, some symbols express the truth more precisely and more deeply than others. Voegelin calls this advance from vague to more precise symbolism "differentiation". The next moment of differentiation came with the reimagining of society on moral lines in ancient Greece. Rather than order in general, it was now thought that society should conform itself to the order of the soul. At the same time, men began to understand themselves as beings confronted by the demands of morality and justice. Voegelin calls this the "discovery of the soul" and the ideal state was thought to embody the truth of the soul ("psychological truth"). The most complete articulation of the human condition to date came with the arrival of Christianity and its doctrine of grace. Christianity is seen here as a differentiation of the truth of the soul, where now the soul is not only confronted by a divine standard of justice, but transformed through God's initiative. This introduced "soteriological" symbolism into society, so that a new organization, the Church, became the primary social embodiment of the truth of the soul.

There was a danger inherent in the new symbolism, however. The state was almost entirely stripped of its sacral character. There was no longer a "civic theology", so the interests of a temporal polity no longer had any necessary connection to God or one's soul. Only the Church and the holiness of individual souls had this connection. Many men could not stand to have ultimate meanings pushed to such ethereal realms; they demanded a more "solid" congress with the gods. Thus arose Gnosticism, beginning with Joachim of Fiore in the twelfth century, as an attempt to resacralize the temporal sphere. According to Voegelin, the Gnostics attempt to immanentize the Christian eschaton by reimagining the Kingdom of Heaven as a future utopia to be constructed by human effort. All modern revolutionary doctrines, particularly Marxism, can be seen as versions of this Gnostic fallacy. The Gnostic utopia replaces heaven as the ultimate end of mankind, so that any crime or tyranny is justified in realizing it. The burst of chiliastic energy released by Gnosticism may be credited with the rapid advances of the modern world, but they ultimately destroy their own foundation. The Gnostic counterfeit of the Christian eschaton debases and falsifies the truth of the soul, and so it must ultimately erode the human spirit.

Any one page summary of this book will fail to do justice to it. One finds in its pages a study of Sir John Fortescue's theory of the state, an account of Mongol emperor Kuyuk Khan's correspondence with the pope, an analysis of Aeschylus's play The Suppliants, a comparison of Varro, Cicero, and Augustine on civil theology, etc. Most importantly, it should convince readers on two essential points: to understand a society one must understand its symbolization of truth, and understandings of society are intimately connected to understandings of the soul.

The Philosophy of Right

By G.W.F. Hegel, 1821, translation & notes by T.M. Knox, 1952

Hegel's Philosophy of Right is arguably the greatest work of political philosophy produced in modern times. Most of the interesting ideas put forward by liberals, conservatives, and socialists—before and since its publication—are to be found in it. Why then isn't Hegel a fixture of political discussions, the way Marx and Rawls are? That's no mystery to anyone who struggles to actually read this book. While the book is not absolutely unreadable, opaque pronouncements about "the self-actualization of the Concept", "the will in and for itself", "the unrestricted infinity of absolute abstraction", etc come at the reader hard and fast. If you're like me, you'll need to consult Professor Knox's notes after every paragraph and read the main parts at least twice. If you want to understand the logic embodied in the modern state, it is an effort worth making.

For Hegel, the point of public life is freedom, rationality, and self-consciousness—three words which are more or less synonymous for him. Who or what is it that is to be made free, rational, and self-aware? First-time readers are apt to be confused by Hegel's abstract style, which sometimes seems to suggest that some disembodied will is actualizing itself by spinning off political bodies through history. In fact, it is primarily the individuals in the society who are to enjoy freedom and rationality, although the organization of the society itself is both a necessary condition and an expression of the people's freedom and rationality, and so it can be said to, in a sense, enjoy these qualities itself.

How is this supposed to work? Let's start with the lowest meaningful idea of freedom —being able to enforce your will on some domain. We can imagine a society that acknowledges this idea of freedom as one where each person has some recognized private property on which he can impress his decisions. It may be simple, but Hegel sees that this idea of freedom contains a valid insight—that private property gives me an acknowledgement of my own unique will and personality, and that I need this for my self-development. The trouble is that if I just have rights but no responsibilities, then I'm not really free; I'm a slave to my desires, passions, or caprices. The will may be driving the car, but it's still getting directions from the outside. Hegel believes that, for the mind to be really free, it must not only be able to make decisions, it must be able to supply the content of those decisions by itself, i.e. without "outside material" from non-rationally formed desires.

So what kind of content could reason itself (i.e. uncontaminated by self-interest or desire) supply to the will? We might expect to get universal rules and maxims, like Kant's categorical imperative: always act so that your action could be a universal rule. This introduces us to a new idea of freedom and self-consciousness: I am a moral subject who has a conscience and is responsible for his actions. The trouble with this is that it's still too vague. As Hegel points out, just about any act can be self-consistently universalized into a maxim, even if the maxim is something like "always act so as to destroy all life on Earth". All we get is the bare idea of duty, without any way of figuring out my duties in particular. The truth is that I never get up in the morning and think to myself, "Given the current situation of the human race, what is it that somebody needs to be doing?" and then act accordingly. No, when I get out of bed, I get to work on my particular duties. How are these derived?

The answer, of course, is that I find myself in a number of structured communities, each of which has an explicit division of duties which assigns to me particular tasks, and each of which is oriented towards some common good with which I can associate my actions. Hegel calls such a community an ethical substance, and he claims that they are crucial for ethical life (and are, indeed, the very embodiment of ethical life). Unlike the abstract idea of having rights or the abstract idea of having moral duties, the ethical substance is concrete, and it determines what my rights and duties actually, concretely are. It also ties the two together, so that my rights and responsibilities are rationally correlated. The ethical community also reconciles—to some degree—my duties and desires. My love or patriotism for the community allows me to subjectively identify its common good with my own, and objectively it is also true that my good is contained in the common good. Most importantly for Hegel's scheme, an ethical substance allows me to reconcile the universal with the particular. For example, "enforce justice" is a nice universal command of "pure reason", but it's not one that I can personally execute in my day-to-day life. It is something that the State should try to execute, though, and as a member of the state, I can do my bit to enforce justice by doing my own humble public duties. Of course, this reconciliation of universal and particular can only work 1) if my duties really do contribute to some universal, rational goal, and 2) if my duties can be seen by me to be so related to such a goal. That is to say, the organization must be really rational. If it isn't, that's something that should be fixed.

Hegel identifies two ethical substances: the nuclear family and the state. The family is based on the love of the spouses, the complementarity of the sex roles, and the family's corporately-owned property. An aggregate of families buying and selling goods with each other forms a civil society, by which Hegel basically means a market. Through the market, separate families become connected and interdependent. This interdependence is, however, not based on any conscious good will between buyers and sellers; it is an invisible product of the law of supply and demand. As pointed out above, to have a truly ethical life, one's actions must not only serve the common good, but must consciously and visibly serve the common good. The market is "ethicized" by two factors. First, there are the profession-based corporate bodies (i.e. guilds) which promote fraternity within a profession. More importantly, there is the state, which regulates the economy for the public good. The state itself is composed of three branches: the monarch, the legislature, and the executive (which includes the civil service and the judiciary). The monarch is needed to represent the unity of the state's will. The legislature, according to Hegel, should be divided into estates. Thus, farmers are represented by the agricultural deputies, and businessmen by the business deputies. This way, the professional corporations are themselves incorporated into the state so that they can be visibly seen to be ordered to the common good. When a citizen votes, he does so as a member of his profession, not as an atomic individual. This is, I think, an insightful point.

Hegel was not a good writer, and he had some screwy ideas about metaphysics and history, but you shouldn't let that keep you from his incomparable analysis of the modern state.

The Revolt of the Elites and the Betrayal of Democracy

By Christopher Lasch, 1995

Christopher Lasch, who I have elsewhere called the "conservative Marxist", was one of America's most independent thinkers. Like most intellectuals, he started out as a Marxist, mostly (I think) to oppose what he regarded as the dehumanizing effects of wage labor and overspecialization, but his opposition to these things eventually led him to conclusions much different from those of Karl Marx and his followers. By the end of his life, Lasch was calling himself a "populist". Rather than reacting against wage labor by trying to make the government the universal employer, his ideal—which he insisted was the reality in the USA for the first century of its existence—was a nation of independent small property holders, of craftsmen, small farm owners, and the like. Like others who hold this dream, such as Distributists and guild socialists, Lasch has little to say about how we are to recover this state of affairs. The goal of this collection of essays is to describe how the populist ideal was lost and to keep it from being forgotten altogether. United by this theme, the essays in this book cover economic, political, cultural, and even educational issues. They are all relevant because, as Lasch tells it, preindustrial Americans prided themselves for their independence of mind and spirit as well as for not having employers. All of these self-employed laborers were supposed to be educated citizens, real participants in the national political debates. The sharp division between manual and intellectual labor was considered a feature of European despotism. One can then see why Lasch feels compelled to attack two ideas common among his liberal friends and former allies. The first is replacing the goal of dignified labor with the goal of upward mobility. The second is the growing tendency toward rule by experts and judges, based on the belief that the common people are too ignorant or bigoted to make good decisions. Closely connected to this tendency is an excessive emphasis on "objectivity" in the press and in the schools. Lasch thinks that these institutions have made themselves boring by trying to hold themselves above and outside of political and philosophical debate. Even worse, the "objective information" they convey is sometimes just the questionable beliefs of whoever are regarded as "experts". Lasch encourages us to reconsider the interest-generating and knowledge-spreading power of real public debates of the kind we used to have before the "objective" media started directing them.

The essays themselves were originally published separately, and so they can be read independently. *Opportunity in the Promised Land: Social Mobility or the*

Democratization of Competence? is a good summary of the book's main points. In this essay and also *The Common Schools: Horace Mann and the Assault on Imagination*, readers are introduced to the great but unjustly neglected nineteenth century essayist Orestes Brownson. In *Racial Politics in New York: The Attack on Common Standards* Lasch shows real courage in criticizing the post-King civil rights movement. In their mixed promotion of universalism and tribalism, he believes that the liberals have gotten things backwards. Instead of smashing ethnic and cultural enclaves to prevent them from fostering racism, distinct neighborhoods should be preserved as the only genuine embodiment of cultural particularism. On the other hand, liberals do minorities no favors when they attack universal standards as "racist" and sharing the riches of Western culture as "cultural imperialism."

I also recommend the essay *Communitarianism or Populism? The Ethic of Compassion and the Ethic of Respect*; Lasch criticizes communitarianism in ways that I never thought I'd hear come from an alleged man of the Left. First, their claim to oppose both free market capitalism and welfare statism is mostly bogus—all of their hostility is directed towards the former. Second, they surrender to liberal libertinism on issues of family and sex.

> *"The authors of The Good Society assure their readers that they 'do not want to advocate any single form of family life.' It is the 'quality of family life' that matters in their view, not its structure. But quality and structure are not so easily separable. Common sense tells us that children need both fathers and mothers, that they are devastated by divorce, and that they do not flourish in day care centers...We need guidelines, not a general statement of good intentions."*

This has also been my experience with communitarians; they only oppose liberalism on a very abstract level, never on any practical point. Lasch goes on to complain that our obsession with tolerance has led to moral indifference, and one is struck by what a wonderful reactionary he would have made.

The Revolt of the Masses

By Jose Ortega y Gasset, 1930

A century of security and prosperity (the nineteenth, that is) has produced a populace of spoiled brats. That's the main contention of Ortega y Gasset's famous book. The new type, which he calls "mass man", is distinguished above all by ingratitude and complacency. He has grown so used to stable government and a rising standard of living that he has come to imagine that these exist automatically without any human effort. Being oblivious to the effort needed to maintain and run a civilization, he certainly feels no responsibility to contribute to the endeavor, but rather settles for demanding a greater and greater share of the spoils. Mass man has no interest in the science that gives him his technology or in the history and culture that form his civilization. The mass calls on the state to gratify its desires by bullying those who stand in its way, oblivious to the ruin this will eventually bring.

The noble man always serves some good or outside himself and judges himself by a harsh external standard. (*Noblesse oblige*.) Mass man is satisfied with himself as he is. (He has *self-esteem*, we might say.) He has opinions, picked up from the prejudices and buzzwords of his surroundings, on every topic. He has no interest, however, in investigating whether his opinions are actually true. He doesn't feel the need to have what he regards as good reasons, much less to investigate the reasons for and against each view before coming to a decision on a particular issue. He thinks his opinions have value just because they are his. This is only a particularly obnoxious example of mass man's total self-complacency. Experts in narrow technical fields are some of the worst mass men, as their expertise in one field makes them even more smug and incurious in their ignorant appraisals of everything else.

This does indeed sound like an accurate description of the dominant character, at least in the West. However, Ortega y Gasset's recommended solution is catastrophically wrongheaded. To re-moralize Europe, he claims that Europeans need a goal, a project, to inspire them. The best projects he imagines to be the consolidation of peoples into larger and larger aggregates, and so he recommends Europeans devote themselves to European Union. What Ortega doesn't realize is that the process of consolidation is more responsible than any other factor for the creation of mass man. Centralization is a destructive, not a creative force. A dozen cultures, a dozen histories, a dozen governments are reduced to one. At each stage, the locus of decision making and creative activity becomes more remote from the average man. Self-government is only meaningful at the city and county level. Average people can only be involved in maintaining and advancing local culture. To the extent that globalization produces a world culture, or even just a European culture, each of us, unless he is a rare genius, is reduced to being a mere consumer of this culture. The reason mass man is indifferent to the work of maintaining a civilization is because centralization took away his opportunity to contribute so long ago that he no longer remembers what he's missing.

The True and Only Heaven: Progress and its Critics

By Christopher Lasch, 1991

Christopher Lasch is the most unusual of creatures—a conservative Marxist. Like Marx, he hates wage employment and the division of labor, and he blames these things for most of the world's ills. However, among those ills, he is especially bothered by moral and cultural breakdown. Weakening of the family and attacks on "lower middle class" morality horrify him. Lasch thinks that the "bourgeois" morality he admires is disappearing because we have lost the economic order to which it corresponded. This order was one of widespread ownership of productive property: family farms, self-employed artisans and craftsmen, etc. The ownership of productive property fostered discipline and independence; indeed it was once universally believed that the existence of a large wage labor class is incompatible with American freedom, and Lasch thinks there was something to this belief. What most upsets him is that we have lost, not only the reality, but the very ideals of proprietorship and of disciplined excellence in a craft. He accuses both the political left and right of trading this ideal for an ideal of perpetual "progress", understood in the degrading sense of ever higher levels of material consumption.

The bulk of the book is a retelling of key episodes in the social and intellectual history of the United States. Lasch's disenchantment with the contemporary U.S. (including both its political parties) gives him a particularly good perspective for this. He is able to break free from the standard—one might call it the "Whig"—narrative that all of American history was a buildup to today's New Deal managerial capitalist democracy. Instead of the triumphant march of progress, Lasch sees both gains and losses, unheeded warnings and tragically lost opportunities. I found it a most illuminating tour of American history, and I strongly recommend this book to anyone who wants to understand our country more deeply.

Given his perspective, it's not surprising that Lasch gives a good deal of attention to lost causes like populism, syndicalism, guild socialism, and agrarianism. His distillation of recent research on the populist movement is particularly interesting, in particular by showing how populism had been misunderstood by Marxist historians too eager to fit it into their preconceived narratives. Populism was *not* the first stirring of the incipient working class; it was the last stand of the small producer class. What's more, social agitation became much *less* radical once it did come to be dominated by socialists and wage laborers. Unlike the populists, the unions had resigned themselves to the wage labor system, and only wanted to get the workers a larger share of the spoils. In Lasch's retelling, the roads not taken (e.g. syndicalism) get their due attention, and Cassandras like William Cobbett, Orestes Brownson, and G. D. H. Cole get their due respect.

The book also has some pretty easily identifiable villains. In the mid-twentieth century, educated liberals lost faith in the American people. They came to see the mass of their fellow citizens as ignorant, "authoritarian" bigots who needed to have their lives and their beliefs reconstructed by enlightened experts. Thus was born that obnoxious entity, the therapeutic state, where the government tells the people what to believe rather than vice versa. Lasch reviews the role of thinkers like Robert Lynd, Thurman Arnold, Gunnar Myrdal, and Theodor Adorno in bringing about this therapeutic mentality.

Finally, let me especially recommend the chapter on the Civil Rights Movement. According to Lasch's analysis, the movement was successful in the south because it was build on the strong black communities organized around the black churches. The movement floundered when Martin Luther King began agitating in Chicago and found no such social capital to build upon. Instead of making an attempt to build social capital in the ghetto, King turned left—essentially turning into a communist—and began demanding that the government step in to smash white ethnic communities and radically redistribute the country's resources. In this, King was betraying his earlier and better instincts.

No question about it—you should get this book.

What is the West?

By Philippe Nemo, 2004

What is the distinctive characteristic of Western civilization? According to Philippe Nemo, the West is defined by liberalism, by which he means classical liberalism: democracy, freedom of speech, capitalism, etc. The bulk of the book is a description of five historical "episodes" that contributed decisively to the West's character: ancient Greece (which gave us science and citizenship), ancient Rome (which gave us the rule of law), ancient Israel (which gave us our moral code), the papal revolution (what most people call the "Investiture controversy", which produced the first synthesis of Greek and Jewish culture and began the desacralization of the state), and the liberal revolutions proper of the eighteenth and nineteenth centuries.

This equation of Western civilization with classical liberalism raises several questions. Are the five episodes events in the life of one civilization? Is this the story of an essentially liberal society articulating its essence more and more fully? Or did western society only come into existence with universal suffrage and the free market? The latter would appear to be Nemo's opinion, since he claims that Russia, Israel, and Latin America do not belong to the West because they are insufficiently liberal. But couldn't other civilizations adopt liberalism? If so, would they lose their own identities and become Western? Nemo does address this issue. He believes western liberalism has universal value. However, it only functions in a society with certain ethical beliefs. In the West, these were originally provided by the Jewish and Christian religions; in other societies, something else may play this role. Nemo also acknowledges that other civilizations have strongly communal ethical systems, and that these communal elements have value. He hopes for a dialog of civilizations leading to a synthesis containing the best of each. In this dialog, however, the West only offers individualism. Nemo doesn't mention that Christendom had its own communitarian tradition before it was murdered by liberalism.

I'd say the highlight of this book is chapter five, Nemo's discussion of liberal democracy. He gives an intriguing account of the difference between classical liberalism and its rivals: conservatism and socialism. Liberalism, in Nemo's view, is based on spontaneous order which emerges from the free actions of a multitude of individuals: the free market of goods and ideas being quintessential examples. Conservatives want to organize society according to natural orders, like the family. Socialists believe in artificial order, a society directed by central planning toward ideologically fixed goals. Nemo thinks that spontaneous order is both more efficient than and morally superior to its rivals. The former may be true, but I question the latter. There is a reason those on the "right" and the "left" are disgusted by a society organized on pluralistic, free market principles. Natural and artificial orders address man as a rational and moral being by illuminating his duties; the market treats man like a walking stomach and addresses him only through his private desires.

The Works of Joseph de Maistre

Selected, Translated, and Introduced by Jack Livery, 1965

De Maistre is probably the most famous continental counter-revolutionary. He has a reputation as being the crazy reactionary in comparison with Edmund Burke, his more moderate-seeming English equivalent. Like Burke, de Maistre is concerned with defending long-established customs against reckless innovation. However, while Burke's defense of tradition was very general, de Maistre focuses almost exclusively in his political writings on the issue of authority. He regards established political sovereignty as literally miraculous. To be superior to men's wills, it must not be the product of men's wills, but rather the work of God through long history. *Philosophes* and constitution-writers will thus be unable to replace what they are destroying.

De Maistre was a strong supporter of papal authority. He preferred the pope as a check on the despotism of princes to a right of rebellion on the part of subjects. When the pope dispenses the people from their duty to obey the temporal sovereign, he implicitly recognizes the normal validity of this duty. De Maistre also devoted a great deal of thought to theodicity in his *Saint Petersburg Dialogues*. All suffering, he believes, is a punishment for sin. However, rather than punishing individuals for their personal sins in this life—an arrangement that de Maistre thinks would render virtue meaningless— God punishes the human race as a whole. The sacrificial offering of the innocent for the guilty is, he believes, a truth recognized by all religions. The *Dialogues* also contain an extended attack on the writings of John Locke and a defense of the existence of innate ideas, by which de Maistre seems to mean ideas that cannot be derived from the senses. It is perhaps a sign that Kant's influence was not yet felt outside of Germany that these writings assume that to prove an idea is innate is to prove that it is absolutely true.

To summarize these writings is to miss the main attraction, which is the striking ways that de Maistre manages to express his delightfully grim view of the world. Here is a sample:

> *Government is a true religion; it has its dogmas, its mysteries, its priests; to submit it to individual discussion is to destroy it; it has life only through the national mind...What is patriotism? It is this*

national mind of which I am speaking; it is individual abnegation. Faith and patriotism are the two great thaumaturges of the world... Do not talk to them of scrutiny, choice, discussion, for they will say that you blaspheme. They know only two words, submission and belief; with these two levers, they raise the world.

People complain of the despotism of princes; they ought to complain of the despotism of man. We are all born despots, from the most absolute monarch in Asia to the infant who smothers a bird with its hand for the pleasure of seeing that there exists in the world a being weaker than itself.

Thus is worked out, from maggots up to man, the universal law of the violent destruction of living beings. The whole earth, continually steeped in blood, is nothing but an immense altar on which every living thing must be sacrificed without end, without restraint, without respite until the consummation of the world...

And yet all grandeur, all power, all subordination rests on the executioner: he is the horror and the bond of human association. Remove this incomprehensible agent from the world, and at that very moment order gives way to chaos, thrones topple, and society disappears.

I thank God for my ignorance still more than for my knowledge; for my knowledge is mine, at least in part, and in consequence I cannot be sure that it is good, but my ignorance, at least that of which I am speaking, is His, therefore I trust it fully.

Book Reviews: Religion

A Key to the Doctrine of the Eucharist

By Abbot Vonier, 1925

This is the best theological investigation I have found on the idea of a sacrament, of God acting through sensible signs. In contrast to what one might expect from a book on this subject, the author—a French-English Thomist—has an almost mathematical insistence on precision. Catholics who for years been told nothing but how they should *feel* about this or that doctrine (rather than what it actually *means*) will find this insistence on clarity and rigor as refreshing as I did.

The "key" promised in the title is the idea of a sacrament as a sign that does exactly what it signifies, nothing more and nothing less. Vonier discourages any understanding of a sacrament which would see the ritual appearance as a sort of mask underneath which God does something essentially unrelated to what is seen and heard. Instead, he emphasizes the following points:

1. The unity of sign and reality. According to Vonier, God's action in a sacrament is to make the sign be true. "*The sacrament must signify in words and deeds and things...to the point where it will be necessary, if a lie is to be avoided, that the sacrament should even contain what it signifies...The inward reality of the sacrament is the prolongation of* [its] *signification...*"

2. The difference between sacramental and natural efficacy. In a sacrament, God acts through signs; He does not give a natural being an intrinsic hidden power commensurate with the sacrament's effect. The sacramental world is "*reality without fixity of being.*"

3. Each sacrament signifies the past (Christ's passion), the present (the grace being communicated), and the future (the hope of eternal life). A non-sacramental gift of grace, wonderful though it is, does not refer to anything outside itself. In the sacraments, however, "*historical events of centuries ago are renewed, and we anticipate the future in a very real way.*"

4. The sacraments glorify God as well as aiding man. "*Let us cling to the old maxim* '[sacraments are for the sake of man]', *provided we realize that nothing is so useful to man as to adore God...We must ever remember that the sacrament is a res sacra—a sacred thing—given to man so as to enable him to approach God...In the sacramental system man is active, not only passive; in it he gives back to God God's own gifts.*"

Applying these points to the case of the Eucharist, Vonier points out

1. It is the presence of Christ's Body and Blood that are the direct "divine prolongation" of the Eucharistic ritual, and the ritual separation of the Body and Blood constitutes the sacrifice because it recalls Christ's sacrifice on Calvary. Jesus' Soul and Divinity are also present in the Eucharist, but by concomitance, i.e. because they are united to His Body and Blood. Therefore, if one of the Apostles had celebrated the Eucharist on Holy Saturday, while Jesus was dead, His human Soul would not have been present in the host, because it was separated from His body.

2. Vonier insists that Jesus is present under the accidents of the transubstantiated host in a different "mode of being" than that of His natural glorified Body. I'll admit that I'm not entirely sure what Vonier means by this. I found the two chapters on transubstantiation somewhat vague and confusing, in marked contrast to the rest of the book.

3. The Eucharist is not a new sacrament to make up for some kind of deficiency in Christ's sacrifice on Calvary. That sacrifice was the one and only offering needed for our salvation. In the Eucharist, this one unique sacrifice is re-presented, i.e. made present. Such a thing would be nonsense from a natural point of view, but it is a natural thing for a sacrament.

4. In the Blessed Sacrament, Christians share in Christ's sacrifice. The Eucharist is given to man not only to heal his soul, but to satisfy his desire to do justice to God. In this sacrament, the Church is given a sacrifice worthy to be offered to God.

The Fullness of Being and A Most Unlikely God

By Barry Miller, 2002 and 1996, respectively

If you're going to do analytic philosophy of religion, this is how you do it. These two books form part of a trilogy in which Dr. Miller provides a powerful, modern restatement of the claims of classical theistic metaphysics. (I haven't yet been able to get access to the other book, *From Existence to God*.) In most cases, his arguments vindicate the positions of Ibn Sina and Thomas Aquinas, but to me at least, Miller's reasoning seems clearer and more precise. To sum up Miller's main points,

1. He argues that existence is a real property of individuals. In this, he dissents from the popular view, going back to Frege, which regards existence as a second-order property, i.e. a property about properties, namely, how many times they are instantiated. On the contrary, Miller argues, we certainly do refer to the existence or nonexistence of individuals, not just the instantiation of properties. The alleged paradoxes attending this view are shown to be only apparent.

2. Existence is unlike all other properties, though. Other properties inhere in a subject, i.e. they add something to a subject which is logically prior to them. Existence can't be like that, since there is no subject until it exists. In fact, Miller argues that one cannot even speak of an individual (as opposed to a bundle of properties) until he exists. Therefore, the subject is logically posterior to its existence, so the metaphor of "inherence" is inappropriate. In its place, Miller proposes the metaphor of a bound: the subject (e.g. Socrates) bounds or limits his existence. His existence gives the subject its actuality; the subject gives its existence individuality.

3. Existence is the source of all actuality: there is not one act of existence—the same for all beings—and then other acts on top of it. Socrates' existence is that by which he exists, that by which he is a man, that by which he is wise, etc.

4. One can meaningfully consider the limit case of unbounded existence, an existence that doesn't need a bound to be individuated. Miller claims this is equivalent to the limit case of a bound with its own actuality. This limit-case being is, of course, God, the only subject who is identical with His existence.

5. Miller emphasizes the difference between a limit simpliciter and a limit case. In the former case, the limit of a series is the member of the series; in the latter case it is not. As an example of the latter, the limit case of a series of circles of diminishing radius is a point, an entity which is not itself a circle. God is a limit case of existence, and so he is not just greater, but radically different from other existents. This distinction between types of limits allows Miller to explain some otherwise perplexing aspects of Divine Simplicity. This doctrine asserts that God is Subsistent Existence, Subsistent Goodness, Subsistent Power, etc, and furthermore that all of these properties are identical in Him. How can this be, since existence, goodness, and power are obviously different things? They are indeed different, but that doesn't mean that their limit cases have to be. For example, a point is the limit case of shrinking circles, but it's also the limit case of shrinking rectangles, even though circles and rectangles are different for any finite size.

6. I quite like the discussion of God's power. According to Miller, greater power means being to create from less reliance on previously finished material, and its limit case is creation ex nihilo. Here we see a clear case where the limit is radically different from the members of the series leading up to it. God should not be said to act on things, as if things had existence and propensities prior to his creative action. Instead of "God causes x to do y", one should say "God causes (x does y)". Formulated this way, it is easier to see how God can be the primary cause of all actions without compromising the existence of secondary causes, even those that are free acts.

7. One of the big challenges to Divine Simplicity comes from the fact that God has knowledge about contingent things, i.e. the universe that He freely created. God necessarily knows about Himself and contingently knows about the universe. As the challenge goes, since the former act of knowledge is necessary and the latter is contingent, they must be separate acts of knowledge. Therefore, God has multiple acts and is not simple. One can make a similar argument based on God's necessary will of His own God and His contingent will to create the universe. Miller, on the contrary, sticks by the assertion that God has one act of knowledge that includes both Himself and all of His creative acts, and similarly one act of will that wills both Himself and the universe. Thus, if the possible universes are A, B, C, etc, then the possibilities for God's knowledge and will are (Himself and A), (Himself and B), (Himself and C), etc. While it is a contingent truth that God wills to create our universe, we can't infer from this that He wills our universe in a contingent way, as if He has an unrealized ability to will something else instead. Unrealized abilities imply potentiality, and Miller will admit none of this in God. Instead, he is willing to say that God does not have abilities,

strictly speaking. He has free will, but not choice. It is impossible that we could change His mind.

I myself remain undecided on the strong version of Divine Simplicity embraced by the scholastics. I'm not entirely convinced that it is necessary. On the other hand, these books have convinced me that the doctrine does not lead to the paradoxes and contradictions that might seem to follow from it. I also liked, and largely agree with, the analysis of existence put forth. My disagreements are on fairly minor points. I disagree with the assertion in *The Fullness of Being* that matter can come into existence with no cause whatsoever; I will argue elsewhere that this is a philosophical misinterpretation of quantum mechanics. Also, in *A Most Unlikely God*, after demonstrating that God causes free actions, Miller tries to excuse Him for responsibility for evil actions by saying that it is the intention, rather than the act itself, that causes the evil. However, this doesn't help at all, since a wrongdoer's intention is also an act, albeit a mental one, and hence also an effect of God's creation. God is ultimately responsible for evil actions; let's just deal with it.

Discovering God

By Rodney Stark, 2007

This is a very nice and readable introduction to the history of religion for those with no prior knowledge of the subject. Stark discusses the studies of anthropologists on primitive religions, giving particular emphasis to the findings of Andrew Lang and Wilhelm Schmidt, which suggest that the most primitive religions include belief in a supreme ("High") God, and they are neither crude nor amoral. Stark reviews the major world religions, focusing particularly on the archeological and historical evidence regarding their origins. Unlike most sociologists of religion, Stark seems to delight in showing ancient scriptures to be more reliable than their ill-informed nineteenth and twentieth century detractors. So, for example, some used to say, with supreme confidence backed by no evidence whatsoever, that Confucius, Buddha, Jesus, or Muhammad never really existed, or that our records of them are totally unreliable. Stark marshals the evidence to put these claims to rest. In discussing primitive, historical, or modern believers, he always questions explanations that assume the people in question to be total idiots. He also likes to attack popular misconceptions, for example by showing that pagans and Muslims could be just as hostile to Jews as Christians could be.

The limitations of this book come from the ideas Stark does use to explain religious history. I appreciate his respect for believers. (Stark seems to be a deist himself.) One of his recurring claims is that humanity might not be just inventing new conceptions of an imaginary God, but rather discovering better conceptions of a real God; some at least of his subjects, he says, might have had genuine revelations. The actual explanatory apparatus used in the book, though, suggests that people tend to accept whatever image of God is most psychologically appealing or socially advantageous. These are the reasons he gives, for example, for the triumphs of polytheism and of Christianity. Stark is also big on economic models of religion, and he thinks that religions are only healthy in a pluralist environment, where they are forced to compete with rival religions. Of course, there can be little evidence of this from pre-modern societies, since, for example, the ancient Babylonians and the medieval Catholics didn't carry out surveys to see if they were really as godless as Stark thinks they were. More importantly, I think he concerns himself too much with agitation and proclamation, not enough on taken-for-granted belief. For example, nobody doubts that it's wrong to eat babies, and so nobody talks about it. People would only start loudly embracing this belief if other people were to publicly question it. What established religions have going for them is this sense of being part of the eternal order of the world and being infused in every part of public life. One objections Stark notes is that Western Europe is today a godless place even though freedom for religious entrepreneurship is officially allowed. He replies by citing a study by Grim and Finke which rates countries by their degree of religious freedom and lack of favoritism for one religion. They find most European countries to be no freer or more neutral than Afghanistan. To me, this suggests that the index being used is crazy. I could only justify it by claiming that atheism is as established in the EU as Islam is in Afghanistan, and unfortunately establishment doesn't seem to do any harm to atheism.

God, Freedom, and Evil

By Alvin Plantinga

Alvin Plantinga is one of the better-known analytic philosophers of religion. The distinguishing feature of analytic philosophy, as far as I can tell, is an annoying insistence on labeling everything with letters—I suppose to make philosophy look like mathematics. Sure enough, in this book one has to slog through a lot of prose like "S is included in W and includes neither P's performing A nor P's restraining from performing A". It's not too hard to mentally translate this into regular English. Still, I've yet to encounter a philosophical problem where pseudo-math-speak works better than plain English.

In this book, Plantinga addresses two of the classical problems of natural theology: theodicy and the ontological argument. The first part analyses a project of what he calls "natural atheology", namely, can one use the existence of evil to disprove the existence of an omnipotent, benevolent God. Plantinga sets out to show that one cannot. His goal is not to explain why God really does allow evil; he only wants to show that the propositions "God exists", "He is all-powerful", "He is morally perfect", and "There is evil in the world" don't contradict each other. To establish this, he only has to provide some possible scenario in which all are true. His solution is a variation on the famous free will argument. This argument says that God allows evil in the world as a necessary consequence of creating beings with free will. Having free creatures in the world is a very great good, and by definition even an omnipotent being cannot control a will without it ceasing to be free. He considers an objection: since God is omniscient, He knows what every person's free choices in every situation will be. So why didn't He just pick to create precisely those people and those situations such that—of their own free will—no one ever happens to sin? Plantinga introduces the concept of "transworld depravity". A person is transworld depraved if he will freely sin at some point in every possible world in which he exists. It is possible, Plantinga argues, that everyone has transworld depravity, in which case even God couldn't create a world with free rational creatures and without sin. Since this is possible, we can't say that the existence of evil is inconsistent with the existence of God. Plantinga also briefly questions the belief that God is morally constrained to create the best-possible universe, because it is doubtful that a best-possible universe can even be imagined. (You could always imagine adding more good things to it.) Of course, he doesn't stress this point, because transworld depravity allows him to argue that maybe this really is as good as things could be.

Plantinga's natural theology project is the ontological argument. After quickly reviewing and dismissing the cosmological and teleological arguments, he comes to Anslem's famous idea: God, the greatest possible being, must necessarily exist, because existence is a necessary quality of greatness. The ontological argument certainly sounds like a ridiculous piece of sophistry, but philosophers are still finding new subtleties to it. Most of the famous arguments against ontological-class arguments (including, as Plantinga explains, Kant's) are question-begging. Other philosophers have set to work to fix the proof and make from it a really valid proof of God's existence. One such attempt was made by Norman Malcolm, who suggested the following: the existence of a greatest possible being is possible, i.e. He exists in some universe. Now, necessary existence is one aspect of maximal greatness. Therefore, in some possible world, there is a God who exists in all possible worlds, including ours. Plantinga points out that this version only proves that a being exists in our world that has the properties of God in the possible world. I don't think it would be too hard to argue that if God exists in a given world, that he carries his Godly properties with Him. Instead Plantinga restates the argument so that this comes directly from the proof. His trick is to switch from talking about possible beings to talking about qualities, in particular the quality of "maximal greatness"—the property of having the maximal degree of all excellences in every possible world. The premise of the proof is that there is a possible world in which maximal greatness is instantiated, from which it pretty easily follows that this being exists in the actual world. Plantinga admits that this proof probably won't convince many atheists, because they can just deny the premise. I myself agree that a lot of work would have to be done even to make it plausible to non-theists.

This book is a worthwhile contribution to the philosophy of religion, but I wouldn't recommend it to someone just starting on the subject. The writing style is unnecessarily complicated, the conclusions are rather meager (atheism isn't necessarily true, and theism isn't necessarily false), and the issues discussed are not necessarily the most interesting ones.

Islam and the Destiny of Man

By Gai Eaton, 1985

I found this book by accident roaming through the library, but I'm very glad that I did. This book is an ideal introduction to the religion and civilization of Islam. The author, Gai Eaton, is a western convert to Islam with an obvious love for his new faith, but with a marked respect for the other Abrahamic religions as well. In fact, one of the attractive features of this book is that Eaton realizes that Christians aren't his primary enemies. One of the few rebukes in this generous book is directed at liberal Muslims who, he says, are stripping away what they imagine to be impurities in Muslim society and replacing them with western Marxism. He thinks that, if the Israel-Palestine conflict had not distorted the perspective of so many of his co-religionists, it would be obvious that Islam should stand with the United States against the godless Soviets, and with the Christians against revolutionaries of all sorts. His respect for Christianity allows him to make some interesting observations. For example

> *As* [others] *have pointed out, the only legitimate comparison would be between the Prophet and Mary on the one hand and on the other between the Quran and Jesus. For Christians the Word was made flesh, whereas for Muslims it took earthly shape in the form of a book, and the recitation of the Quran in the ritual prayer fulfils the same function as the Eucharist in Christianity; at the same time, Mary gave birth to Jesus without passing on to him any taint of earthly sin, and Muhammad acted as a channel for the Word without lending it any taint of merely human wisdom.*

Speaking of the Quran, we have all heard that Muslims regard only the Quran in Arabic as the inspired word of God, and that one can't really understand it in translation. Eaton explains why this is. Every Arabic word has a verbal root of consisting of three consonants. One forms a word by taking a root and then adding vowels, prefixes, and suffixes. All of the words built up from a particular root are understood to be related to each other as variations on a theme. Therefore, each Arabic line of the Quran contains allusions, built into the word structure itself, which a translation couldn't hope to capture.

Islamic civilization desires that every aspect of life should be placed under God's sovereignty. According to Eaton, Muslims reject the idea of a secular realm:

> *...the nearest equivalent we can find in the West to a society of this type is the monastic community...One of the things that Christians and occidentals in general seldom understand is this mighty effort, this jihad, waged to prevent any element of earthly life from escaping and taking on a separate existence of its own, or flying off...into the empty space which we call the secular or profane realm. Even men and women quite lacking in natural piety are, through integration into this theocentric community, carried along the road which leads to salvation, their daily lives penetrated by a transcendent perspective which, as individuals, they may be incapable of perceiving, let alone of understanding.*

Eaton claims that the desire to affirm God's sovereignty also explains why the occasionalism of Al-Ash'ari has been so popular among Muslim philosophers. To admit secondary causes and "laws of nature" would invite the danger of giving things a separate intelligibility apart from God. Eaton is even pleased that Islam has not "succumbed" to science like the West.

These are just a few of the fascinating observations in this book. Go out and buy it now so that you too can learn to admire the magnificent religion and civilization of Islam.

Islam in the World

By Malise Ruthven

This is the best book on Islam written by a non-Muslim that I have found. The trouble with many books on Islam–like the awful ones by Karen Armstrong–is that they're not about Islam at all. They present an idealized image of Islamic society and then use that image as a stick to beat the Catholic Church (their real object of interest) with. We've all heard about how enlightened, literate, diverse, tolerant, creative, peaceful, etc, etc medieval Islam supposedly was compared to you know who. Ruthven doesn't seem to have an agenda in this book; her view of Islam is generally positive, but not apologetic. She doesn't hide or excuse aspects of historical Muslim societies that we would find objectionable, but her focus is, as it should be, on understanding Islam rather than judging it by a foreign liberal standard.

Ruthven goes through the whole history of the Muslim umma. Along the way, she makes some fascinating observations. First, she is quite frank about Sunni orthodoxy's connection to occasionalism (God as the only real cause) and divine comman ethics (things are wrong just because God says so). I mention this because you'll remember how a few years ago everyone said the pope was an idiot for making the same observations. Second, as I've mentioned before, she claims that Shari'a is more individualistic than Western law. In particular, Muslims reject the construction of legal personality, i.e. of the State, the Church, or a business corporation as a legal person that can own property and make decisions for which it, rather than its members, is responsible. This, she speculates, comes from the more corporate nature of the Catholic religion, in which we are saved, not in isolation, but through membership in the mystical body of Christ. Third, after making the commonplace observation that Muslims don't separate "church" and "state" (and how could they, given that they don't have either in our sense?), she points out that they do have a somewhat comparable separation, at least since the end of the caliphate and largely before: namely, the separation between law and politics. The law (shari'a) is given directly by God, and earthly rulers have no right to usurp His place by assuming a directly legislative role. Rulers are accepted for practical reasons (keeping the peace), but they claim very little divine sanction, certainly nothing like divine right. Fourth, she explains the role of Sufi practices in the Muslim world. In fact, she thinks the revival of Sufism is the cure to Islamism. Westerners tend to imagine Sufis as New Age hippie-like figures. While there was a little of that in the beginning, Sufism was brought within the orthodox fold by Al-Ghazali, who showed how the exterior fulfillment of Shari'a law is to be combined with interior love and reverence for God. Fifth, Ruthven relates the rise of Islamic modernists. Their shenanigans will sould very familiar to Christians; Islam supposedly has a bland inner meaning of inner niceness which must be separated from the 7th-century cultural trappings, which include everything (distinct gender roles, etc) that 20th-century liberals don't like. 7th-century Arabic culture is not normative, but 20th-century American culture is. You know the drill.

The last page is a bit disappointing. Ruthven expresses hope that Islam will make peace with modernity because it could be used to encourage responsible treatment of the environment. It's not clear why we need Islam for that. I think Muhammed has more important things to say to us.

Metaphysics

By Aristotle

This is one of the most important books ever written, but my experience has been that a good deal of the literature on Aristotle either mistakes his beliefs or at least doesn't quite appreciate the motivations behind his ideas. Therefore, I'm going to explain the Metaphysics to you. As I've found, there's no substitute for the actual text, so I recommend the Penguin Classics translation by Hugh Lawson-Tancred as the clearest, best organized English version. Be warned that my understanding of Aristotle's position is very different from the one given in Lawson-Tancred's introduction.

What is the most fundamental reality? What things are really real? By Aristotle's time, there were two popular answers. There was the materialist answer: matter is the only ultimate reality. "You" are really just a heap of atoms that we imagine to be a distinct thing. The other answer was given by Plato: what are ultimately real are ideas. This may sound crazy, but think about it. An idea like "Humanity" has a more solid existence than an individual person like you. "Humanity" exists eternally and necessarily, which is more than can be said for you. Also, there obviously couldn't be individual humans if there was no such idea as "Humanity", so individual material things seem to depend on their ideas, a fact that makes the ideas "more real". Aristotle disagrees with both of these positions. He spends a lot of space attacking Plato's theory of ideas. Plato seemed to think of ideas as separate beings that exist independently of their instantiations. But if you and "Humanity" are two separate beings, it's hard to explain the relationship between the two. Plato says that you "participate" in "Humanity", but he never explains what that means. In fact, Aristotle claims that the idea of separate forms explains nothing; it just postulates a secondary world in addition to our physical one, a world filled with things like the idea of justice, the idea of grass, the idea of headaches, etc.

Aristotle also disagrees with the materialist position. His reason, although he doesn't explain it very clearly, is the key to his thought. The materialists say that the world is just made out of stuff—there are a certain number of atoms in each place, and that's all to be said about anything. Aristotle points out that the world doesn't just have stuff; it also has things. What do I mean by a thing? The best example would be a biological organism, say a cat. A cat certainly isn't just a bunch of atoms that we have arbitrarily decided to refer to as a single thing. We think of a cat as a single thing because it has a real principle of unity. It is made of atoms, but these atoms are united by being engaged in a single pattern. This pattern, the life processes of the cat, can continue—

and continue as the same pattern—even as the matter of the cat changes through digestion and excretion. The world is made of things (Aristotle uses the word "*substance*"), and things are marked by the property of having unity (which Aristotle calls "*thisness*"—note that he means something entirely different from what Duns Scotus means by this word). No explanation of reality can be right that ignores things.

Aristotle says that the way to understand things/substances is to realize that both the materialists and the Platonists were partly right. A substance is a combination: it has a principle of unity, called a "form" or "essence", which is like one of Plato's ideas except that it exists only as part of the substance. Substances also have matter, the material in which the form instantiates itself. So what makes something a substance, ultimately? A substance is an instantiation of an essence. The essence is what gives the substance unity, what makes it identifiably one thing. The essence also makes it possible for a substance to change in various ways while still remaining its identity through time. So Aristotle can and does summarize his metaphysics with the following formula: being = substance = essence. Unfortunately, when he says things like "being is essence", it tends to cause confusion. People think that Aristotle is saying that essences are like Plato's ideas and that they exist on their own apart from the substances that "participate" in them. If this were what he meant, Aristotle would look pretty silly for criticizing Plato so harshly and then adopting basically the same theory. But this isn't what Aristotle means. He means that a substance is an instantiation of an essence.

So I am an instantiation of the essence "man". On the other hand, I'm obviously very distinct from the essence "man". I have all sorts of qualities, like the fact that I'm sitting down and the fact that I'm dressed, that are *inessential* i.e. the essence "man" doesn't specify anything about my clothing or by body position one way or the other. On the other hand, I don't have all that is implied by my essence. Rationality is an essential human trait, and one that I often fail to exhibit. My eyesight is bad, which means that my eyes aren't behaving the way that my essence allows me to infer that they should. I do not fully actualize the essence "man", although I actualize it enough that it's clearly my essence, i.e. the essence by which to judge and understand me. There must be a principle which separates being from essence. Aristotle identifies this principle, although he doesn't quite realize that it represents a "gap" between substance and essence. The principle is called "potency" or "potentiality". Basically, it means that something could be different in some way or other while still keeping the same identity and essence. In material things, Aristotle identifies matter with potency and form with "act" (i.e. actualization of essence).

Are all beings material beings? Not according to Aristotle. There is also one or several beings that are pure act and hence nonmaterial. (No being could be pure potency.) The *Metaphysics* argues that the ultimate source of change in the universe must be such a being, an Unmoved Mover that drives the action in the world. The argument given is the first clear formulation of the cosmological argument for the existence of God.

Reading this book is a big investment of time and effort. You will often find yourself flipping back and forth between the text and the editor's notes, hoping for some help. Still, if you're interested in these questions, it's worth it. In my opinion, the Aristotelian position is basically true.

On the Incarnation

By Athanasius of Alexandria

Each Christmas, I re-read a bit of St. Athanasius's brilliant but short On the Incarnation to get me in the holiday mood. Some things that jumped out at me this time:

> *For the solidarity of mankind is such that, by virtue of the Word's indwelling in a single human body, the corruption which goes with death has lost its power over all. You know how it is when some great king enters a large city and dwells in one of its houses; because of his dwelling in that single house, the whole city is honored, and enemies and robbers cease to molest it. So it is with the King of all...*

We have recently had cause to discuss this solidarity of mankind in the context of original sin. Athanasius points to the more important application of this principle to our collective redemption.

> *When God the Almighty was making mankind through His own Word, He percieved that they, owing to the limitation of their nature, could not of themselves have any knowledge of the Artificer, the Incorporeal and Uncreated. He took pity on them, therefore, and did not leave them destitute of the knowledge of Himself, lest their very existence should prove purposeless...How could men be reasonable beings if they had no knowledge of the Word and Reason of the Father, through Whom they had received their being? They would be no better than the beasts...But, in fact, the good God has given them a share in His own Image, that is, in our Lord Jesus Christ, and has made even themselves after the same Image and Likeness. Why? Simply in order that through this gift of Godlikeness in themselves they may be able to perceive the Image Absolute, that is the Word*

> *Himself, and through Him to apprehend the Father; which knowledge of their Maker is for men the only really happy and blessed life.*

To be truly reasonable beings, he says, we must know God, and in particular His Word, which is the rationale of all things. Mankind is made in the Image of God. The Son/Word/Chist is the Image of God. Therefore, man is made in Christ, that is, by Christ and after Christ. We often think of the Incarnation as God making up a body for Jesus based on what we were already like, but that's backwards. We were already made in His image. Thus, when he came "in our image", it was no disguise, but the true bodily incarnation of the Son, the template after which we were made.

> *It was by surrendering to death the body which He had taken, as an offering and sacrifice free from every stain, that He forthwith abolished death for his human brethren by the offering of the equivalent. For naturally, since the Word of God was above all, when He offered His own temple and bodily instrument as a substitute for the life of all, He fulfilled in death all that was required...*

> *The same writer goes on to point out why it was necessary for God the Word and none other to become Man: "For it became Him, for Whom are all things and through Whom are all things, in bringing many sons unto glory, to make the Author of their salvation perfect through suffering." (Heb. II 9)*

The hardest thing to understand about the Atonement is how one person (Christ) can legitimately pay the debt for the sins of someone else (me). How is that fair, when Christ and I are two separate people? It can only make sense if there's some connection between us. It may make no sense for a stranger to pay my tickets for me, but it makes a little bit more sense for my father to pay my tickets for me. As Athanasius tells it, there was an intimate connection between us and the Word even before He became incarnate. We were made through Him and in His image. We are also for Him, in that (c.f. the earlier quote) we only fulfill our purpose by apprehending Him. So we are directly connected to the Word by our efficient, formal, and final causes. For a being who is my creator, the model for my creation, and my final destiny to take my sins upon Himself begins to sound less arbitrary. He was necessarily involved in my salvation or lack thereof regardless.

Perfect Being Theology

By Katherin Rogers, 2000

Professor Rogers provides an accessible introduction to and defense of perfect being theology. This is the program, initiated by St. Anselm, of defining God as the most perfect conceivable being and then seeing what consequences for God's nature logically follow from this definition. Among contemporary analytic philosophers, it's become popular to chuck many of the qualities that have traditionally been associated with a perfect divinity: simplicity, necessity, eternity, immutability, omniscience, etc. Rogers defends most of the claims of classical perfect being theology regarding the divine attributes. She reminds readers of the reasons for these claims and answers most of the criticisms directed against them.

Perhaps the most bizarre claim made by Anselm, Aquinas, and the rest is that God is utterly "simple". This means that, not only are all of God's qualities (power, wisdom, justice, etc) mutually consistent, they are actually identical in Him. Also, not only does God possess these qualities essentially (i.e. by His very nature), they are each identical with His very being. This sounds weird. If goodness is a property, and God=goodness, it would seem that God is a property, rather than an actual being. Rogers says that this criticism misunderstands what the doctrine of divine simplicity is saying. Classically, the divine attributes were not seen as static properties, but as acts. For example, His wisdom is the act of knowing everything, His omnipresence is His act of being everywhere, etc. Divine simplicity claims that these are all ways of describing one single act, an act which is also identical with God's act of existing. Stated this way, the doctrine isn't obviously crazy, but there's another problem. It seems that some of God's acts/qualities are necessary (e.g. His existing) while some are contingent (e.g. His creating me and knowing that He has created me). By creating me, it seems that God has altered His knowledge (by adding the fact that I exist), but if God's knowledge=God's nature, it would seem that God has altered His very nature. Rogers is willing to accept this conclusion. I'm not sure. I wonder if one could assert a weaker version of divine simplicity (e.g. God has a unitary essence that includes all of His perfections) that would still rule out God being a composite or being dependent on external standards (this being the motivation for asserting simplicity) without all the baggage of strong divine simplicity. Sometimes it seems like even Rogers doesn't hold to the doctrine, such as when she insists that the moral law proceeds from God's nature rather than His will. I agree with her and think this is an important point, but can we make such distinctions in a simple God? Perhaps it's just we must think of morality coming from God's nature, because nature and will are distinct to our limited minds.

Rogers does an excellent job defending the doctrine of God's eternity—that He doesn't just live forever, but that He is outside of time. All times are always equally present to Him, and He is entirely present at each times. This doctrine is frequently attacked, but the attacks all fail. For example, it's sometimes said that if all times are present to God, they must all be present to each other, in which case time would be an illusion. As Rogers points out, one could make the same argument about God's omnipresence in space. Each point in space is present to God (meaning that He is present at each point), but this doesn't mean that every point in space is physically touching. Rogers acknowledges that God's eternity only makes sense if one accepts the B (eternalist) theory of time, i.e. that the past and future have real existence but just aren't present to us right now. She finds this acceptable, as do I. She points out that only such a conception can reconcile divine foreknowledge with free will understood in a non-compatibilist way. If the future doesn't exist for God to just see, than the only way He could know what I'm going to do would be if my actions are predetermined. If the future is there to be seen, no such conclusion need follow. Rogers is committed to a libertarian understanding of free will, i.e. that free choices are not causally predetermined, because it helps her get around theodicy problems. Surprisingly, she feels less need to defend this sort of freedom for God Himself. She more or less agrees with Avicenna and Leibnitz that God is constrained by His own goodness to create a best-possible world. I myself am more inclined to grant libertarian freedom to God and not to His creatures.

Another useful part of the book concerns the relationship of God to creation. She begins with an analogy. The best way to understand the relationship between God and His creatures is to imagine the relationship between me and my thoughts. My thoughts are distinct from me, but totally depend on me for their continued existence. I can imagine a story where, say, character A kills character B. Who caused B's death? From the point of view intrinsic to the story, it's A. However, from the wider perspective, I wrote the story where B does this, so I'm the ultimate cause. This is a good way of understanding primary and secondary causation. Rogers decides to take this idea even farther, and asserts that the things in the universe really are just God's thoughts. I really don't think anything is gained by this move from analogy to univocality, but fortunately it doesn't make much difference for the points she's making.

As I said, this is a nice short introduction to the classical theory of God's attributes. It's not a book about God's existence, which it takes for granted. It's also not a book about how these attributes square with the God revealed in the Bible, although she mentions ways that they can be understood to be compatible.

The Beauty of the Infinite

By David Bentley Hart, 2003

Try to guess what the following have in common: 1) a man comes up to me and kicks me in the shins; 2) a mother reminds her daughter that it's not ladylike to spit; 3) a group of friends form a club for Chicago residents of Polish descent; 4) a philosopher proposes an explanation of reality; 5) an essayist claims that America's history has been one of expanding freedom. If you're a postmodernist, you've probably guessed that these are all instances of "violence". Those of you who haven't afflicted your sanity by reading Nietzsche, Lyotard, Foucault, etc. are no doubt confused—surely only #1 is violence? Here's the claim: the philosopher in #4 and the essayist in #5 are proposing "metanarratives" or "metaphysics", which means they're trying to impose their view of the world on everyone else and crush other legitimate worldviews. All attempts to explain a multiplicity of facts under a unitary scheme, we are told, are instruments of "violence". Similarly, the mother in #2 is using rules of etiquette to assert her will to power and crush the spirit of her daughter. Okay, so if unity is oppressive, multiplicity must be good, right? Nope, despite what they sometimes say, postmodernists hate particularity too. The friends in #3, by limiting the membership of their club, are excluding the "other" out of sheer hatred for non-Poles. Only their weakness keeps them from committing genocide. Well, then, if all of these things are violence, what isn't violence? Nothing—the will to power is the only reality.

I have trouble regarding postmodernism even as a species of error. To me, it's a species of paranoid insanity, a matter of interest only to psychologists. Eastern Orthodox theologian David Hart, however, has decided to dignify their critique with a theological response. Christianity, he says, provides a new paradigm for understanding unity in difference. In God—whose inner life is the complete and eternal self-giving love between the Father, Son, and Holy Spirit—the two are equally fundamental, and they combine not in violence of any sort, but in peace and charity. When God created the world and fashioned a multiplicity of beings, this was no violent rupture in an original unity of being. The heart of being Himself already contains interpersonal plurality; the "distance" between God and creatures is prefigured in the "distance" between the divine Persons. Therefore, finite creatures are actually images of God by their very finitude. The ultimate reality is not violence, but love. This may sound naïve, the sort of thing a postmodernist would dismiss as a comforting illusion. Hart, in a somewhat surprising move, turns the tables and accuses the modern and postmodern views as the comforting illusion, in fact a return to a distinctly pagan illusion. In Greek tragedy and in the ideology of the polis, evil and chaos are primordial forces, ineradicable facts of life which must be accepted but can be held at bay by the violence of the state. For the Christian, evil is not primordial, it does not even have positive existence, and it is not necessary. This, in fact, makes it more unbearable. Thus, Hart criticizes efforts to read the crucifixion in a Greek-tragic light. The resurrection does not vindicate the crucifixion, but rather the One who was crucified, and it awakens hopes that a merely tragic wisdom would have us put aside. Similarly, Hart rejects the claims of some contemporary theologians that the crucifixion was somehow necessary for God's self-actualization, a view that would remove the gratuity from creation and make us a means to God's own end. Nor will he stand claims that suffering and death have been assumed into the divine nature: the point of the Incarnation was to share God's Trinitarian life with us, not to contaminate God with our problems. Hart also briefly critiques the moronic (but very common) assertion that God became man and died so that He could see how tough we have things and cut us some more slack.

For me, the most interesting parts of the book are where Hart is defending or attacking other theologians. Part of the enjoyment comes from the fact that I usually agree with him. For example, he points out that Rene Girard, in his claims that Christianity has overthrown the pagan order of sacrifice, has a grossly oversimplified idea of sacrifice. Christ's crucifixion may have exposed the inadequacy or injustice of sacrifice as transaction and sacrifice as expedient to maintain the social order, but it exemplifies and establishes another order of sacrifice, that of self-giving. Hart notes that this type of sacrifice is prefigured in the Old Testament; I would say traces of it are also found in paganism. As a second example, it was quite gratifying to read Hart's response to Karl Barth's claim that the analogy of being is a doctrine of the Anti-Christ: Hart's response is, basically, that Barth doesn't know what he's talking about. I also appreciated Hart's refusal to play the game of contrasting Eastern with Western Christianity. I never thought I'd live to read an Eastern Orthodox theologian defend Augustine's Trinitarian metaphors or Anselm's theory of the Atonement, but Hart does so ably. Indeed, he thinks the whole East vs. West/patristics vs. scholastics dichotomy is overblown. (For example, most of Anselm's claims about the Atonement are prefigured in Athanasius.) Without a doubt, the favored Father of the Church in this book is Gregory of Nyssa. Gregory was the first one to imagine in God a being that is infinite but not indeterminate—not a formless expanse, but an infinity with form and beauty. Near the end of the book is a discussion of Gregory's universalism—his belief that everyone eventually goes to heaven. What drove this was not wishful thinking (the usual source of modern universalism), but a profound sense of the unity of the human race. In the final kingdom, Christ must gather all things to Himself, God must be all in all. Every person is an irreplaceable part of the Body of Christ, so heaven can't be heaven without everybody. Let us hope that Gregory turns out to be right.

At the end, the book returns to the postmodern hermeneutic of suspicion. Hart ably carries out the standard conservative rebuttal: the postmodern claim that all metanarratives are masks of the will to power is itself a metanarrative—it is, hence, self-refuting. Furthermore, it is a particularly destructive ("violent", one might say) narrative, because it erodes every community of shared meaning and leaves individuals naked and adrift in the value-free market and helpless before undisguised power. Of course, if Hart had made this argument at the book's beginning, he wouldn't have needed to write the theological sections, but since these were the most interesting part, it's good that he didn't.

This book's main drawback is the writing style. From years of reading continental philosophers, David Hart seems to have been contaminated by their habit of writing impenetrable prose. Here's an example:

"What, exactly, after all, is the 'moral' interval that Christian thought imagines the soul to possess, if not precisely an interval, an opening or delay, where will doubles back upon itself or divides, where thought hesitates between identity and difference, where desire pendulates from delight to delight ('delectatio quipped quasi..." as Augustine says...), and where the self finds itself always subject to the bearing over (metaferein) of metaphor? Is not such an 'interiority' merely an intensity, an inward fold of an outward surface..."

What the hell is any of that supposed to mean? (Perhaps if I could read the Latin and Greek parts, it would help, but I doubt it.) Fortunately, not all of the book is like that. My recommendation: when Hart starts with the philoso-babble, skim.

The Genius of Christianity

By Rene Francis Augustus, Viscount de Chateaubriand, 1802

The Enlightenment actually produced very little in the way of arguments against Christian truth claims. Its main accomplishment was to convince its readers that Christians themselves are stupid, unimaginative, boorish, and cruel. *The Genius of Christianity* is an important refutation of the Enlightenment, one which made a sensation in Napoleonic France. Like his adversaries, Chateaubriand chooses not to focus on arguing the reality of things like Hell, the Trinity, or the Resurrection. Instead, he argues that we recognize the *beauty* of Christianity: its doctrines, its mores, its ideals, and its general sensibility. One might say that Chateaubriand treats Christianity as a particularly excellent species of paganism. The Bible contains the truths of the world's mythologies, but without the philandering gods and other nonsense. The Bible has its own literary style which bears comparison to Homer's. (Chateaubriand spends a great deal of space comparing Homer and Virgil to Milton and Racine. This does little to advance his thesis, but it is a pleasure to read because of his admiration for all four.) The Christian moral sense adds seriousness and poetry to life; its expectation of conflict between duty and desire and its promises of eternal rewards and punishments provide great material for the dramatist. The code of chivalry is superior to the martial virtues of antiquity, and the Mass is morally superior to pagan sacrifices. The mixture of joy and solemnity in the Christian marriage rite, the simple pleasures of the family together for Christmas, the sight of churches and their graveyards, and the sound of bells—all of these things have something so poetically *right* about them. These things should be taken into account when judging Christianity; they're not as simple as they appear. Chateaubriand and de Maistre loved to mock the revolutionaries by saying that they could never establish feast days embraced by the people like the Church has. Chateaubriand even defends the popular superstitions of uneducated country folk. There are distinctly Christian superstitions which carry spiritual and moral truths, and he worries that, if the peasants should ever lose these beliefs, they would only replace them with immoral superstitions. Anticipating Chesterton, he says, "He who believes nothing is not far from believing everything."

In perhaps the strongest part of the book, Chateaubriand argues that Christianity has created a new kind of hero—the missionary. In reviewing the exploits of the missionaries in China, Paraguay, Canada, and elsewhere, one is reminded how really remarkable the missionaries of the Counter-Reformation era were. How often has any endeavor succeeded in calling forth so much courage, ingenuity, and generosity as did this drive to save souls for Christ? One suspects that, if these men had been Oriental pagans rather than Catholics, the *philosophes* would have praised them to the skies. Of course, other religions and cultures have had their own remarkable heroes and public benefactors. However, the Christian missionaries combined courage and charity in a way which I think we may follow Chateaubriand in saying was unique. Christianity has a unique *style* or, to quote the title, a unique *genius*.

In the end, this line of apologetics has the same weakness as the attack it is answering. Just because Christians are dumb doesn't mean Christianity is false. Conversely, just because Christianity is beautiful doesn't mean it's true. On the other hand, I think *The Genius of Christianity* has value apart from this argument. It is valuable as a description of Christianity, seeing this religion in terms of the way of life it fosters rather than its formal tenets.

The Idea of the Holy

By Rudolf Otto, 1917

What do we mean when we say something is "sacred" or "holy"? Well, from the way we use these words, we certainly seem to mean something positive, so a first guess might be that "holy" means "supremely good" or something like that. This guess would be wrong, or at least gravely inadequate, insists Rudolf Otto in this book. Holiness is an entirely distinct category from moral value, and indeed from anything other than itself. It can't be explained or even described in terms of other things, any more than sight can be described in terms of sound or smell. This would seem to make Otto's task of describing holiness impossible from the start. And, indeed, if we readers had no faculty for apprehending holiness, the task would be as impossible as that of explaining color to a blind man. Otto insists that we do have such a faculty, though. It is undeveloped in most of us—we may be unconscious to certain aspects of holiness, and our idea of the sacred may be mixed with foreign ideas, but this book attempts to prompt us to experience the sacred for ourselves. It tries to evoke various aspects of the holy by analogies from other aspects of human experience. Because the word "holy" has been too moralized in our languages to suit his purposes, Otto usually refers to the quality he is describing as the "*numinous*" or, occasionally, the "*mysterium tremendum*".

The presence of numinous can be a terrifying experience. According to Otto, the most primitive apprehensions of the numinous are associated with feelings of dread and creepiness. Ghost stories represent a degraded version of this experience, and we can understand an aspect of what it means to say "this place is holy" if we were to say instead "this place is haunted". The numinous is supremely mysterious; it gives the impression of being "totally other", of being utterly outside of nature and beyond the power of our reason to comprehend. In this connection, Otto gives a fascinating exegesis of the Book of Job. When God describes his power and providence to Job, the examples given are not meant to show how God's wisdom is seen in the teleological ordering of nature. Instead, the examples include what seem to be absurdities and monstrosities. What these aspects of nature indicate, according to Otto, is that God is utterly beyond our ideas of what is reasonable. What reconciled Job to his fate was his realization that it is a good thing that God is above our reason: His "wildness" is part of His divinity. The numinous is also connected with an intense sense of power and energy. Indeed, this overpowering force can be a source of terror. Thus we hear of God's "wrath"; He is the "living God", a "consuming fire", and to look on Him is death. These are all, Otto insists, analogies from other experiences used to describe something for which there are no words. For example, experiencing God's wrath doesn't always mean His literal anger, but rather a forcefulness of His presence that can be described in no other way. When confronted by the power of His presence, by His sheer plenitude of being, the creature is struck by its own comparative nothingness. Otto calls this "creature-feeling", which is related to Schleiermacher's "feeling of absolute dependency" in that the former gives rise to the latter. Finally, as the rational aspect of religion is developed, the aspect of the goodness and absolute value of the numinous come to the fore. What had once seemed like a ghost or a demon is now seen to be the source and sanction of the moral law.

Otto believes that religions can be judged against each other according to how well they capture the sense of the numinous. Since he's a Lutheran theologian, it is not surprising that Christianity comes out on top in his estimation. From this, one might get the impression that Otto is a pious Lutheran. However, towards the end of the book and in the appendices he reveals that he doesn't actually believe in miracles or the Resurrection. How has someone so sympathetic to the religious impulse been led to such disastrous apostasy? Perhaps it is because he regards the numinous aspect of religion as not only qualitatively distinct from other experiences, but as actually non-rational. True, by "non-rational" he doesn't mean "irrational", but the effect is still that we can't take numinous expressions literally, and we can't reason from them logically. The point is always to get the "spiritual" message, which opens Otto to the liberal Protestant temptation of dismissing the "carnal" messenger. First distinguish the physical claim of the Resurrection from its spiritual "meaning". Then accept the latter and discard the former. Finally, claim that people who accept the physical fact are thereby denying the spiritual meaning. In the liberal Protestant mind, the two are first distinguished and then, inexplicably, opposed. Far better to accept the classical Christian view, the sacramental/incarnational view that the physical and spiritual are inseparably united.

The Nature of Love

By Dietrich von Hildebrand, 1971 (trans. 2009)

To really understand love, a couple of errors must be avoided. The first is to see love as a form of selfishness, that the beloved is a mere means to the lover's own happiness or self-actualization. The second is to think that love must be entirely altruistic, and that any desire for a requital of love and for union with the beloved is a sort of selfish corruption of love's true nature. One thing to be said for these errors is that they've inspired a number of Christian philosophers—including C. S. Lewis, Josef Pieper, and Pope Benedict XVI—to write some really beautiful meditations to refute them. In my opinion, the best of these (although I strongly recommend them all) is *The Nature of Love* by the Catholic phenomenologist Dietrich von Hildebrand. The basis of von Hildebrand's philosophy is his value ethics developed in his book *Christian Ethics*. In that work, he identified three ways that a person may perceive something as important: it can be merely subjectively satisfying, it can be an objective good for that person, or it can be a value—something objectively good and deserving of esteem. Ethical behavior is a matter of appropriate value response to those values that von Hildebrand identifies as morally relevant. Ethical behavior does promote one's deepest objective good, but that can't be why a morally good person does it; the value must be the main consideration. One can respond to values both with one's will and one's emotions; veneration and enthusiasm would be examples of the latter. Although our emotions are not totally under our control, we can be morally required to endorse or reject a feeling based on the objective value or disvalue of that feeling's object.

What then is love? Above all else, love is a value response to a person. The lover recognizes and responds to the inner beauty and preciousness of the beloved. Love can be inspired by attractive qualities in a person, but love itself is a value response not to these qualities or even to the person's overall spiritual beauty, but to the person himself. We legitimately tend to assume the best of one we love, and when presented with a moral fault of his, we regret it but see it as a betrayal of his true self. Von Hildebrand insists that this is not an illusion but the actual truth: love makes us more objective. Love is an affective value response, i.e. a matter of emotion as well as will. It is also a superactual value response, meaning that we maintain our love for the beloved even when we're not consciously thinking of him.

All of the above is basically an application of the categories of von Hildebrand's *Ethics*. Next, he breaks new ground by saying that love takes value response to a whole new level; it's a "super value response". In love, I make the one I love a matter of my objective good, and not just a matter of disinterested value response. I allow my happiness to become contingent on him returning my love and maintaining a relationship with me. I concern myself with his objective good to such a degree that I come to relate to it in a way similar to how I respond to my own objective good. Now, von Hildebrand insists that this new level of interest is not an intrusion of selfishness but an organic development of love. The desire for union always bases itself on recognition of the beloved's intrinsic value, and the value response and concern for the other's good always take priority. In fact, this "giving one's heart away" so that one's own happiness is tied to the beloved is the greatest tribute one could make to the other's value.

The final highlight of the book is von Hildebrand's discussion of charity. It has been suggested that the difference between "eros" and "agape" is that the former has an element of selfishness in its desire for union while the latter is wholly self-giving. Earlier chapters have shown why this idea reflects a misunderstanding of the desire for union. Charity, i.e. supernatural love, really is distinct from natural love, though. First, charity is based on love of God. God is the primary object of charity, and when we love another human with charity, we respond to him primarily as one created in the image of God and loved by Christ. Charity enhances all the categories of natural love, but it also gives rise to a new kind of love, love of neighbor—the only kind that can be directed to strangers. Love of neighbor is different from natural benevolence, which does not value the person himself, but limits itself to a desire to alleviate pain or fulfill one's moral duties. The most interesting claim made about charity is on its unique relationship to morality. According to von Hildebrand, a heathen can love deeply and be a very moral person, but natural love and morality exist independently of each other, and can sometimes even be in conflict. There is no contradiction in naturally loving one person while hating another, but charity can't work like this. Nor can a charitable love drive one to unjustly favor someone we love or be indifferent to his moral faults. Our love of God also transforms our responses to impersonal moral values by giving a face to the world of values, as it were, and inspiring us to respond to the call of morality with the ardor of love, because all moral deeds glorify God and all evil offends Him.

Arguably von Hildebrand's greatest contribution to philosophy is his analysis of affective value responses, so arguably this book on love is the one he was born to write. I agree with all his main points, except that I'm still not sure if I believe that one can love a stranger even by supernatural means. The book is longer than it needs to be: you can get all the good stuff if you just read chapters 1, 2, 3, 4, 6, 7, 11, and 12. I think the discussions of spousal love give too little emphasis to its orientation to children, admittedly a strange criticism to make of someone who wrote a book defending the Church's prohibition on birth control. I myself would have named parental love as the supreme natural love, rather than spousal love, as von Hildebrand does. These are minor criticisms, however, which don't touch the core analysis of the book, which shows with incomparable clarity that the different aspects of love—what Lewis called "need love", "gift love", and "appreciation love"—do not contradict, but rather reinforce each other.

The Sacred and the Profane

By Mircea Eliade, 1957

This is one of my favorite books. Renowned anthropologist and historian of religion Mircea Eliade attempts to describe how religious people experience the sacred. He also gives a fascinating explanation of primitive religions. The popular image of the religion of primitive peoples is pretty unflattering: they worship rocks, animals, and whatnot; their rituals are just attempts to extract favors from imaginary spirits; their myths are laughably bad attempts at scientific explanations, etc. Eliade shows that these are complete misunderstandings. Primitive people don't worship natural objects, but they believe that natural objects can be revelations of the sacred, and that one can worship the gods through them. Primitive men certainly do want help from their gods (who wouldn't?), but they are also driven by what Eliade calls an "ontological nostalgia", a desire to live in the presence of the gods who are the preeminently real and the source of all being. Nor do their myths seem so silly when one understands the function they serve and the universal symbolism they employ.

The first chapter is on "sacred space." According to Eliade, religious men experience space differently than nonreligious men due to the presence, for the former, of sacred spaces where the gods are especially present. The existence of a sacred place breaks the homogeneity of space and becomes a "center of the world". Since it is a point of access to the gods, the sacred place is also symbolically the highest point in the world (because high regions are closer to heaven). In some cases, the sacred place connects to the underworld as well, and so it is also represented as a pole connecting the three realms. For religious people, the establishment of a sacred place is necessary to give order to the world; indeed, it is a reenactment of the creation of the world, when God brought order out of the primordial chaos. Therefore, the establishment of a home is a sacred act, the act of centering one's world and establishing an access to the gods.

The second chapter is on "sacred time." Sacred time is the time of the creation of the world, the time in which the archetypical acts of the gods "live". It differs from profane time in that it is reversible. By imitating the archetypical acts done by the gods "in the beginning" or by reciting the myths of these sacred acts, the religious man is connected to gods and their creative potency is made present. Before Judaism, religious people tended to regard time as cyclic. According to Eliade, the Christian liturgy is also an example of sacred time, but with the difference that the Incarnation has "valorized" history, so that now it is a particular point in history (the time of Christ) that is made present.

In the third chapter, Eliade explores the sacredness of nature. For a religious person, everything in nature is a symbol of some aspect of God, some modality of the sacred. The sky represents transcendence, the earth fertility, the rock permanence, the moon mutability, and so on. These symbols are universal and account for the commonalities of the world's mythologies: its sky gods, earth goddesses, etc. A particularly interesting symbol is water—water represents unformed potentiality. The world was formed out of the primordial waters. Immersion in water evokes a return to the unformed state of the beginning; it thus symbolizes death and rebirth, and it washes away sins.

Eliade makes it clear that the universality of these symbols does not mean that all religions are the same or teach the same things. It does mean that they all partake of the same symbolic vocabulary; one might say that they are like different books written in the same language. A religion may add a new meaning to one of these symbols, as the Christian sacraments do in relating them to the life of Jesus Christ, but it does this not by negating the prior meaning, but by building upon it.

This book will enhance your understanding and respect for any sacred literature and ritual, from the most primitive to the most advanced.

The Spirit of Catholicism

By Karl Adam, 1927

In this book, German priest Karl Adam tries to identify the "spirit" or essence of Roman Catholicism, that is, the basic principles that make sense of her dogmas, rituals, and organization. Adam is convinced that such a spirit exists, that the Catholic Church is not just a collection of unrelated parts. He seems particularly interested in identifying the main difference between his Church and the Protestant churches, so the basic doctrines of Christianity—Trinity, Incarnation, and Atonement—are taken for granted throughout rather than being explicitly defended. This book is, as far as I know, the best book there is for explaining the Catholic Church to a Protestant.

The spirit of Catholicism turns out to be something one may call communalism or corporatism. It is the idea that Christ came to redeem men not as disconnected individuals but as a united whole. This supernaturally established unity of men is the Church. The Church is the Mystical Body of Christ because it is the primary dwelling place of His Spirit, a Spirit that dwells in individuals only through their incorporation as members of the Body.

> *"The Spirit of Jesus is objectivised and introduced into our earthly life, not through the medium of specially gifted personalities, but exclusively in and through the community, in and through the union of the many in one. So the Church possesses the Spirit of Christ, not as a many of single individuals, nor as a sum of spiritual personalities, but as a compact unity of the faithful...This union, this community, is...not a thing created by the voluntary or forced association of the faithful...but a thing which is antecedent to any Christian personality, a supra-personal thing, which does not presuppose Christian personalities, but itself creates and produces them."*

This idea of a corporate spiritual unity of mankind illuminates all of Catholic belief and practice. It explains how all men could fall with Adam and be redeemed with Christ. It also explains the structure of the Church, since the Body of Christ is, like any other body, an organic union in which the parts perform complementary but distinct functions. Adam discusses the role of the Pope and bishops in representing and maintaining the unity of the Church. He also examines the relevant part of the New Testament to show that the Papacy is in accord with Christ's plan for the Church. There are, however, even more profound manifestations of the interconnection of the faithful. My favorite part of the book is the two chapters on the communion of saints. Here Adam describes the connections between the Church Militant (on earth), the Church Suffering (in purgatory), and the Church Triumphant (in heaven). Catholics and Protestants agree that God is the source of all grace, but Catholics believe that God works through his saints, elevating them through grace so that they can become sharers in God's work of salvation. Because of the supernatural links between souls in the Church, one can even speak of a common store of grace and of a flow of grace from one member to another. (Hydraulic metaphors seem to be hard to avoid here.) The saints in heaven intercede for the souls on earth, and the souls on earth intercede for the souls in purgatory. Of course, God could do His work without any mediation, but he chooses to work through His creatures so that they may be more perfectly bonded in love. God even uses His saints to show us aspects of His own nature. This is particularly true of the Virgin Mary:

"When a Catholic speaks of his Heavenly Mother, his heart is full with all the strength of feeling that is contained in that word. Mary is as it were a gracious revelation of certain ineffable and ultimate traits in the nature of God, which are too fine and too delicate to be grasped otherwise than as reflected in the mirror of a mother."

Finally, if the Church really is the spiritual unity of mankind restored, then her mission must be to draw all people into this union which is their birthright. And not only all people, but everything of human value—everything good in antiquity and foreign cultures, in profane philosophy and pagan piety—must find its place in the Church. Indeed, these things, so far as they are good, must be championed by the Church, as they were when the Church preserved the pagan classics during the Dark Ages. If the Church really is the Body of Christ, it must be unique, and it must be necessary for salvation. Hence "outside the Church, there is no salvation." Adam defends this belief, although demanding that it be understood in what he (and, I think it's fair to say, the Magisterium) understand as the proper way. First, it means that no religious body outside the Church has saving power. This only applies in its entirety to non-Christian bodies, since the Orthodox and Protestant Churches have maintained large amounts of Catholicism, and so the Church has always recognized at least some of their sacraments as valid. Second, it means that belief systems that contradict the Catholic faith are wrong, and so they exclude their adherents from salvation through the Church *in so far as those adherents fully understand these beliefs and how they constitute a rejection of the true Church of Christ.* It is when one switches from talking about belief systems to talking about individuals, from "theology" to "psychology", that the maxim "no salvation outside the Church" becomes more difficult to apply. On this subject, Adam has a very good discussion of baptism of desire and the possibility of invincible ignorance. He does admit that the Church was not always conscious of this distinction between a belief and how it is psychologically appropriated by its adherents (not that the Church used to reject the distinction but now accepts it—the Church never reverses her teaching—but that it was simply not considered), and this was the cause of religious persecutions during the Middle Ages. However, this was due to the "logical" rather than "psychological" temperament of the time (the habit of judging ideas rather than people), rather than the actual dogmas of the Church.

Adam hits all of the points that a Protestant would be likely to find confusing or objectionable: the hierarchy, purgatory, indulgences, Marian devotion, veneration of saints, ecclesiastical exclusivity, and the Inquisition. It would seem that he has done a good job of identifying the distinctive essence of Catholicism.

Tradition and Traditions

By Yves Congar, 1960

I've found that all of the most interesting books about tradition are written either by Catholic or Eastern Orthodox theologians. This is because these traditional Christian bodies are committed to the following two not-easily-reconcilable propositions: 1) revelation ceased with the death of the last Apostle, and 2) doctrines like that of the Trinity are parts of the Christian revelation, even though we have no records of them being explicitly promulgated by the Apostles. How can this be? Here is where tradition comes to the rescue: the traditions of the Church have come down to us from the Apostles, and these traditions contain, at least implicitly, some theological content beyond what could be directly inferred from the New Testament. Therefore, the development of doctrine through Church history is not a case of continual revelation. Nor is it a case of a primitive revelation being corrupted by merely human additions. Rather it is a case of knowledge already embedded in some way in the life of a community being extracted into propositional form. This is the Catholic/Orthodox view, and even if it were not true, it would still be the most interesting description of description out there. It asserts straight up one of the most intriguing features about tradition: it has real intellectual content, but this content is not (at least, while it remains traditional) being transmitted in written/conceptual form.

Congar's book is largely a review of Catholic speculations on tradition. The two thinkers from whom he draws most frequently are Johann Moehler and Maurice Blondel. Congar shows that the Church has always asserted the existence of a body of tradition received from the Apostles. Sometimes this meant information passed down by word of mouth rather than writing, although a number of actions (e.g. liturgical practices) were also understood to be part of the tradition. Since the nineteenth century, the Catholic understanding of tradition has grown more subtle. Traditions communicate something greater than bare information; they make a person part of a collective life. For the Catholic, this collective life, the Church, is also the mystical body of Christ, so it is a direct experience of the reality to which revelation refers. Traditions refashion one's character and sensibilities. They provide a context, a milieu, within which information like doctrines are to be understood. For the Catholic Church, two of the great "monuments" of tradition are the liturgy and the writings of the Fathers, or rather the spirit one extracts from them.

Though we may lose consciousness of some of the riches of the faith, so long as we preserve tradition, these treasures will be preserved for our rediscovery. As Congar writes in 1960,

"But we need only step into an old church, taking holy water, as Pascal and Serapion did before us, in order to follow a Mass which has scarcely changed, even in externals, since St. Gregory the Great, or we may open our missals at the pages which give the Paschal Tridiuum...Everything has been preserved for us, and we can enter into a heritage which we may easily transmit in our turn, to those coming after us. Ritual, as a means of communication and of victory over devouring time, is also seen to be a powerful means of communication in the same reality between men separated by centuries of change and affected by very different influences. Both as a lived action and as a ritualized action, the liturgy preserves and hands on to us elements which are much more numerous than were realized by those men who performed and preserved the rites, and actually handed them on to us: many more, even, than we ourselves can know. The whole Eucharist is given to me in its celebration, I myself possess it in its entirety, although I understand and could express so little of it...The whole of our love is expressed in the liturgical kiss, even if we do not really attend sufficiently to what we are doing. The whole of our faith is in the most ordinary sign of the cross, and when we say 'Our Father' we already imply all the knowledge which will be given to us only when we embrace it in the revelation of glory."

Oh, wait...thanks a lot, spirit of Vatican II.

Tradition: Concept and Claim

By Joseph Pieper

In the debate over whether tradition is something you believe or something you do, German Thomist Joseph Pieper definitely comes down on the side of belief. Tradition is a teaching which has been handed down to us, and which we have a duty to pass on unchanged and uncorrupted. Pieper is the opposite of those (most of whom take the tradition-as-action view) that the point of having a tradition is to tinker with it. What interests Pieper is how tradition can have this authority. If it were a mere accumulation of human wisdom, there would be no reason not to add to it or correct it. No, the authority of a tradition rests on its claim to come from God Himself. The sayings of "the ancients" are treasured not out of reverence for our elders, but because "the ancients" means "those who received the revelation from God and passed it on to us". A new revelation (like Christ) generates new ancients (the Apostles) and a new tradition. Pieper acknowledges the usefulness of purely secular traditions, i.e. customs, for common life, but these don't interest him much. They don't have the authority of sacred tradition; we only avoid tinkering with them for prudential reasons. Because a tradition is from God, it is superior to what human minds can achieve, and it must be passed down uncorrupted. Pieper does not admit any change at all in the content of sacred tradition—as a Christian, he wants to believe exactly what the Apostles believed. What changes is the translation of the tradition into the language, concepts, and categories of each time. This is the arduous intellectual work of theology, which he calls the science of tradition.

A particularly interesting part of the book is Pieper's speculation about where sacred tradition can historically be found. Being a Catholic, it's not surprising that he finds it in the Old and New Covenants. However, he also suspects the existence of a general revelation to all mankind, pieces of which are contained (though corrupted) in the myths of all peoples. Pieper entertains the idea that Christianity will gather up and purify the pieces of this general revelation scattered throughout the world, and the resulting shared tradition would form the basis for a substantive world unity. This prospect is threatened by the movements in the world today that are seeking global harmony through the attenuation or destruction of the world's particular cultures. I'm not sure whether I buy this idea of general revelation, that the heathen myths contain truths above those accessible by human reason and imagination. It is certainly not a possibility that a Christian would reject lightly. I must say that Pieper's vision of world unity, unity through rather than against tradition, is the only one I've ever found attractive.

Book Reviews: Society

Family and Civilization

By Carle Zimmerman, 1947

Zimmerman, an American sociologist, examines the evolution of the family during the course of Greek, Roman, and Western history. His focus is on the relationship of the family to the larger society as measured by the former's authority and independence. He identifies three family types:

1. The trustee family. When the state is weak, the extended family or clan is the primary social power, and the state itself is seen as a union of families rather than individuals. Rights and property belong primarily to the family itself, and its current living members see themselves as mere trustees, charged with passing along what they have received. The family is the primary instrument of justice: the family itself is held accountable for the misdeeds of its members, and each member has a duty to avenge wrongs against his kinsman. Trustee society is naturally polytheistic, with each clan having its private gods. Greece, Rome, and the Germanic barbarians all began with the trustee family system.

2. The domestic family. As the state gains power, it takes over the role of enforcing justice and tries to stamp out the private justice of the trustee family. Universal religions extend moral duties to non-kinsmen. With the spread of trade, it becomes useful for a family to be able to sell the property which it had been holding in trust. Out of these pressures arises the domestic family, the type which Zimmerman believes constitutes the best balance of family and society. The domestic family consists of the living members of the nuclear family unit: father, mother, and children. Family property belongs to the paterfamilias; the living no longer hold it in trust. Rearing children is the family's primary function. Religion provides strong social sanctions against divorce, childlessness, and sexual immorality.

3. The atomistic family. As individualism and impiety spread, the ideological foundations of the domestic family are undermined, leading to the atomistic family. In an atomistic society, marriage is seen as a temporary and socially unimportant contract between independent individuals. As atomism spreads, divorce becomes common, adultery loses its stigma, sexual perversions of all sorts come to be accepted and even celebrated, children rebel against their parents, childbearing comes to be seen as a burden, and the population implodes. A society cannot survive without the will to produce a next

generation, and so the decedent society is eventually replaced by a new civilization embracing a more virile (trustee) family type, and the cycle begins again. Greece after the Peloponnesian War, Rome during the late empire, and the contemporary West have the atomic family as their dominant type.

Zimmerman sees Western civilization headed for destruction if it cannot revive the domestic family. One of the heroes of his story is the Emperor Augustus, whose anti-adultery and anti-celibacy laws can be seen as a rational attempt to protect the Roman family and hold Rome's destructively atomistic tendencies at bay. This history's most important hero, however, is the Roman Catholic Church, which was forced to fight a war for the domestic family on two fronts, against both Roman atomism and barbarian trustee-ism. By the High Middle Ages, the Church had established her own sacramental version of the domestic family as the primary type in Christendom. This work was undone by the smart-aleck partisans of divorce and immorality of the Renaissance and Enlightenment.

The family is a key to history too seldom considered, so I strongly recommend this book.

Kinship and Marriage: an Anthropological Perspective

By Robin Fox, 1967

Anthropologist Robin Fox takes it on himself in this book to systematize what anthropologists have observed about the family structures in the many societies they have studied. He thinks that anthropologists have been too shy about generalizing, so that the field has accumulated a wealth of isolated case studies without enough theory to give them context. According to Fox, the various family structures are based on four universal, or nearly universal, principles:

1. The women have the children.

2. The men impregnate the women.

3. The men usually (i.e. for all societies up till now) exercise control.

4. Primary kin do not mate with each other.

These are the given parameters. Families are what people do with these facts, how they use them to form social bodies which can outlast individuals. There are basically three ways that a family can propagate itself from generation to generation; it can be matrilineal (inheritance through the female line), patrilineal (inheritance through the male line), or cognatic (inheritance through both parents). Fox argues that each of these choices has its own intrinsic logic that influences the relationships between family members, and he cites a number of examples to show how these tendencies play out among actual tribes. So, for example, the role of sister is crucial in matrilineal societies, since they produce the family's next generation, while in patrilineal societies, the important female role is wife/mother. On the other hand, the husband/father is central in patrilineal but not matrilineal organization. In fact, Fox argues that husbands aren't really necessary at all for the matrilineal family. The mother's brother fills the role of male authority figure, so women could be impregnated by random strangers, and the system would still work fine. Indeed, it does seem that marriage and adultery are taken much less seriously in matriarchal societies. His concentration on such cases leads Fox to believe that the role of husband/father, and therefore the nuclear family itself, are not natural in the way the four main principles are. However, I don't think that the facts he cites support such a radical conclusion. Nearly all of the matrilineal societies Fox discusses do have important father/husband roles, even though they do indeed clash with the logic of matrilineality and present a rival to the authority it vests in the maternal uncle. Of course, the majority of peoples are patrilineal, so for them these problems don't arise.

Cognatic inheritance is another beast entirely. If a person belongs to both the family of his mother and the family of his father, then people will have multiple kinship groups. This means that cognatic descent groups can't focus like unilineal descent groups. There are societies that operate on this principle, however, and it functions surprisingly well for some purposes. To complicate matters, some tribes use unilineal descent when determining family connection for some purposes and cognatic descent when assigning it for other purposes. There's also a distinction to be made between descent groups, which have a corporate life of their own, and ego-centered groups (the set of my first cousins, for example), which cannot. Unlike descent groups, ego-centered groups are intransitive: just because A is my first cousin and B is my first cousin doesn't mean that A and B are first cousins. This group is entirely "me-relative". Fox additionally distinguishes lineality from locality, i.e. which parent you inherit your kinship group from vs. which parent you live with after marriage, but this was more detail than I was interested in.

Of course, there's more to kinship than just deciding who counts as the next generation. One can ask what happens when a family becomes too big and needs to be broken up. One can study how groups of related families form clans. One can look at the ways that neighboring families form alliances by trading women in marriage each generation. Fox devotes space to all of these issues and others besides.

In order to keep the book on track, Fox doesn't devote much space to describing the beliefs the people he describes have about their family roles. For example, I get the impression that in many cases wives in patrilineal societies are "adopted" into the family of their husbands, but this never seems to happen to husbands in matrilineal societies. Are these observations generally true? It doesn't affect which family the children belong to, but it does affect how spouses understand their stake in their children. I think the lack of emphasis on beliefs (ideological superstructure, if you will) weakens the chapter on the incest prohibition. Fox examines the common explanations and finds them unsatisfactory, but his own speculations seem inconclusive too. I think the prohibition can be best understood by looking at how the acknowledged possibility of incest threatens peoples' understandings of their family roles. These are issues for another book, however. Fox was right not to sacrifice the unity of his book, which is an excellent introduction to family structure based on simple descent rules.

Modern Culture

By Roger Scruton, 1998

Culture has long had a double meaning. For the anthropologist, culture is the common stock of stories, beliefs, and customs that unite a people and make a common life possible. On the other hand, culture can also mean high culture—the great works of art and literature. High culture is not the common possession of all the people; it takes a great deal of study and training to become "cultivated". What the rest of the people have is called common or popular culture, which is art that is more accessible but less profound. In this book, Roger Scruton is examines modern culture in both its senses. His primary interest is in how the two relate, namely how high culture helps fulfill the functions of culture identified by anthropologists.

According to Scruton, the original heart of culture (in the anthropological sense) is religion. Religion taught people not only how to behave, but how to feel, because he insists that our sensibilities need training no less than our minds if we are to live full human lives. Religious rituals, especially the act of sacrifice, gave people a tangible sense of the community. Important life transitions, such as those to adulthood and to marriage, were marked by rites of passage. Death itself was reinvisioned as a passage to another state, with accompanying rites. Even after death, one was still a part of the community. Religion encouraged man to see himself as a free moral subject, and his choices assumed an awesome importance.

Then the Enlightenment came and overthrew religion. It's not clear if Scruton thinks that the Enlightenment actually disproved religious beliefs, but he is certain that they will never again be taken for granted, which means they can no longer fill the social functions once assigned to them. Even to present a rational defense of belief is to take a position outside belief, so we can never return to the faith of our ancestors. This claim seems bizarre to me; both doubt and the rational defense of belief certainly existed long before the eighteenth century. Nevertheless, let us agree with Scruton that there are many people alive today for whom religious belief is not a live option. The trouble is that the needs that were served by religion are still present, so something new must satisfy them. That something, according to Scruton, is high culture. Art also provides training for the emotions and the imagination. (Of course, to really make us grow in this regard, art must challenge us. It is not something that can be digested easily—hence high art's relative inaccessibility.) Of course, art can't satisfy all of religion's functions, and even those it can, it can do for a very few. Indeed, one of high culture's functions is to mourn the loss of religion and traditional community. However, art has this in its favor: it makes no claims on our beliefs. What we get out of it, Enlightenment can't take away.

Scruton defends bourgeois society as a valiant effort to salvage what could be saved from the religious consciousness while embracing the benefits of Enlightenment rationalism. In his view, bourgeois society means the rule of law, private property, monogamous marriage, science, and the market, but it also means the death of Christianity as well as permanent loneliness and alienation. He insists that this deal is worth taking; it is better than any alternatives. Although Scruton is arguing against leftist enemies of this order (particularly Foucault and all those who promise to liberate us from "domination"), his willingness to take the deal offered by modern life means that he's no reactionary. Needless to say, I disagree that we must or should accept this evil, impious culture in which we happen to have been born.

Nevertheless, it is clear that Scruton himself doesn't think highly of most modern culture. Those in charge of preserving high culture have decided to court favor with the mob by attacking the classics as elitist. Most popular culture is either violent or pornographic fantasy, or it's what he calls "kitsch". Youth culture consists of bad music, drugs, and promiscuous sex. Worst of all, adolescence is no longer considered a stage towards adulthood, but is considered an ideal in itself. There are no longer rites of passage to mark the ascendancy to a higher and more responsible state. Because it denies standards and responsibility, the communities that youth culture tries to create are inevitably fake.

In the end, Scruton points us in an unexpected direction, towards Confucius, the sage who exhorts us to piety and reverence without (it is claimed) making any demands on our faith. I agree that this would be a step in the right direction, although hardly the final destination. The book is full of aesthetic and ethical side discussions that are as thought-provoking as we expect from this author. I was rather disappointed that he didn't explain what he would regard as a healthy popular culture. I realize that he regards the one we've got as crap (and I suspect Scruton would regard everything I like as kitsch), but it's not clear what could be both generally accessible and avoid his disapproval. This contrasts with Scruton's other recent work on aesthetics, *Beauty*, that spent some time addressing the humble ways we express our desire for "fittingness". I wonder if he misinterprets some aspects of modern culture, because he doesn't realize that some of us aren't looking for a substitute religion in our art.

Natural Symbols

By Mary Douglas, 1970

In 1967, the Catholic bishops in England abolished the rule of abstinence from meat on Fridays. The abstinence rule had become a meaningless ritual, it was believed. It made Catholics stand out from other Englishmen, something the Bishops regarded as bad. True religion, it was felt, should be a more spiritual thing and a more individual thing. Beneath it all was the belief that progress in religion meant less emphasis on ritual and more on ethics. Shortly afterwards, renowned anthropologist Mary Douglas wrote this book to refute the bishops' superficial understanding of their own religion. Rituals that receive widespread obedience are never meaningless. They function as "condensed symbols" which carry a wide range of implicit meanings about society and the cosmos. A ritual like Friday abstinence expresses solidarity among all Catholics, both living and dead. It's supposed to make them stand out. The bishops don't understand how rituals function because they grew up in relatively unstructured (non-hierarchical) homes without developed symbolic means of communication, and so they are deaf to the significance of condensed symbols for their own flocks.

What about the claim that the replacement of ritual by ethics is the good and true progress of religion? Douglas claims that it is an error to believe that all primitive people are ritualistic. The pygmies, for example, have essentially no interest in ritual, and seemingly even little interest in religion itself. So Douglas changes the question to "why do men abandon ritual as they become more scientific?" to "why is industrial Europe reverting to the spiritual state of the pygmies?" "Science" and "moral progress" can't be the answer. What Europeans and pygmies have in common, she suggests, is a weak social structure: weak loyalty to group and weakly defined social roles.

Douglas believes that a society's structure is reflected in its understandings of the cosmos and the human body. The cosmos and the body are always symbols of society. She credits Durkheim with this idea, but she seems to have the opposite preferences as Durkheim. Douglas classifies societies according to two variables: "group" and "grid". "Group" means the strength of group bonds, how much loyalty and sacrifice they command. "Grid" means the importance of role differences, things like gender roles, age roles, and status. This point, that social strength is two-dimensional, has certainly helped to clarify my thinking on these matters. A people can have strong group and weak grid, and vice versa. Based on these variables, there are four possibilities:

1. Weak group, weak grid—the state of pygmies, university students, and the urban proletariat. Since bonds are weak, people feel that their lives are controlled by impersonal (natural or bureaucratic) forces. The world seems an amoral arena controlled by chance, and there is little interest in ritual or religion. The case of such a people being embedded in a more structured society is considered below.

2. Strong group, weak grid. Here "us" vs. "them" is the category that eclipses all others. Such peoples tend to have dualistic cosmologies (i.e. to see the cosmos as a battleground between a good and an evil power), and fear of contamination is the most potent bodily symbol. People are particularly interested in rituals that ward off the influence of witches.

3. Weak group, strong grid—the world of individualist capitalism. Here status (often represented by wealth) is king. The universe is seen as generally amoral, but it rewards hard work and cleverness. Ritual magic is used primarily to get ahead. The losers in this system tend to sink into a weak group, weak grid existence.

4. Strong group, strong grid—the world of Catholic Europe. Since people's lives are controlled primarily by personal forces (i.e. authorities), the world is seen to be infused with morality—a good God or gods reward good, while demons and witches (if they exist) punish evil. The body (representing society) is regarded positively as a mediator of spiritual values, so religion is strongly sacramental or "magical". Dogmas like the Incarnation and Transubstantiation also affirm the body's role as mediator of God, and therefore symbolize society's benevolent mediating role.

A particularly interesting case is what happens to the mass of losers in a weak group, strong grid society who fall into an undifferentiated (weak grid) existence. These tend to be subject to millenarian fantasies. The body (larger society) is contrasted with the spirit (the un-integrated minority), with the former despised and the latter extolled. Douglas suggests that the best thing to do for these unfortunate souls would be to organize them so that they can have the spiritual benefits of a strong grid and so they can take effective collective action. Instead, she points out that their leaders prefer to engage in mass marches and protests, to despise forms and hierarchies, and to harbor ridiculous fantasies of creating a utopia just by overthrowing the existing order. What is going on here is that the alienated members of society are trapped in the bodily symbols of their alienation. Rather than reintegrating "body" and "spirit", they imagine that the latter can overthrow the former.

"How to humanize the machine is the problem, not how to symbolize its dehumanizing effects. When bureaucrats hear the catchword 'equality' (a symbol of non-differentiation), they should beware. The way to humanize the system is to reject equality and to cherish the individual case....Instead of anti-ritualism it would be more practical to experiment with more flexible institutional forms and seek to develop their ritual expression. But this would mean going into the world, mixing with corruption and sin, dirtying oneself with externals, having some truck with the despised forms, instead of worshipping the sacred mysteries of pure content."

Old Wine in New Skins

By Jorge Gracia, 2003

In this short book, based on the 2003 Aquinas Lecture at Marquette University, Professor Gracia tries to explain what traditions are and how they function. Gracia assumes that a tradition must be either a "belief" or an "action". Since traditions seem to be more flexible than beliefs (that is, they have a greater capacity to change while maintaining their self-identity), he reasons that tradition must be a species of action. In particular, it is an action which is also a conscious reenactment of a previous action. Since reenactments don't have to be precise to count as reenactments, this definition explains the flexibility of tradition. Gracia thinks this property of identity through change is necessary if tradition is to fulfill its role of binding people across space and time. Applying his definition to the Catholic faith, which he takes to be a tradition, Gracia concludes that being a good Catholic consists entirely of making the correct ritual responses at Mass, that beliefs have no meaning except for their implications for ritual, and that the only way to be a heretic is to disrupt the ritual functioning of the Church. Thus Gracia seems to adopt the absurd position that an atheist could be a perfectly good Catholic as long as he says "Amen" on cue with everyone else at Sunday Mass. What would Gracia say about this case? This lecture suggests that he would recite some mumbo-jumbo about the "Hermeneutic Circle" to claim that belief in God has no meaning except to tell us how to reenact rituals.

When one reaches an absurd conclusion, one should reexamine one's premises. Either traditions have a greater belief component than Gracia admits, or Catholicism is more than a tradition. I think that we must admit a strong belief component to traditions. The Eastern Orthodox theologian Jaroslav Pelikan has compared tradition to a religions icon: its function is to point to something beyond itself. This, I believe, is the key point Gracia is missing. Tradition does indeed solve the problem of the Hermeneutic Circle and make communication possible. However, once communication is possible within a tradition, it becomes possible to make real statements about God, the world, or whatever. Of course, only people inside the tradition will understand these statements, but that doesn't change the fact that they are statements about these things themselves, not just statements about how we talk about them. One might say that that the creed, scriptures, and rituals of the Catholic Church form a single complex designed to make special forms of communication possible. Living as a Catholic gives one a certain understanding of mysteries like the Incarnation. And when two people are living under this umbrella of shared meanings, it certainly is possible for one to know that the other is a heretic. In fact, I'd say the truth is the opposite of what Gracia claims. It is only because of tradition that we can confidently identify and denounce heretics, because when one says "The Resurrection just means that Jesus' memory lived on in his disciples" or some other such crap, we know damned well what he means.

Primitive Man as Philosopher

By Paul Radin, 1927

I wanted to like this book, but the flaws are too great. The author, Paul Radin, wants to prove that the tribal peoples of the Americas, Africa, Australia, and the Pacific have developed well thought-out philosophies, but nearly all that he can come up with are myths, ethical maxims, and other folk sayings. I don't doubt that these have value in themselves, but they are only raw material from which one might begin to philosophize. Radin presents little evidence that the natives themselves, even their intellectual elite, have done this. Instead, he engages in some amateur philosophizing himself, trying to systematize the reported cultural material rather than report the systemizations of his subjects. Not surprisingly, he comes up with "principles" of primitive peoples' thought–such as "respect for the development and expression of individual personality" that sound like the sort of ethical axioms an early 20th-century American with ties to the pragmatist movement might lay down. (This book sports a forward by John Dewey–that in itself should have scared me off.) The primitives themselves are never quoted explicitly formulating these modern-sounding principles. Perhaps this is evidence that they have some philosophical acumen after all.

Given the paucity of explicitly philosophical material, Radin makes some rhetorical moves intended to offset criticism that actually undermine his credibility. He dismisses concerns about a lack of systematic speculative thought, saying that systemization is just a Western preoccupation. Has the man never heard of Ibn Sina, Samkara, or Zhu Xi? Then there are the attempts–annoyingly common in anthropologists–to make his primitives look good by denigrating Christianity. Do the natives' ethical codes leave something to be desired? Well, they're still better than Christian morality, in which (Radin seems to believe) it doesn't matter how you treat people as long as you go around saying that you love them. This doesn't make me think any more highly of the Winnebago; it just makes me question Radin's reliability. If he's such a boneheaded critic of his own culture, how well could he really understand another?

The highlight of the book, for me, was the two chapters on primitive man's understanding of God. Radin accepts and presents evidence for Andrew Lang's thesis that the most primitive peoples are at least incipiently monotheistic. In addition to their lower dieties, they posit the existence of a Supreme Being.

From the Maori comes the following impressive description of the Supreme Being. Reading it, I feel certain that it is the true God they are describing.

> *Io-te-wananga (Io-the-omnierudite) of the heavens is the origin of all things. These are the things tat Io-mata-ngaro (Io-the-unseen-face) retained to himself; the sprit and the life and the form; it is by these that all things have form according to their kind...*

> *All things were subservient to Io-the-great-one, and hence the truth of the names of Io:*

> *Io-the-great-god-over-all, Io-the-enduring (or everlasting), Io-the-all-parent, Io-of-all-knowledge, Io-the-origin-of-all-things (the one true God), Io-the-immutable, Io-the-summit-of-heaven, Io-the-god-of-one-command, Io-the-hidden-face, Io-only-seen-in-a-flash-of-light, Io-presiding-in-all-heavens, Io-the-exalted-of-heaven, Io-the-parentless (self-created), Io-the-life-giving, Io-who-renders-not-to-man-that-which-he-withholds...*

> *Now, it is clear that all things, the worlds and their belongings, all gods of mankind, his own gods, all are gathered in his presence (i.e. proceed from him). There is nothing outside or beyond him; with him is the power of life, of death, of godship. Everything that proceeds from other than Io and his commands, death is the collector of those. If all his commands are obeyed and fulfilled by everyone, safety and well-being result therefrom.*

> *Now, it is obvious that all things of life and death are combined in the presence of (or are due to) Io-the-hidden-face; there is nothing outside or beyond him. All godships are in him and he appoints them their places; the gods of the dead and the gods of the living. All things are named (i.e. created) by the god of the worlds, in the heavens, the plances and the water, each has its own function. Even the smallest atom, such as grains of dust, or pebbles, has its place—to hold the boundaries of the ocean or the waters.*

Few primitive peoples have carried their speculations this far, but it seems that at least the Maori have had among their number some genuine theistic philosophers.

Purity and Danger

By Mary Douglas, 1966

Mrs. Douglas seems to have written this book to combat an idea, still popular at the time, of what distinguishes "primitive" from "advanced" religions. Primitive religions were supposedly concerned with magic, i.e. with following arbitrary rituals or observing arbitrary taboos in order to manipulate supernatural powers for one's own benefit (or at least to keep them from causing one harm). Advanced religions put aside all that mumbo-jumbo, and only concern themselves with morality. As Douglas points out, these characterizations really just carry over Protestant polemics into the science of anthropology, and they don't describe real primitive peoples any better than they describe real Roman Catholics.

This book focuses on the idea of impurity. While this might seem like a purely religious concern, Douglas argues that we have it even in modern secular society, except instead of calling things "impure" we call them "dirty". An example would be getting food on one's clothes. This doesn't really cause anyone any harm, and we don't regard either clothing or food as inherently evil. Still, we object to their combination, because we like to have things in their proper place: food here, apparel there. Douglas insists that, rather than seeing this as irrational, we see it as a positive thing—as human beings establishing an order in their world. We all feel the need for systems, both as individuals and as collectives. When something doesn't fit the system, we call it "impure" or "dirty".

Douglas does not deny that there is a meaningful distinction between primitive and advanced religions, but she finds it not on the level of doctrines or spirituality, but on the level of how the religion functions in its society. She is a follower of Durkheim, and accepts his distinction between primitive and modern societies based on how extensively the division of labor is developed ("mechanical" vs. "organic" solidarity). Modern society, with its extensive and complicated division of labor, has developed vast and powerful means of social control—of monitoring citizens and punishing bad behavior. Primitive societies don't have so many means of control, so religion has to pick up the slack. That's the big difference between primitive and modern religion, according to Douglas. The former had a responsibility to maintain social order that the latter doesn't have. Hence it needed stronger ideas of taboo and more stories about how people get smitten for their sins, just to keep people in line.

Much of the book consists of examples of how ideas of impurity promote good behavior or discourage bad behavior. For example, the Nuer believe that if a woman commits adultery, it will cause her husband to have back pains if he sleeps with her. The Nuer don't seem to take adultery that seriously in itself, so adding the idea of physical suffering for the aggrieved husband helps them to work up more indignation against infidelity than they might otherwise muster. In another series of examples, Douglas notices that authority figures are often thought to have supernatural powers under their control (e.g. the ability of fathers to curse their sons), while people in roles that effectively give then power without formal authority are more often imagined to be practicing witchcraft without intending to (e.g. through unexpressed feelings). Here we see that these beliefs don't just reinforce the social order; they in some ways represent it. This will be the major theme of Douglas' later book, *Natural Symbols*.

The most famous and interesting chapter is on the prohibitions in the book of Leviticus, such as that against eating pork. Douglas examines and rejects several proposed explanations of these Mosaic rules: that they're intended to prevent disease, that they symbolize moral lessons, that they're just there to distinguish Jews from pagans, or that they're totally arbitrary. What reason does the Bible give for these rules? Here's an example: "Whatever pars the hoof and is cloven-footed and chews the cud, among the animals you may eat....you shall not eat these: the camel, because it chews the cud but does not part the hoof, is unclean to you..." What the devil does that mean? Douglas speculates that the Hebrews had definite ideas about what constitutes a proper land animal, fish, or bird. An animal that had some but not all of the qualities of its type was ambiguous, and therefore unclean. This is because their idea of the Holy consisted not only in being set apart from the profane, but also the idea of unity and completeness. Thus, the exemplars of each of the classes of being were symbols of God, each in its own way. The Jewish dietary rules expressed their vision of the order of the universe and of God's perfection. Douglas has since recanted this theory, but I still find it suggestive. At least, I think the true explanation of these laws would have to be something of this sort.

There are many interesting parts of this book; I particularly recommend the chapter on Leviticus. On the other hand, I think there are some gaps in Douglas' arguments that someone should try to fill. For example, she claims that we all need to systematize the world, but that our systems are all, to some extent arbitrary. I think the latter claim is a larger concession to nominalism than is philosophically warranted. I admit that the systems of the primitive peoples she discusses seem to have arbitrary elements. However, that's another unexplained problem: why did they feel obliged to introduce rigid categories where it's not needed? I can understand why one needs to have a limited number of social roles and have them rigidly defined, but why did these tribes feel the need to do the same thing with animal species? For example, the Lehe are thrown into mystic confusion by the pangolin, a land animal that looks scaly like a fish.

They have a cult to this animal, who represents to them formlessness and, ultimately, the God who contains within Himself all forms. That's nice, I guess, but it seems like a slightly finer classification scheme could have accommodated this animal rather easily.

The Hero with a Thousand Faces

By Joseph Campbell

I have an abiding interest in mythology, so whenever I find a new bookstore, I always stroll down to the "myths and folk tales" section. Usually there's only a few things there. Half are anthologies (Bullfinch, etc.); the other half are Joseph Campbell. Campbell never interested me; from what I'd heard, his explanations of myths were entirely individualistic–symbols of the journey each (self-absorbed) individual must take–ignoring myth's crucial social function, as if the functionalist revolution in anthropology had never happened. Still, while I was separated from my books and needed something to read, I thought I might as well see what it is that the general public has been feeding itself. I bought a used copy of Cambell's most famous book, *The Hero with a Thousand Faces*. Having read most of it, I can now say that the book isn't as banal as I'd thought it would be. In fact, it is deeply evil.

Campbell has two keys that he uses to interpret myths (or, rather, two Procrustean beds on which he mutilates them). The first is that myths represent forces of our subconscious. From Freud, Campbell got some bizarre ideas. He thinks that we each have a subconscious that is dominated by our desire for our own mother. Mother-lust is the steam pressure that makes our psychic engines go. At critical role-changing moments in life, we have to dip into the subconscious to redirect our primordial desire to nurse. Everything that's wrong with the world comes from the fact that we got angry at our mother the first time she wasn't there to feed us. For some reason, Campbell imagines that the first occasion for feeling an emotion is the only occasion, so that every form of discontentment we subsequently feel is deep down a rage against our mother for not letting us nurse whenever we wanted to. (Does this sound absurd? Read the book, and give me a less crazy-sounding exposition of Campbell's psychological musings.) From our mother-rage, we got the erroneous idea that there is a real distinction in the world between good and evil. Campbell calls people who believe that some things are good and others are evil (i.e. everyone but a moral inbecile) "infantile". To one who's let go of his mother-rage, such distinctions are meaningless, because the destruction of one form is the creation of another. So, for example, if I were to set fire to a schoolbus full of children, infantile Christians might find this "evil", but to Campbell, it would be just part of the joyful dance of being, whereby one form (children) gives way to another (ashes). Anybody who thinks differently must want to screw his mother.

Freud is one half of Campbell's brain. The other half–the worse of the two–is Buddha. Campbell insists that we all renounce Christianity, with its vindictive God who draws very definite distinctions between good and evil, and embrace the evil, false, repulsive religion of Buddhism. According to Campbell, the true point of every myth (although he has to reinterpret most of them to the point of unrecognizability) is when the hero in a moment of intuition realizes the illusary nature of all distinctions: evil=good, being=nothing, man=woman (Campbell is particularly enthused by sexually ambiguous gods), god=man, me=you=everybody. In otherwords, the hero acheives Buddhist enlightenment and becomes both a moral and an intellectual imbecile.

Campbell is, of course, quite impressed with Buddha's doctrine of anatman–that there is no self. Like other superficial commentators, he imagines this to be merely a help in overcoming egoism. Not being a philosopher (or a serious thinker of any sort), Campbell never stops to think about the consequences of dissolving the sense of personal identity. Not only self-regard, but personal responsibility (e.g. the obligation to keep promises I made yesterday) disappears. Not only do I cease to love myself, I cease to love others–since they don't have enduring selves either, according to the wicked and inhuman doctrine of the Buddha.

Some of Campbell's promotions for Buddhism are inadvertently funny. For example, it is a bit much to hear someone so enamored of the great religion of renunciation condemning Christianity for being insufficiently life-affirming. Then again, there's his constant whining about how Christians are so much crueler towards other peoples than anyone else, evidently forgetting his earlier claims that such concerns are infantile.

Categories are bad. Logic is bad. Forms are illusions that we have to get behind to acheive Nirvana. It's so easy to poke holes in Cambell's thought. (No doubt he would regard the desire for logical consistency as infantile.) What could drive any man to believe this rubbish? There must be some deep motivation at work here.

Christopher Dawson points out that all religion begins in the intuition of Being. There are however, two such intuitions, corresponding to what Aristotle identified as the two types of being: being in act and being in potency. Both potency and act possess a sort of universality that can bewitch the mind. The better religions derive from the idea of pure Act, the confluence and coincidence of all positive perfections that we call God. Being in act has a special intelligibility. As Aristotle pointed out, the law of contradiction only applies to actual being. (For example, a cup of water may be both potentially hot and potentially cold, but it can actually be only one or the other.) The worse religions (Buddhism, gnosticism) find actuality limiting because of its intelligibility–the fact that it's always just one thing, and not also its opposite. For Campbell, the great intuition is to see what he calls "being" as the thing underneath all forms, the thing that endures as it sheds one form and takes on another. Fellow Aristotelians will recognize this principle (which he takes to be ultimate) as matter, i.e.

potency. Pure potency (primary matter) has a sort of universality to it. It is, in a sense, everything and nothing at once. In its all-encompassing aspect, it mirrors its opposite, the pure actuality of God.

Joseph Campbell is possessed by a metaphysical sickness. He hates the intelligibility of being. He dismisses the actuality of things that makes them one thing and not another, and therefore he strives to look away from the aspect of things by which they resemble God. To have a nature, an essence, is too restrictive. He has a nostalgia for the primordial waters that covered the Earth when it was "without form and void" before God said "Let there be light." Understandably, he resents the God who spoke those words.

The Natural Family: a Manifesto

By Allan Carlson and Paul Mero, 2007

The defense of the patriarchal family has arguably been conservatism's most important and enduring cause. However, it's strangely underrepresented among what we usually think of as the conservative "great books". In fact, if an open-minded liberal were to ask me for a good book to read on the conservative/classical/religious idea of the family, I'm not sure where I'd point him. This book by Allan Carlson and Paul Mero is a pretty good attempt to fill this gap, or at least parts of it. The authors aim to defend what they call the "natural family", by which they mean the arrangement of father, mother, and children in which 1) the father and mother have committed to lifelong marriage; 2) the father is the only one with an outside job; and 3) the family produces internally a significant amount of what it consumes. They argue that this arrangement is natural, in the sense that it is found universally across cultures, it corresponds to real biological differences between men and women and the real needs of children, and that it is the only arrangement that can survive without major outside subsidy (as opposed to, say, single mothers, who usually need the help of extended family or the state). They are even brave enough to say that this family structure is the only natural one, and that all others are, to the extent that they deviate from this model, deficient. They also argue that the natural family is beneficial to the spouses, the children, and society at large. Most of these points are made by referring to studies in the sociological and historical literature, so interested readers will want to check the sources for themselves.

The scope of this book is limited. In particular, it's not an ethics book. The writers are not directly interested in sexual morality or the intrinsic disvalue of divorce. They only briefly discuss the biological/psychological/endocrinal differences between men and women, and they don't present any detailed arguments for how these facts acquire moral meaning. If that's what you're interested in, check out my *Defense of Patriarchy*. Unfortunately, this book aims for a wide audience, so detail and rigor of argument is sacrificed in several places. On the other hand, the book really shines in the attention it gives to the economic functions of the family and how government policy can strengthen or weaken these. They point out that countries like France and the United States (under the New Deal) used to have "family wage" regimes, meaning that it was thought that the responsibilities a man has to his wife and children should be reflected in his wages. Married men with children were paid more accordingly, with government grants sometimes being given to avoid incentives against hiring men with families. Hiring women for men's work was actively discouraged. Carlson and Mero claim that these policies were actually pretty successful in helping fathers to support their families so that mothers could stay home with the kids. Of course, from the 1960's onward, these arrangements were considered "sexist", as it was thought that only an animus against women could explain the husband-breadwinner model. Women entered the workplace and stopped having children. They also stopped being involved in household production, leading to an "invasion of the home" by industrial capitalism; families lost their productive activities and became passive consumers. No-fault divorce laws destroyed the sense of marital commitment. Tax laws and Social Security benefits were revised to indirectly penalize marriage or childrearing.

Unlike most books on this subject, Carlson and Mero have some policy recommendations. They mostly involve tax credits to remove disincentives to marriage and family and adjusting Social Security credits to reflect the contributions of raising the next generation. (These reform are to be revenue-neutral, meaning that childless adults would have to pay more taxes.) They also want to remove mortgage and zoning rules that discourage home businesses, gardens, and the like. They would like to replace permissive divorce laws and give local communities greater power to suppress pornography.

It's hard to dislike a book whose authors openly claim Louis de Bonald as one of their heroes. Indeed, it's quite refreshing that they are honest about the history of their movement, tracing it back to French reactionaries, social Catholicism, and the like, rather than trying to disguise it as progressive. The book's greatest strength is its understanding of the clash between the family and industrial capitalism. They show how government can throw its weight behind one or the other, and they make it clear that most liberal/feminist policies effectively make government the ally of capitalism against the family. This can't be emphasized enough.

The Riddle of Amish Culture

By Donald Kraybill, 1989

The destructive work of individualism in society and of centralization in government and the economy has been going on so long that we take it for granted. When we hear about a traditional society somewhere in the world, we assume it must be on the way out. The children will go to school, be taught to despise the provincialism of their parents, and give themselves over to atheism and fashionable sexual perversions. New technology or changing world markets will disrupt established communities, forcing people to leave the land of their ancestors to find work. Local culture will be pulverized by the standardized mass entertainments flowing through each family's television and stereo.

Is there any way for a community to fight this process? Donald Kraybill's book, *The Riddle of Amish Culture*, would suggest that the answer is "yes", but only if a society is willing to make great sacrifices in comfort and freedom. Kraybill is a sociologist whose focus is on this very issue. He seems to have a great admiration for his subjects, one that readers like myself have come to share. He gives the impression of being someone who's lived in a modern cosmopolis his whole life (or perhaps he just assumes that this will be his readers' background), and he treats the advantages of gemeimschaft like fresh discoveries.

The Amish are an Anabaptist sect, and their success in creating a religious community separate from profane society is quite impressive. The average Amish family has 6.6 children. Although they do not make a formal commitment to the requirements of Amish life until their baptism at age 16-21, some 88% of Amish youth choose to be baptized and remain in the community. The Amish deliberately foster an attitude of what they call "Gelassenheit", meaning submission, self-denial, and humility. Their speech, dress, and possessions are regulated to exclude any hint of worldly vanity and individualism. There is a rigid code of conduct, called the "Ordnung", which violates liberal principles in just about every way. For example, it enforces patriarchal gender roles, and it forbids divorce and fornication. Birth control is forbidden or at least strongly frowned upon (I couldn't tell which from the short discussion of this issue).

How have the Amish been so successful in resisting the modern world, when Catholics and mainline Protestants have failed so utterly? Here are some keys to the Amish success:

1. Separation. The Amish live in their own separate communities. Extensive contact with outsiders is discouraged. The primary language of the Amish is Pennsylvania Dutch, a dialect of German; this impedes the easy communication with the "English", as they call outsiders. Telephones are forbidden in homes. Other electronic contacts with the outside world, such as televisions and computers, are also forbidden. The Amish wear distinctive clothes to further mark their separation from the English.

2. No high school or college. Amish children are educated in one-room private schools by Amish teachers, and formal schooling stops after ninth grade. In the 1950s, many Amish fathers were sent to jail for refusing to send their children to high school. In 1972, the Amish were vindicated by the U.S. Supreme Court. Thus, Amish escape the atheist brainwashing the rest of us undergo.

3. Discipline. Those who violate the rules are subjected to varying durations of public ostracism. The worst offenders who refuse to repent can be permanently shunned.

4. Control over technology. The Amish screen new technology; if the use of a device would significantly disrupt their way of life or compromise their separation from the English, its use is forbidden. The fact that the new device would save labor or increase efficiency does not override the primary concern of protecting a way of life. When I read about this, I was surprised that nothing like it had ever occurred to me. I have always assumed that new technology must always be accepted, no matter how disruptive its effects, so long as no direct immorality is involved in its use. The Amish have decided that they will control technology, rather than being controlled by it. Of course, they would have a much harder time with this if they hadn't limited themselves to a few occupations, primarily subsistence agriculture.

Kraybill concludes by wondering if there could be a society with a better mix of freedom and community than the lopsided moderns, on one hand, and Amish, on the other. Of course, most societies before the advent of liberalism were such mixtures. The question is whether a traditional community can survive in the face of aggressive liberalism without taking drastic steps like those of the Amish. I suspect it cannot.

The Wayfinders

By Wade Davis, 2009

I suspect that anthropology can serve as an ideal "gateway drug" to conservatism. Take this book, subtitled "why ancient wisdom matters in the modern world". On the surface, it seems like a pretty standard bash-whitey book, and, indeed, Professor Davis' philosophy could be aptly summarized "all cultures are equally superior to the Christian West." Much of the book is given to lamenting bad things that white people have done to non-white people, all allegedly because of greed or racism. Liberals eat that stuff like catnip. But Davis' concerns are not the standard Leftist issues of inequality and exploitation. He is worried less directly with the fate of individuals as that of cultures. The world's cultures, he points out, are being destroyed at an alarming rate. In our lifetime, half of the world's languages now spoken will likely disappear. With each of those languages will go an entire worldview, centuries of wisdom and expertise, a distinct and irreplaceable "way of being human". Davis takes the reader on a tour across the world to survey the accomplishments of some of these tribal peoples. It is indeed remarkable, what ingenuity it took the Polynesians to explore the entire Pacific Ocean on canoes or for the Inuit to survive in the Arctic. Not only have these peoples found ways to survive, they have built cultures that give dignity and meaning to their lives. Davis can be (unintentionally) quite conservative in his appreciation for tradition and mythology, so long as they come from cultures other than his own. Among the destructive effects of the West, he lists not only colonialism, but also Marxism. The lack in the West of the virtues he praises in other people he attributes to Descartes and the Enlightenment.

Davis is right. These natives should be proud of their cultures. They should strive to preserve what their ancestors entrusted to them, and it would be wrong of us to hinder them. The logical ultimate conclusion is that we too have a right and duty to preserve our traditions against Enlightenment corrosion. That is, we should be conservatives. That, of course, is not the conclusion Davis reaches. In the last chapter, perhaps to preserve his liberalism, Davis seems to revert into Enlightenment thought. Consider the following:

"Were I to distill a single message from these Massey Lectures it would be that culture is not trivial...It is a blanket of comfort that gives meaning to lives. It is a body of knowledge that allows the

individual to make sense out of the infinite sensations of consciousness, to find meaning and order in a universe that ultimately has neither."

No doubt my fellow conservatives were nodding along happily until that last phrase, when the author admits his belief that the cultures he's been praising are all ultimately nothing but lies. These great visions of unity held by Amazonian tribesmen and Buddhist nuns are just imagination. If that's true, then why should they be preserved? Why not be honest and face the abyss of nihilism, as Dr. Davis himself apparently has? I'll let him answer: "B*ut to sum it up, two words will do. Climate change."* That's it; these mystical and mythological beliefs about man's place in the world should be preserved because they can be used to motivate man to take better care of the environment. Don't get me wrong—global warming is a very big problem, but we know this because of Western science, not because the universal Mother of Indian belief told us. If that's all culture is good for, then we really don't need it. In the end, it is the religious conservative who can offer a better justification for the natives than the anthropologist, because we believe that their intuition of a greater reality is, in a fundamental sense, actually true.

Tradition

By Edward Shils, 1981

Max Weber famously divided all organization into the categories of traditional, charismatic, and bureaucratic/rational. For him, modern history is the story of rationalization: the replacement of tradition by bureaucracy. Sociologist Edward Shils is a disciple of Weber, but he thinks that Weber underestimated the ability of traditions to resist the pressures to rationalize. He doesn't deny that anti-traditional forces have made tremendous advances in the past centuries, but he doubts that their victory can ever be complete. Men will always want a connection to their past, a collective memory which extends before the lifetime of the individual. Shils differs from many sociologists in that he regards this desire for connection with the past as basically legitimate and good, although he doesn't regard all traditions as worth preserving.

Shils defines a tradition as anything that's been passed down for at least three generations. This leads him to identify some unexpected things as traditions, including the anti-traditional traditions of rationalization and emancipation, because the proponents of these things generally didn't come up with them themselves, but inherited their ideals from a previous generation of liberals. There is even a tradition of technological invention, because the idea of trying to preserve techniques is given to us rather than continually re-discovered, a necessary factor since most cultures in most times have not had this idea. Shils therefore distinguishes substantive traditions from other traditions. Substantive traditions are conscious of themselves as traditions and explicitly value their connection with the past. Thus, the struggle in modern times is between substantive traditions and anti-traditional (rationalizing or emancipating) traditions, and it's a struggle that can never end in a final victory by any side.

This book is very hard to summarize. It's not clear what the point of it is. It seems that a general sociological analysis of tradition is less interesting than an analysis of a single tradition. The latter is what most books about traditions really are. They are generally written by Catholic or Eastern Orthodox apologists who investigate whether their Church is in some sense carrying forward the same tradition as the Apostles, always of course reaching the answer "yes". Shils isn't committed to any such proposition, so his discussion of the maintenance of identity of a tradition in spite of changes is rather bland. He discusses the ways that traditions maintain themselves and the things that can push a tradition to change in various ways. Some of it is obvious, and some is insightful. Traditionalists should not regard this book as necessary reading.

Essays

Can there be an American conservatism?

This is a dilemma I've often seen posed on the internet, particularly at center-right sites. The United States is a fundamentally liberal country. It was founded by deist freemasons—in an act of rebellion against their legitimate monarch—deliberately for the purpose of creating a Lockean republic. All our traditions are liberal. Since the purpose of conservatives is to preserve tradition, in America, the job of conservatives is to preserve liberalism. Thus traditionalism in an American context is shown to be logically impossible.

Needless to say, I disagree with this conclusion, but it does raise an interesting issue. What exactly are American conservatives trying to conserve? The standard right-liberal, Republican answer is that we're trying to preserve freedom, which is a sort of American essence. But is it true that freedom is all there is to the American nation? Is there nothing more to our heritage than the right to do as we please, so long as we don't get in each other's way? To a conservative, the answer is known a priori. America is not constructed on a social contract based on nothing but individual rights because we are sure that no society could be thus constituted. Americans pay lip service to freedom, but freedom is not, and cannot be, the principle that orgainizes our common life. Nor is the proposition that "all men are created equal." No, the reality of American common life is not freedom, but authority.

People in other nations may be as free as we are, but an American is someone who is subject to a particular set of authorities. The first of these is the government, whose sovereignty is divided into its federal, state, and city incarnations. Americans use Lockean theories to justify their subjection to their State, but this is just sophistry. Americans are morally bound to obey their federal, state, and local governments not because they have consented to it, even implicitly—for to withhold consent would be an immoral act—but because they recognize these authorities as legitimate. This acknowledgment of legitimacy is what makes an American an American, and it is a primary goal of conservatives to establish this sense of legitimacy on its true basis.

It's these sort of unspoken, unchosen, compulsary "givens" that American conservatives try to identify and defend. So, for example, another taken-for-granted fact is citizenship: some people are Americans, and other people aren't. A foreigner can only become an American if the state chooses to grant him citizenship. Americans vocally espouse the principle of treating all people equally, but our unwritten constitution endorses the principle of particular loyalty. Another given is the judiciary. America's laws don't just reflect the will of the current legislature, but reflect a legal tradition developed over centuries. Through precedent, this tradition is another legitimate authority to Americans. A final accepted authority is that of parents over their children. This is so taken for granted that we never mention it in discussing America's constitution. Yet, when a child runs away from home, the police will forcibly return the child to his parents, and nobody asks how to reconcile this with our creed of "freedom" and "equality". Wisdom makes us hypocrites, because if we were to take freedom and equality seriously—as the liberals wish us to do—it would destroy our society.

The Founders were liberals who hated tradition and piety, but since their deaths, the natural instict of a people to revere its founders has siezed upon them and created the memory of the Founding Fathers. From this word "Father", one can see that the attitude assumed by the population is one of piety. Piety is an important part of any community, and so the conservative endorses these sentiments, but his reasons are subtle and far different from those given publicly. The public reason for revering the Founders is that they fought tyranny and established freedom and equality. These are not reasons that will recommend themselves to conservatives; nor are they the real reason the populace reveres the Founders. A true believer in freedom and equality despises piety; at most he may agree with some of the Founders' beliefs and approve some of their actions. No, a conservative knows that piety is ultimately a religious sentiment. We feel awe for our parents and ancestors because they are the source of our being, the channel through which we were created. Every act of creation confronts us with the mystery of Being; creation is where God touches the universe, and those beings that God uses as his instruments of creation become icons of Him. What the Founders succeeded in doing was to establish a legitimate authority. In doing so, they created a principle of order in the minds of their subjects. Symbolically, they repeated God's act of ordering the universe in the first chapter of Genesis. Americans feel awe for the Founding because the moment that the nation was created and ordered is for us an iconic event. One notices that the act that receives the most reverence in the minds of Americans is not some practical decision the Founders made or some brilliant idea they had, but a purely ritual event they performed. I refer to the signing of the Declaration of Independence, an event painted and eulogized countless times. These freethinkers certainly didn't see themselves as ritualistic men, but to found a nation, they performed a ritual. Writing names on a piece of paper is something that has purely symbolic effect, but it's that symbolic effect that was the most important thing for American piety.

One can now see the ambivalence we conservatives have toward the Founders. Seeing them as men, from the standpoint of objective history, they were traitors who deserved to be hanged. Their ideas about the origin of government were ridiculous; their encomia to freedom were reckless. Thomas Jefferson, for example, was a practical anarchist who endorsed permanent periodic revolutions. If anyone were to take his ideas seriously, he would be a threat to the social order. But people don't take his ideas seriously. Nor do they take Jefferson the man seriously. In the minds of the public, the man has been replaced by the symbol, the object of patriotic piety. Jefferson has been "digested" by the social order. No doubt he would have regarded this as a fate worse than death. To the conservative, however, this is all to the best.

What about the rhetoric that Americans use to justify their devotion to the Founding—all that crap about "throwing off the dead hand of tradition", "creating the world anew", of being a nation "concieved in liberty", "founded on the proposition that all men are equal", etc? We don't take it that seriously. We know that ordinary Americans lack a vocabulary to express the piety they feel, so they borrow the language of liberalism to justify it. Our ultimate goal is to give them a fuller vocabulary, so that they can express their devotion to their *patria* without the unnecessary ideological baggage. In the meantime, we must be very careful in critiquing these false ideas so that we don't harm the true sentiments hiding beneath them.

Preliminaries to Catholicism

Chapter 1: Escape from subjectivity

What is distinctive about the Catholic mind, that Catholics believe things that no one else believes? Identifying specific differences is not hard; what is tricky is figuring out which one is the ultimate cause of all the others. For example, many would say that the authority of the Pope is what makes Catholicism unique, and hence we are called "Papists". However, the papacy is for Catholics a conclusion rather than an axiom. We accept it because we see the modern hierarchical Church as the historically legitimate development of the Apostolic Church. But looking at the same historical and scriptural data, Protestants and Orthodox see corruption rather than development. What underlying difference causes us to read the data so differently? Again, one could cite specific dogmas that are distinctive to the Catholic faith: the assumption of Mary, Purgatory, the *filioque*, the immorality of contraception, etc. But why do Catholics believe these things when others don't?

What do you say Catholics have too much of?

On what authority are the above dogmas based? Depending on the issue and who one asks, one will get an appeal to *Tradition*, to reason (or, in the Catholic-speak I prefer, to *natural theology and natural law*), or to ecclesial *authority*. And indeed, Catholics are noted for their distinctive attachment to all three of these, as we are often accused of corrupting religion with our blind adherence to the past, our unscriptural rationalism, and our unfettered authoritarianism. This is a rather odd thing in itself, don't you think? I mean that the Church should go (or at least be seen as going) so over the top on all three things. For, on most people's understandings, these three things are entirely independent. We would thus expect them to contradict each other at times. Tradition is understood as uncritical acceptance of inherited practices, justifiable if at all only on prudential grounds ("established practices must have some adaptive value...", etc). Not being able to make any sense of classical metaphysics, "reason" to the modern ear means scientism and utilitarianism, while the picture of authoritarianism is just lawlessness at the top. Putting these things together should make an incoherent muddle, but actually the Catholic worldview is strikingly coherent and interconnected. In fact, the Catholic understandings of tradition, natural law, and authority are very different from the non-Catholic ones. These three things are seen more as different manifestations of a deeper underlying principle than as autonomous and antagonistic principles. The success of

Catholicism in creating a coherent worldview should be taken as a sign that our understanding of these principles is the better one.

The Church also goes overboard in other areas, according to her critics: she is excessively *ritualistic*, *hierarchical*, and *dogmatic*, they say. Once again, the intriguing thing is that these are seemingly independent ingroup-identifiers. Why should a single organization feel the need to over-emphasize all three? If correct belief is the important thing, why bother so much over rituals and obedience, and vice versa. (Catholics, of course, will see in this criticism a case of the perverse "if distinct, then opposed" modern mentality.)

What do you say Catholics have too little of?

To avoid the impression that Catholicism is just religion to excess, imagine asking the Church's critics what Catholics have too little of. In the first place, they will say *freedom*. In their different ways, liberals, Jews, Protestants, and Orthodox will all say that Catholics' relationship with God is over-regulated, that stifling and unnecessary uniformity is being imposed from the top. But why are such constraints not only unnecessary but bad? Here we come to the crux of the matter. The intuition is that such formalities are ill-fitted to genuine spiritual life, and everybody agrees that Catholics are not particularly "spiritual". Pretty much every opponent of the Church defines itself in some way or another as the more spiritual alternative to Catholicism. Let's accept that and try to make sense of it: on the "religious" versus "spiritual" divide, Catholicism is most people's idea of the high religion/low spirituality extreme, while they all compete to fill the other extreme.

What the heck does this really mean, though? When some New Age hippie claims that he's "spiritual but not religious", what is he getting at? (I won't ask what he literally means by it, since conceptual clarity is not to be expected from that sort of person.) Obviously "spiritual" is being opposed to dogma, to ritual, and in fact to anything public and non-subjective. The ideal of spirituality is unmediated communion of the private soul with ultimate reality. Now, doctrines, ritual, ecclesial membership, and authority are intrinsically public. Even to express religious beliefs in language is to give them a sort of public existence, an existence outside of one's mind. In the "religious" vs. "spiritual" dichotomy, the public world is seen as less spiritually significant than the private world, and indeed often as a totally meaningless interplay of material and biological forces. Public acts are "formalities", empty of meaning but for the contingent spiritual acts that sometimes accompany them. From the "spiritual" perspective, authentic religion is a matter solely of feelings and authentic morality is a matter solely of intentions. Consider a man who feels guilty after having committed a wicked act; seeking to purify himself from moral defilement, he dumps water on his head. A silly superstition to think this would do any good, right? After all, what God really wants is perfect contrition, and this is an entirely spiritual–i.e. private, mental, and unscripted–act. Such is the spiritualist's case. Of course, Protestants and Orthodox are in many ways closer to Catholics than they are to "spiritual but not religious" hippies, but they also in their own ways accuse Catholicism of slighting the subjective sphere, of being the overly-objective (ritualistic or rationalist) variant of Christianity.

Against spirituality

Given that one can have spiritual Christianity, why would anyone choose carnal, superstitious Christianity? Let me for a moment speak for myself. When I probe into my psyche, what I find is not Descartes' repository of clear meanings, but a house of mirrors and fog. My own true feelings and intentions are never clear to me, and my capacity for rationalization is boundless. I doubt that I have it in myself to be perfectly contrite; nor could I ever know if I had succeeded. My motives are always mixed and unworthy, and my intuitions are too unreliable to base something as important as a relationship with God. Although I'm as much driven to find meaning and authenticity as the next man (at least I think I am–not that I really know or care), for me this drive takes the form of a quest to get out of my own head.

Public meanings

The public world, on the other hand, is suffused with the Logos, filled with intelligibility, meaning, and purpose that human minds find rather than invent. We confront this extra-mental intelligibility in the objectivity and beauty of mathematics, in the precision and simplicity of the laws of nature, in the intrinsic teleology of living organisms, in our apprehension of the beauty of the natural world. The human world, too, is imbued with an order we find rather than create, despite the fact that we are its subject. The basic goods of human nature are not a matter of choice, and they color bare biological facts like sex, kinship, and death with unchosen meaning. We may rebel against those meanings (as our age has chosen to do), but we don't have the option of starting from a blank slate where our acts have only whatever meanings we give them. Even our imaginations seem to participate in universal forms unchosen by us, as seen in the recurring archetypes and symbols that inform the worlds' mythologies. At the level of human aggregates, too, we see neither chaos, a mere mechanical balance of strife, nor consciously engineered structure; rather we see emergent order in the form of communal identities, authority recognized as legitimate, and the inherited traditions of peoples. Such things do, of course, emerge from a history of human acts, but they are, and must be, bigger than any particular conscious choices of individuals or even communities themselves (which, after all, are constituted by these things).

The above examples of "public meanings" may seem very different. Some may be surprised that I count mythic symbolism as an aspect of objective reality, or that I say that nations cannot be engineered into being when we Americans are proud of our "Founding Fathers" for supposedly doing just that. However, all these things are bigger than the individual human mind in a way that pure human artifacts are not. For a speech, a short story, or a corporate logo, we can ask what the author was thinking when he made it and what he meant to convey by it. For things discovered rather than purely invented, or for emergent rather than consciously engineered order, we cannot even in principle hope to thus get to the bottom of the thing and find a human idea or perspective. This makes public meanings not less intelligible than private meanings, but more. Our minds can absorb their truths partially, but because there is a lack of fit between the truth grasped and the mind grasping, our contemplations are never exhausted, never "hit bottom". This same "lack of fit" provides an opening for us to transcend the limits of human rationality. Ironically, the very unintelligibility of matter–its *ambiguity*–in making things less than spiritual, at the same time makes it possible for material beings to be vehicles of the more than (humanly) spiritual.

God Himself is the author of public meanings. The order of the cosmos speaks to us, and yet it is no creaturely intelligence speaking, but God speaking in the truths of His creation. And when we participate in objectively meaningful acts, God Himself speaks through us.

Catholic authenticity

My deepest sense is that real meanings are not what is inside my head, but what is outside of it. The task is to appropriate these objective meanings, to allow them to inform the soul. On its own, my soul is just a chaotic jumble of desires; its purpose is to receive order from outside rather than impose it. A true, good, and authentic response to the order of the world would be complete receptivity, a response to things as they really are and not as my internal jumble of desires and fantasies color them. Thus, when I want to really make contrition to my Creator, I am not left to my own internal devices. I can appropriate the symbols of the public world and speak with a depth of meaning beyond my native power. The superstitious man in my example above had the right idea. He knew that, in his wretchedness, no attempt to make things right by his own spiritual purity will suffice. To ascend to God, he must in a sense lay aside his very self, approach God's throne as an archetype rather than an individual, and speak only with the pure words that God Himself gives him. Water is a universal symbol of formlessness, purification, and rebirth. This symbol is not our creation, but His, and in His words He places great power.

I am a Roman Catholic, and dumping water on people's heads is one of the most important things my Church does.

I don't expect you to be convinced yet; this is only part 1 after all. However, you can already begin to see the advantages of carnal, superstitious religion (of which, remember, Catholicism is *the* exemplar). It promises escape from the prison of subjectivity. It promises to reconcile reason, natural, tradition, and authority, so that the compatibility of these indispensable guides becomes clear. Most importantly from a Christian point of view, it allows a natural appreciation of the central facts of salvation history, for although many Christian sects boast of their spiritualism, spiritualism itself is problematic for the Christian story. If the private soul is everything, how could we justly be condemned by Adam and justified by Christ, justified what's more by a physical–not merely spiritual–sacrificial event? It is to this question that I will turn next.

Chapter 2: The sign of the cross

The key to understanding Catholicism is our attitude toward symbols. In naturally symbolic acts like sexual intercourse or animal sacrifice we find the meaning to be partly embedded in the nature of the act itself and independent of the performers' intentions. The signification achieved is *suprarational* in that the performer needn't be able to articulate fully the meaning of his act; nor need such a full articulation even be possible. The performer need only affix his assent to the given meaning of the act; he is able to "say" more than he can think. The signification of a natural symbol is also *suprapersonal* in that it is part of the public world rather than of the performer's intentions, in some cases making it possible for others to affix their assent as well. Even conventional symbols display this suprapersonal nature, e.g. so that a company saluting a flag is a single act of the company itself, whereas the interior patriotic feelings of each soldier are necessarily individual and incommunicable. Thus, participation in these symbols allows a soul to transcend itself in a twofold way: beyond its nature as a limited intellect and beyond its person as a single individual.

The central dogmatic claim

Catholicism also contains in its essence a central dogmatic claim: that Jesus Christ, fully God and fully Man, has, by his sacrificial death and resurrection two millennia ago, freed mankind from slavery to sin and opened the possibility of communion with God as His children.

Now, I don't expect this dogma to sound attractive or plausible or even sane on a first examination. Accepting it too easily means you probably haven't understood it. You'll need to have a good grasp of the key words "God", "sacrifice", "sin", and "children". Perhaps you don't feel particularly in thrall to "sin", or you don't see why God has to be such a vindictive jerk about such things, or you don't see how what happened to another person two thousand years ago could affect your spiritual state regardless. If you are a fellow Christian of the Protestant persuasion, on the other hand, you will accept the above "core Catholic dogma" as your own, but you may understand it differently, and it is possible that we can learn from each other.

Man's alienation from God

To understand Christianity, one must first understand the problem it is meant to solve: alienation from God, not being His children apart from Christ's atoning sacrifice. This alienation is conceived as both *moral* and *ontological*. The moral part is what was most often emphasized by the Latin Fathers: we are alienated from God by our sins. This is a matter of great misunderstanding between Catholics and modernists. The latter often express consternation over "Catholic guilt" while being convinced that they themselves are already basically good people, or good enough anyway. The question, though, is "good enough for what?" If one just means "good enough not to be a nuisance to the social order" then probably many people clear this low bar. However, here we're talking about communion with God, so "good enough" must mean "pure and fit to stand in the presence of the All-Holy". Many socially unimportant vices in my soul—the vanity, selfishness, and vengefulness restrained to petty infractions merely by social pressure and lack of opportunity– positively contradict an all-Holy presence. We often hear that God is merciful, but this cannot mean that God chooses to ignore the offense of our sins, that is, that His mercy is a mere deficiency of justice. To ignore sin would do the sinner no good, at least as far as communion with God is concerned. The impurity must be removed, the debt paid, and the sinner redeemed. This is God's mercy.

Even apart from the moral faults of mankind, an ontological chasm separates us from God. Naturally speaking, we cannot be God's children–even by adoption–because we are limited intellects and He is unqualified Being, subsistent Truth and Goodness, and necessarily incomprehensible to us. God cannot induct us into the distinctive goods of His own Nature, as a father by definition does with his children. At best, we might be His beloved pets. Our intellects are made for objects in the world, but God is not an object in the world (i.e. an instance of some limiting nature), making it impossible for us to genuinely conceive and relate to Him.

Sacrifice

The religious response is to offer God a sacrifice, in which payment is offered in reparation for sins. As blood is (symbolically) the principle of life, the shedding of blood is a fit recognition that it is the sinner's very life that is owed and vicariously offered. Meanwhile, in being consecrated to God, the blood of the victim acquires sacramental power, and through the existence of a sacred space (the temple and victim), God condescends to be treated as a part of the world, a resident of a particular place with whom transactions can be made. This arrangement, instituted by the Lord Himself in the Torah, does not involve any anthropomorphizing error about God, because the offering proceeds by way of public, suprarational signification (the symbolism of blood as life–cf. Lev. 17:11). Its participants never need imagine that they have any kind of adequate conceptual understanding of what the offering accomplishes or to Whom it is offered.

Many objections have been raised to sacrificial religion. Most recently, Rene Girard has tried to reduce the whole thing to a matter of mob pathology, an accusation the Catholic mind naturally rejects. More serious is the old Anselmian claim that no homage to God by mere men can atone for sins, because we owe all that to Him anyway. What's more, even if we say that the sacrifices of men succeed in bringing God down to our level (allowing us to treat Him as a being in the world), they certainly don't bring us up to His level.

Or do they? Worship may be a meritorious act, but it would seem to be a distinctly un-Godlike one. After all, assuming monotheism, who would there be for God Himself to worship? The whole experience must be alien to Him. However, in Christian orthodoxy, God is a Trinity of persons, each one eternally engaged in perfect adoration of the other two. Indeed, all of the virtues of religion–piety, gratitude, obedience–are present in exemplary form in God the Son, Who enjoys a genuinely filial relationship with God the Father. Sacrifice in the sense of self-offering to God thus belongs to God's own inner nature, as does the communion Christianity claims He offers us.

We can now see how the sacrifice of Jesus is uniquely fitted to reconciling God and man. As the physical, suprapersonal act of a man, Christ is able to offer Himself, not just as an individual, but as Man, for all mankind. A symbolic event in the public, human world, it is a thing suited for the appropriation of other men, in a way that the eternal filial devotion of the Son for the Father, absent the Incarnation, is not. Given Christ's humanity and divinity, though, a participation in His divine sonship is possible. As a suprarational act, Jesus' self-offering is, while a genuinely human act, not limited in its significatory power by human concepts. It's meaning can reach so far–indeed, given Who He is, it must reach so far–as to include the Son's self-offering to the

Father, the act that constitutes the Son's very identity. A divine "word"–one identical to the Logos Himself–has been put in the human world for our appropriation.

Note that the meaning of Christ's sacrifice is contained in the physical act itself, in His physical murder. Christ's perfect interior obedience to the Father and love for us are in themselves insufficient, because without the public action (His physical execution), Christ's interior obedience would be incommunicable, would be His alone rather than all humanity's. Of course, Christ's private moral goodness in allowing Himself to be tortured to death for our sakes is still very important! Given His omnipotence, our Atonement could not have happened without his assent. Also, to be a valid sacrifice, Christ must affix His subjective assent to the act.

(Compare: consent of both partners is needed to validly consummate a marriage, but the bride and groom just thinking consensual loving thoughts about each other is itself insufficient to consummate a marriage. What is needed is the symbolic physical act of intercourse to whose meaning the participants affix their assent.) No doubt, two millennia of Christian devotion were not wrong to draw inspiration and devotion from the memory of our Savior's love and fortitude unto death. However, we must avoid the temptation to over-spiritualize His work, lest we make the Incarnation seem pointless! The crucifixion did not happen just to teach us a lesson or to give us an example or for Jesus to win merit by His private virtue.

Given this unashamedly carnal focus, it is natural that images of Christ's execution play so large a role in Catholic worship and devotion. Walk into a Catholic Church, and you will be confronted by crucifixes and stations of the cross. We place crucifixes on rosaries, necklaces, and holy cards. At the start and end of each prayer, we sign ourselves by the instrument of His murder. In the Blessed Sacrament, we claim to make His sacrifice our own.

Chapter 3: The sacramental life

How to earn salvation? You can't. The idea of a just God rewarding or punishing each soul according to its individual merits is something one must *overcome* in order to understand any of the branches of Christianity. How can it be that the righteousness of Jesus Christ and His own relationship to God the Father are transmitted to other human beings? Catholics approach these questions with our distinctive attitude toward symbols and the public world; our answer comes from our distinctive doctrines on faith and the Church, grace and the sacraments.

Christ's sacrifice, as we have argued, was a public symbolic act, meaning it is the sort of act that can be appropriated by other people via public symbolic signification. This was discussed at some length in part II, but recall the key power of symbols to unite the actions of multiple people into a single meaningful act. Christ's sacrifice doesn't inspire us to offer distinct, lesser sacrifices of our own. Through the sacraments, we participate in His own sacrifice, a sacrifice that itself contains in symbol His whole identity as the Son of the Father. We thus inject ourselves into the life of the Trinity, or, to put it more traditionally, the Trinity becomes present in our souls through grace.

From this understanding, the Catholic doctrines of the Eucharist follow. The Protestants call it a "symbol", and we agree—it is a symbol that God makes true. It is a sacrifice, the very same sacrifice of Calvary sacramentally recalled for our appropriation. Through this symbolic appropriation, the Blessed Sacrament is also a source of grace, the constitutive act of the Church, an establishment of communion with God and all His children in heaven and on Earth.

As with all symbolic signification, both a subjective (private) element and an objective (public) element are necessarily involved. In the objective realm are the sacramental signs that, by their objective symbolic meanings, incorporate us into Christ's death and resurrection. To claim possession of these meanings requires the subjective element—the soul's interior "Amen" of faith.

Symbolism: the objective element of the sacraments

The meaning of the sacraments, that which is "spoken through" them, is given entirely by the acts themselves (which includes words spoken) read through the normative context of salvation history. Thus, to understand what the Eucharist or Holy Orders means, one notes the words spoken and actions performed and asks "What meaning does this suggest, given the story of God's covenant with Israel and revelation through Jesus?" One does not ask what the participants of the sacrament are thinking; nor does one worry about their personal character. The potency of the sacrament likewise comes from God alone, Who acting through the symbol makes it to be a true statement. Hence the Catholic doctrine that the sacraments operate *ex opere operato.*

The suprapersonal nature of the sacraments allows a soul to "claim" Jesus' words to His Father. All those claiming Christ in this way thus make, not many statements to the Father, but a single one (appropriated many times). They speak with a single voice, that of Christ Himself, and so constitute a corporate person. This is the Church, called "the mystical body of Christ". Catholics believe that grace not only unites our souls with God, but also with each other. Grace may "flow" from God to one person through another. This sense of a supernatural connection between those in a state of grace, living or dead, is what inspires those distinctively Catholic practices of offering prayers for the souls in Purgatory and praying for the intercession of the saints.

Faith: the subjective element of the sacraments

Of course, salvation is through faith, a Biblical truth affirmed by both Protestants and Catholics. Faith opens the soul to grace. Its act of trust is an interior, private reality; each person must make his own act of trust. However, the revelation we are to accept is a public thing. I am saved not by accepting my private faith–some set of propositions on religious subjects, understood as I understand them–but by accepting the faith of the Church. To accept the faith of the Church does not mean that one has looked at an exhaustive list of Catholic doctrines and decided that one agrees with every one of them. Of course, knowingly dissenting from a Catholic doctrine does disqualify one from holding the Church's faith, but to have gone through an exhaustive list is neither required nor possible. This is because the faith of the Church really refers to the meaning of her sacramental worship–that which the Mass and the sacraments objectively "say". *Lex orandi, lex credendi.* Because these are suprarational, their doctrinal content is inexhaustible. It makes perfect sense even for a well-educated Catholic to say that he knows little about his own faith. And yet he does believe it, even the part he doesn't know. Such is the nature of trust that one doesn't require a full understanding of what one is believing to really believe it. Faith is the interior "Amen" to the meaning of the sacraments, the conviction of the participant to mean what his acts objectively mean and to believe what they objectively proclaim, even though he grasps their meaning only imperfectly.

Faith is, thus, an open-ended commitment; no one really knows all of what he's "signed up for" at his baptism. For Catholics, this does relate to the authority of the Church, the competence of her teaching office to reliably draw out the doctrines implied by her inherited worship. However, Protestantism's acceptance of the Bible's authority gives it a public character as well. The Protestant accepts the Bible's authority without imagining that he has completely plumbed its depths. Like the Catholic, he may end up surprised by some of the things he's committed to believing. Even for "faith alone" Protestants, Christianity always ends up being an adventure of getting outside one's own head.

And that's a good thing.

Chapter 4: Vows

A sacred vow gives form to a life.

Man loves his freedom but finds no happiness in it. As a miser hordes his gold, so the freedom-lover hordes his options. Both make the same mistake. Just as the only joy in money is in spending it, the only joy in freedom is in casting it away in the act of commitment. This indeed is the ultimate self-mastery, to hold one's entire life in hand and, in one moment's vow, to offer it whole to God. The Church offers man the life-disciplines of marriage, holy orders, or the religious life. In embracing one, he imposes on his life a unity and definiteness, an overarching project to be completed, a narrative to be lived. His life becomes an intelligible thing, now that each episode can be related to the primary plot line.

To make one's life something definite certainly restricts one's future freedom, and some find this frightening. It is also true that to see one's life as a single, definite thing is also to see it as a finite thing; in every ordination or wedding is an intimation of mortality, and many I suspect find this frightening as well. But what is the alternative? An uncommitted life, a formless life, the meaningless expanse of years. Such is the life fashioned by modern man's miserly freedom-hoarding, the clinging to escape clauses that vitiate even those commitments he does (sort of) make. Stuck in indeterminacy, he loses the vow's moment of existential mastery and the subsequent comforts of a meaningful connection to his past and future.

Marriage and ordination are gifts that enlarge the soul.

Marriage and ordination are great blessings, but it would be wrong to think that, just because the free vow lies at their heart, they are blessings we bestow upon ourselves by sheer force of will. A mere private act of will, such as a decision by a man to be faithful to a particular woman, could never order an entire life like a marriage vow can, because one moment's decision can be overturned by any future moment's regret. Why should his will then have authority over his will now? Even to promise himself to the woman is not enough, because she would then be the holder of the promise and could at any moment release him. In marriage, through its power of sacramental signification, God lends the couple His own voice, empowering them to make a sacred vow with a moral force beyond their or anyone else's reach. There is a promise, but God Himself is its holder. It is an act of freedom, yes, but a supernatural freedom bestowed by our Father in Heaven.

What's more, if vocation were a mere act of will, its content could be nothing more than what was consciously willed; whatever was in one's head at that moment becomes the guiding light to one's life. If that were the case, then the Church's enemies would be right to see this as a diminishment of a man. The vow would constrict his spirit, never allowing him to grow beyond the vision of that moment when he calcified his soul. In fact, the three particular Christian vocations, although chosen by us, are not made by us. Each is a great suprapersonal mystery, something larger than the soul that chooses it, something into which one grows. To choose one of these paths is to expand one's soul, opening previously inaccessible spiritual vistas, not to contract it.

Marriage and the wisdom of recklessness

Marriage is the most lowly vocation, but it is nevertheless more beautiful than anything in the profane world. In this station the family, one's role as mother or father, is the main organizing principle of one's life. Reduced to its essence, the marriage contract is a public agreement a particular man shall be recognized as father to a particular woman's offspring, with all the duties to each other that this implies. Contrary to what is often said today, the love of the spouses is not the contract's defining feature. Marriage is, however, the natural fulfillment of romantic love. The Church didn't invent the idea that a man and woman should promise each other exclusivity and permanence–lovers have always promised each other that; love carries with it the impulse to make such vows. The Church is unique only in allowing these vows to mean precisely what they say.

Would any lover be content to make the marriage vows to his beloved while replacing the promise "till death" with "unless I become unhappy"? Surely not. True love scorns such timidity. Even heretics and heathen, who admit divorce in principle, would think it base not to at least pretend to marry in the Catholic way. They call the Catholic way cruel, because it traps spouses in "unhappy" and "failed" marriages. But the vow's "cruelty"–the depth of self-sacrifice it may potentially demand–is inseparable from its grandeur. Moderns are never trapped in unhappy marriages at the cost that to be married now just means to be accidentally not yet divorced. Like soldiers, married Catholics know that their honor is tied to the magnitude of sacrifice they may have to make. Who would be so reckless as to take such a vow? Anyone who has been in love.

For all its sentimentality, the world does not respect romantic love nearly as much as the Church does. Modernity indulges lovers, but it doesn't respect them. It treats them like drunks whose car keys need to be taken away. Yes, lovers feel compelled to promise each other undying love, but this is a sort of madness, and it would be cruel to hold them to it after they've sobered up. The Catholic Church, on the other hand, sees love–and *especially* the urge to make of one's life a gift to another in contempt for one's future freedom or ease–as a special lucidity of mind, and she grants to lovers her supernatural binding power. What modernity calls wisdom, the prioritizing of personal happiness over marital duty as if life were long and eternity short, is where we see a clouding and enfeeblement of the mind.

Career as modernity's replacement for marriage

It is sad to think of a person looking back on a life of hopping from spouse to spouse and family to family. (Like Saint Paul, I suspect that even widowers would be happier not remarrying, although there is no sin in them doing so.) What would such a life be about? Where would be the unity to it? The modern world, which celebrates divorce, does have an answer to this, though more often implied than stated. For the modern man, career is supposed to be the focus of one's life. Career is the ultimate substantive good in the world's dominant ideologies of liberalism, capitalism, and feminism. Career is what liberalism means by freedom and what feminism means by self-actualization. Looking back on his life, modern man on his deathbed can recollect how well he climbed up the corporate ladder. *That* is what his life was about. *That* is the freedom that the destruction of Catholic patriarchy delivers.

The priesthood is not a job.

Vocations to the priesthood and religious life are similar in spirit to marriage, but more elevated in that God is more directly the object of self-offering. Much of the world's confusion about the Catholic priesthood stems from failing to realize that the priesthood is a vocation, not a job (or–Heaven forbid!–a career). Thus, we hear many asinine remarks about how women or married temporary functionaries could perform the same functions as an ordained man. This is false (no one but an ordained man can confect the Eucharist, the main duty of a priest), and the reason is that a man's priestly role has to be his core self-identity.

Suppose one were to say that a revolving sequence of babysitters could take care of a child just as well as his mother could. Of course, the babysitters could do many of the same things as the mother, but the depth of meaning would be lost, because when a mother cares for her child, these acts are the very heart of her life. Priesthood is spiritual fatherhood; we even call our priests "father". What wife and children are to a married man, his parishioners are to a priest.

(This understanding, while somewhat safeguarded by the discipline of celibacy, which deprives the priest of any competing "private life", has been gravely obscured in recent times by the horrible policy of rotating priests from parish to parish every six years or so. Evidently, the bishops have begun thinking of their priests as mere employees, who needn't develop a personal patriarchal relationship with their parish, and the laity have just taking this attitude to its logical conclusion of wanting married/women/pervert priests who can "do the job just as well".)

When, endowed by God with a special sacramental character, the priest stands on the altar and speaks Christ's own words in His place, we see the heart of his life. The perfection of the Eucharistic sacrifice demands that the identity of priest and victim be maintained. The priest must sacramentally identify as Jesus Christ. This must be the core of his life and his identity, with his own personality displaced to the periphery.

Religious life: a deliberate scandal to the worldly

Then there is the religious life, which scandalizes modern men most of all. Marriage they understand as emotional fulfillment, and a priest they imagine to be a funny kind of therapist, but what could be the point of monks and nuns? Some indeed perform secularly useful charitable work, but we should be clear that the purpose of most religious orders is not to staff schools, hospitals, and soup kitchens. It would be closer to the truth to say that their purpose is to give the sort of scandal they give, to present the sort of life that can't be understood, or even (like marriage and the priesthood) misunderstood by worldly minds. The religious stand out as a sign that temporal usefulness is not the ultimate measure of value, that what we call "the real world" is a small and transient thing in the light of eternity. Appreciate why the Church thinks it good that some should devote their lives to prayer, and one can then understand why she thinks it good that others should marry or be priests.

Chapter 5: Moral rules

Five hundred years ago, when somebody said that Catholic beliefs don't make sense, he was probably talking about something like Transubstantiation; today, when somebody says that, he's almost certainly talking about sex. While moral rules are not the focal point of Catholicism, they are closely connected to it. However, to one who holds the Catholic perspective as I have described it–an alertness to the symbolic depth of the public world–the Church's rules on sex, killing, usury, submission to authority, and the like are no scandal to the intellect. They are rather such natural conclusions that the Church's commitment to them is evidence for her reliability.

Morality cannot be reduced to intentions and consequences

Why though do modern men think the Church's prohibitions on contraception, remarriage, usury, etc. don't make sense? It is because they can only conceive of three reasons an act could be wrong: a malicious motive, bad consequences for other peoples' happiness, or an invasion of other peoples' legitimate spheres of personal autonomy (i.e. violating their "rights"). Now, many things Catholicism calls sins are bad for these reasons, but not all. Consider masturbation or assisting someone else's suicide. Why does the Church forbid these things? Did it just never occur to us that masturbation doesn't hurt anybody, that the motive–carnal pleasure–is the same motive I have when I put honey in my tea? Has nobody pointed out to us that to help a man kill himself relieves pain and enhances his control over his life?

No, trust me, we're familiar with the arguments from these sorts of observations, and we've rejected them. They all hinge on a false premise, seldom even stated and always sloppily taken to be coterminous with reason itself. I mean the assumption that the meaning of an act (and, hence, its moral status) can only depend on the intention of the actor and the consequences for other people. Following this assumption, one can say that any act is licit if the actor intends no harm and no one is inconvenienced. However, Catholicism rejects this reduction of morality. I belabor the point because one cannot understand Catholic morality at all without realizing this, and very many people don't. For Catholics, meaning also comes from the embedded symbolism in the material and social world. An act can thus have a meaning independent of its effects on others or its author's intention, and so it can be sinful on account of this meaning.

Man the symbol-bearer; inviolability of human life

This is the true dignity of man–his symbolic potency, the fact that, unlike a puddle of water or a mouse, he can perform acts of the greatest meaning; he can perform true worship or true sacrilege. Our recognition of this dignity differs fundamentally from the Kantian respect for persons based on their status as subjects. Intellect and will are certainly a crucial part of humanity's capacity for meaningful action, but they are not the whole of it. The human body itself participates in this symbolic "charge", as does the community of humans. After all, we participate in God's sovereignty through government, in His act of creation through coitus, and in His great sacrifice through digestion. The whole organism is the bearer of this awesome significance, not just the mind which is a part but most certainly not the owner of the whole.

Thus, the respect due to human persons is not just a respect for their wills, which may be malformed or nonexistent in certain cases. The Catholic prohibition against murder is in many ways stricter than what modern man finds reasonable. It protects all human organisms–the preconscious fetus, the mentally disabled, and the unconscious, every bit as much as those alert enough to object to their own murder. It prohibits suicide and mercy killing because our lives are not our own, and we may not dispose of them at will. Man, in his symbolic potency, is a temple of God, and to destroy him is itself an act of terrible symbolic meaning.

Sexual purity

Similarly, Catholic sexual ethics bases itself on the recognition that sex is a natural symbol with an objective meaning. It is a sort of natural analog to a sacrament given by God to the family to signify and effect the union of two lives in the creation of a third. Sex is not a blank page on which we may write any meaning or lack thereof we like. Its procreative end and its reference to the total commitment of marriage are already given;

these have, as it were, arrived on the scene before us and already made their claims. Our only options are to respect the act's given meaning or to reject it, to vandalize it by reducing it to our own ends. When properly used, sex has the power as a supra-rational signifier to draw the soul out of itself and beyond its native powers. God gives the husband and wife one of His own "words" for their use, so that by affixing their assent to the conjugal act's given meaning, they are able to "speak" through their bodies with a depth and finality beyond the power of spoken words. To reject the act's meaning through fornication, adultery, or contraception, to reduce God's donated word to raw material for one's gratification, is not just a failure to take advantage of something beautiful God offers; it is gravely sinful rebellion.

Social justice

As a final scandal to the modern mind, the Church proposes these truths not only to the individual in his private conscience, but to the community as well. She rejects liberalism not only on the level of substantive morality but also on the formal level of liberalism's commitment to private autonomy via public neutrality. Not only is public neutrality on matters of goodness and justice impossible anyway, so that liberals end up using the state and media to promote licentiousness and careerism; neutrality is undesirable, because it deprives men of one of the greatest goods: membership in communities of shared moral vision. In fact, following Cicero and Augustine, one might well question whether a real community can be said to exist at all without being built around a moral consensus. Here is the source of Catholicism's infamous hostility to democracy and capitalism. Not that elections and markets are bad things per se, but they should not be allowed to control a society's ethos, because their fundamental principle is choice rather than love or duty.

Justice, then, is social as well as individual, in that societies as well as private citizens must render to good and evil their due. The first command of social justice is that the community must recognize God's corporate sovereignty over it. Next, a properly formed moral consensus must be embodied in the community's laws and customs. Sometimes a certain form of wickedness cannot be forcibly suppressed, but it should never be officially approved or culturally celebrated. Thus, for instance, a healthy moral consensus can rightly defend itself by banning pornography and homosexual propaganda. At the very least, it must insist on not ceding control of the public realm—what is taught in schools, what is affirmed by statesmen, what may be said in public without scandal—to such vile influences. Lastly, because elections and markets have in themselves no explicit orientation to the Good, the community must impose such an orientation on them from outside. The form that such regulation takes might vary widely, but it must allow citizens to experience their community as a moral enterprise rather than a libertarian jungle of mutual exploitation and predation against the weak.

Chapter 6: Last things

Being towards judgement

We have seen that the mind is less the ultimate bestower of meaning than the ultimate locus of ambiguity. Everyone is a mix of good and evil; even my good deeds are vitiated by resentment or expectation of reward. My very freedom traps me in ambiguity by making it impossible for me to make an irrevocable choice for obedience to God. To the extent that I control myself enough to choose good today, to that same extent it will be in my power to repudiate good tomorrow.

Once again, the rescue must be to appropriate meaning from without. God it was Who, through the sacrament of marriage, allowed my life to have an overall plot. God it will be Who will give my life an overall resolution. At the end of life, or so Catholics believe, each soul will be judged, and at that moment that life's definitive truth–as a story of transformation in Christ or rebellion to the end–will be established. Death and judgement are the inescapable horizon, marking, as death does for atheists, each life as finite, contingent, and individual. Each of us must suffer his own death and have rendered his own personal judgment. However, we are assured that Jesus has gone before us and by his great sacrifice offered salvation to all.

This is not to say that all will ultimately be saved. For most of the Church's history, the assumption has been that the judgment of most is one of damnation. The Catholic attitude thus tends to be different from the Protestant "assurance of salvation". A Catholic, knowing his own inner indeterminacy and freedom to reject God, expects no such assurance. After all, even if I am in a state of grace now, what's to stop me from choosing mortal sin tomorrow? I can be sure of God's continued assistance, but not that I won't thwart it. True, from God's atemporal perspective, each man is either predestined or reprobate. However, this is not a perspective we can share until death. Human life is, by its nature, the realm of time, uncertainty ("fear and trembling"), and freedom.

The ascent of Mount Purgatory

Yet life's resolution is more than an external judgment. Jesus Christ said that even the least in the Kingdom of Heaven is greater than John the Baptist (Matt. 11:11). To really vanquish sin and erase its hold, the soul must be internally purged and cleansed; the seed of charity in it must permeate and reorder the whole. The saints and martyrs show us what souls ordered by charity can do. Many willingly endured ostracism, poverty, torture, mutilation, and death out of loyalty to God. Reading their stories, I wonder whether I too would have chosen to endure such things if put in their situations. It would be nice to think so, but I don't sense any great reserves of courage in me. I can hope (and am commanded to pray) that God will deliver me while on Earth from intolerable temptations. However, I cannot hope (and nor should I really want to) that this will mean getting into heaven "on the cheap" with my weak character and petty sinfulness intact. Only souls that would endure unimaginable tortures rather than turn away from God are capable of beatitude. And yet we know that such virtue does not come cheaply.

Dante presents a gripping image of Purgatory as a vast mountain whose ascent represents the rectification of the soul, culminating in the recovery of original innocence. The souls in Purgatory undergo penances as extreme as the punishments in hell, but with the crucial difference that they are undertaken willingly and in a spirit of hope. In Dante's telling, the souls of the Church Suffering display an almost superhuman single-mindedness toward their penances; so perhaps shall it someday be with us. Today I know myself to be very weak, barely on God's side at all. How many eons in Purgatory might it take to forge in me the soul of a saint? Yet every Catholic knows that God has the power to make a saint out of anyone, and that He will settle for nothing less.

The Meaning of Conservatism

What does it mean to be a conservative? Let us first dismiss the purely literal meaning of "cautious" or "prudent". Of course, a conservative will avoid needless and reckless change, but so will an intelligent liberal. Does it mean to hold some set of political beliefs? It must be more than that, since we often hear about "conservative" or "liberal" religions, ethical beliefs, and sociological theories. Furthermore, these orientations are sufficiently connected that a person is nearly always liberal or conservative in all areas. No, to be a conservative is to have a certain attitude or orientation towards the whole order of being. It is this orientation which I wish to describe and defend.

Three levels of being

Man experiences the world's order in three levels. The first is inert matter and the empirical or "brute" facts about the world which it embodies. Matter qua matter has neither purpose nor higher meaning; it is raw material which man subjects to his will. The second level is that of subjective will. Man is aware of himself as a being with desires, goals, and opinions, in sum as one who assigns value. As an assigner of values, he can "color" his world with meaning, finding a thing good or bad, useful or harmful, beautiful or ugly. The level of subjective will is also the level at which we encounter the liberal version of morality. Man recognizes that other sentient beings also assign desires and fears, values and disvalues to the things in the world. He realizes that the subjective valuations of others are in some objective sense "equal" to his own and entitled to the same respect.

Inert fact and subjective valuation do not exhaust our experience of order; each of us recognizes that the world is "weighted" with meanings which seem to exist prior to and independently of anyone's will. For example, one can see the distinction between the three orders in the relationship between a mother and her child. On the level of empirical facts, there is the fact that this baby is the offspring of that woman, there is the inability of human young to care for themselves, and there are the many facts about the woman, such as her ability to nurse, which are relevant to child rearing. On the level of subjectivity, there are the feelings of the mother and child towards one another. Finally, there are the stations of mother and child, the un-chosen context which gives meaning to their acts toward each other and the standard by which they are judged. All cultures recognize a duty for mothers to nurture their offspring, and a duty for children to honor and obey their mothers. The nature of these stations cannot be derived by mere logic from any set of empirical facts. On the level of empirical fact, one cannot even surmise a basic fact like that the purpose of the uterus is reproduction, but only that it can be used for this purpose. Objective meaning belongs to an entirely different and higher order of intelligibility. In fact, it is the idea of the station of motherhood which allows a woman to make sense of the many empirical facts of her femininity. Nor does the station of motherhood derive from subjective desires; neither the mother nor the child nor both together have the authority to dissolve the bond between them. Of course, a woman may neglect or abuse her child, but even so she doesn't escape the context of her maternal station; she just fulfills it poorly, making herself a bad mother.

Some of these un-chosen meanings seem to be fixtures of human nature. The basic roles of mother, father, and child seem to be of this sort. So too is the meaning attached to the conjugal act—sex seems to have a meaning which suggests itself to us, independently of what meaning we might want to attach to it. There also seems to be a natural set of symbols embedded in the human mind, as evidenced by the many common motifs in the world's rituals and mythologies (animal sacrifice, earth goddesses, etc).

Some un-chosen meanings are limited to a culture. Obvious examples include a society's customary standards of politeness and modesty. No one in particular chose these norms, and yet they have moral force over the society's members. This moral force is not hard to understand. A society's customs establish a bond between all the members, a bond they feel obliged not to destroy. These customs also allow us to recognize the dignity of individual members in ways which are only possible within the particularity of a given culture. There is no culture-independent way to show respect or acknowledge privacy, even though we feel that these are basic moral obligations. Above all, there is the massive fact of political sovereignty. As a civilized man, I belong to a polity ruled by a political authority. I chose neither to belong to this polity nor to be subject to its sovereign, and yet I am morally obliged to obey its commands. If I refuse, I am a criminal and a traitor. These facts are so inexplicable from an empirical point of view that some liberal theorists like to pretend that political authority is based in some way on consent. But an authority based on consent is no authority at all. As Joseph de Maistre pointed out, the distinctive feature of sovereignty is the very fact that it is un-chosen (that we have a duty to obey whether we like it or not) and instituted by no one in particular (except, perhaps, by God Himself).

Finally, there are religious meanings and contexts. Seen on the third level of intelligibility, the world contains a cluster of objective goods. The man immersed in this world senses that all of these goods are in some way congruent, that to act against one is, in some indescribable sense, to offend them all. He intuits that the laws of nature and morality and custom are all part of a single sacred order. This is the primal religious experience. This unity in the order of the world leads men to consider that all the parts of the world are like organs of a single body, or like children of a single Father.

What liberalism is

The dispute between liberals and conservatives can now be put simply: what public authority should these un-chosen meanings have qua objective values? The liberal grants them no authority. Of course, the liberal does not consider himself to be hostile to family, or religion, or particular culture per se. His sincere goal is to maximize the freedom of each individual to pursue these goods as that individual sees fit. However, he demands that the state and civil society be organized to recognize only subjective beliefs and desires. This is required by the supreme liberal virtue of tolerance. Tolerance, as liberals use the term, means a willingness to abstain from favoring one's own values or "comprehensive account of the good" over other peoples' in one's dealings with them. It means an ability to hold one's own beliefs "at arm's length" when judging others. Applied to the individual, tolerance requires "open-mindedness", lack of favoritism towards those who share one's account of the good, and a radical privatization of one's religion and culture. Applied to the state, tolerance requires neutrality towards competing comprehensive accounts of the good. The state is a machine designed to enable the satisfaction of preferences which it never presumes to judge. There are various algorithms for deciding how preference satisfactions should be distributed among the populace, e.g. the utilitarian system which maximizes total satisfaction, or the communist system which demands equal satisfaction to each. They are all liberal systems, so long as the algorithm does not discriminate between good and bad desires or correct and incorrect accounts of the good. A desire is only thwarted if it interferes with someone else's desires. The only recognized concerns are to maximize freedom and ensure equality.

There are two grave sins against the virtue of tolerance, both inspired by Hegel's account of consciousness. The first sin is called alienation, dogmatism, false consciousness, bad faith, or reification. This means imagining that preferences, values, etc. which are products of your will have some objective validity independent of you. Liberal and Marxist theorists claim that private property, organized religion, and sexual morality are examples of alienation. We made these things, they say, and we have the authority replace them with something better, if only we stop kidding ourselves that they are acts of God or nature. The second sin is called discrimination, hatred, prejudice, or "othering". Any morally significant division of the world into "us" versus "them" will likely be regarded by liberals as discriminatory. Every powerful intra-group loyalty is essentially connected, they believe, with an at least implicit hostility to outsiders and a devaluation of the outsiders' preferences and beliefs. "Racism", "sexism", "nationalism", and "homophobia" are commonly castigated forms of discrimination.

Why liberalism is wrong

Liberalism has won the complete allegiance of the world's intelligentsia. Nevertheless, the claim of the liberal state to be a neutral arbiter between different theories of the objectively good is an obvious sham. Its pretence to abstain from deciding whether something or other is an objective good is almost always practically equivalent to deciding that it isn't. Neutrality between ethical systems turns out to mean always coming down on the side of one particular system, namely utilitarianism, which is erected into an uncompromising public orthodoxy. This can be seen for any controversial issue. For example, the state is actively at war with some moral views, such as belief in ethnic loyalty or gender role differentiation, to the point that it criminalizes any public action based on them as discrimination and indoctrinates school children against them. Nor can a regime which funds abortions be agnostic as to the moral status of prenatal humans.

It should not be thought that conservatives wish to replace liberals' defective system for neutral decision making with a better one. We deny that there can be any such system. The alleged virtue of tolerance is incoherent. I cannot set aside my conception of the good and then, from an "original position", decide a fair arbitration between my beliefs and someone else's. Without my full morality, I have no way of deciding what a fair decision would be. Therefore, for the liberal to reach any conclusions at all, he has to sneak some comprehensive moral suppositions into the original position. John Rawls himself, the liberal who first explicitly formulated this thought experiment, realized this when he noted that men in the original position operate on a "thin" theory of the good, a theory which basically turns out to be utilitarianism.

Since neutrality is impossible, the state must take stands on matters of moral good and evil, so it might as well be honest about it. Of course, simply making the state's implicit utilitarianism explicit would be one choice, but before making it one must ask oneself whether utilitarianism is a true—rather than neutral—system of morality. It is pretty clear that it is not; no moral theory could be true which ignores the things which give human life seriousness and nobility. These relate to the un-chosen goods and meanings we discussed above: filial piety, patriotism, codes of chivalry, chastity, devotion to God, loyalty to particular communities, tradition, communal moral consensus, reverence for ancestors, and so on. These goods are not reducible to the liberal principles of freedom, equality, and happiness. Sometimes their requirements clash with one or more liberal principle. This is because many of these goods can only be pursued in common.

What conservatism is

In every age, men have formed communities which embody a common understanding of an ostensibly objective good or objective order, be it natural, traditional, or divine. These communities exercise a definite moral force on their members. They do not fit liberalism's "mechanical" model of society—they are not mere means for the satisfaction of individual desires. They are ends in themselves, because they are icons, hierophanies, of the goods they embody. As such, they possess authority. We are now ready to define conservatism. It is the defense of common understandings and structures of authority embodied in moral communities. The most important of these moral communities are the patriarchal family, organized religion, the traditional culture of a local community, and the nation-state.

The defense of authoritative communities contains a personal and an institutional aspect. On the institutional side, the authority of the community must be defended against subversion by the partisans of freedom and equality. On the personal side, virtues must be promoted which allow each individual to personally appropriate the goods of the community. Conservatism is indeed a politics of promoting virtue, but virtue of a particular sort. The virtues of self-control (temperance and fortitude) are appreciated equally by liberals and conservatives, since they can be put in the service of any conception of the good. The supreme conservative virtue is reverence, the sensibility towards an order of good which disposes one to appreciate its sacred character and to recognize its claim not only upon one's acts, but even on one's thoughts and feelings. For example, continence is a matter of self-control, but chastity is a matter of perception—it is reverence for the conjugal bond. Piety is the reverence owed to the sources of our physical and social existence. It is owed to parents, to country, and to God.

Objections to the conservative view always fall into one of a few classes. Some deny that there are objective goods, or that we could have knowledge of them even if there are, because they are not empirically observable facts. These objections are based on philosophical schools like empiricism or positivism which no functioning human being can hold consistently, so we needn't be too troubled by them. The Marxist objects that common understandings are mere ideological superstructure, masking the realities of wealth and power. However, the Marxist has no reason but his materialistic prejudices for thinking that beliefs are less real than economics. To most men, beliefs matter far more. Finally, the cosmopolitan claims to approve of an institution, but demands that it abstain from drawing distinctions between insiders and outsiders, so that it can offer its good to the whole human race. This demand ignores the fact that all true love or attachment is directed towards a particular person or community, never to an abstraction like "humanity". For example, the claim "all men are brothers" is a pernicious lie. I cannot love a stranger in the same way that I can love a man devoted to the same parents and with whom I spent my childhood. To demand that I have the same love for strangers that I do for my brother ultimately means that I must regard my brother as a stranger. Equality and inclusiveness are not worth such a sacrifice.

The Audacity of Natural Law

Consider the following statements:

- It is intrinsically immoral to have sexual intercourse with someone who is not one's spouse.

- Parents have a duty to raise their children, and children have a duty to obey and revere their parents. Unless extreme circumstances make it impossible, children should be raised by their biological parents.

- It is intrinsically immoral to deliberately cause a sexual act to be infertile.

- It is immoral to drink live blood.

- Suicide is intrinsically immoral.

- It is always wrong to kill an innocent person, even if he has low quality of life and wants to die.

Setting aside for the moment the all-important question of whether or not these statements are true, what they have in common is that they all belong to the natural law system of ethics. They all take a set of biological facts–coitus, filiation, death–and purport to read moral meanings out of them. The natural law presumes that the human body is charged with meaning, so that biological acts and relations have their significance built into them. The "natural meaning" of the act exists prior to and independent of what the actor understands or intends by that act, and yet he is morally bound by the natural meaning none the less.

I saw a nice example of natural law reasoning in the movie *Vanilla Sky*. (It's not very good; don't watch it.) I don't remember the characters' names, but in actors' names here is the setup: Tom Cruise has been sleeping with coworker Cameron Diaz in an informal relationship, and then he decides to leave her for Penelope Cruz. (When you're Tom Cruise, you can do those sorts of things.) Diaz's character becomes distraught and pleads with Cruise that he can't just leave her like that after they have coupled. "Your body makes a promise even if you don't." This is a natural law way of thinking. We say that fornication is wrong because when you have sex with someone, you make her a promise–whether that's what you and her want to communicate or not–and that promise is the same one a person makes at a wedding ceremony.

This way of seeing things is very different from the modern mentality (although, as we've seen, the old mentality pops up in unexpected places). Modern man is, whether he admits it or not, strongly shaped by Cartesian dualism to see the body as "brute matter", as *res extensa* distinct from the *res cogitans* (the soul). Meaning, it is believed, is a distinctly mental phenomenon. Its origin, and indeed its whole being, is in the mind. What an act means is what the actor intended it to mean and what he knew his observers would take it to mean–no more, no less.

Modern ethics is usually consequentialist or deontological. Sin is identified either as harming someone else or instrumentalizing him (treating him as a "mere means"). Harm and instrumentalization are defined solely in terms of the person's preferences and choices. Natural law agrees that harm and instrumentalization are wrong, but it defines them differently, in terms of man's natural *telos* and natural meanings.

Modern man finds this idea of normative natural meanings foolish and arbitrary. Natural law advocates are said to be ignoring the person to focus on the body, of ignoring intention to focus on biological function. Natural law is accused of committing the "naturalistic fallacy" by hostile philosophers; Catholic heretics accuse it of "physicalism". These accusations have the merit of getting at the essence of the disagreement. It it's "physicalism" to believe that sex, parenthood, etc. don't just mean what we decide for them to mean, then we natural lawyers are physicalists.

The modern critique of natural law has an undeniable plausibility. Biological facts can no doubt affect our and other people's desires and thus indirectly become morally relevant on modernity's terms, but it is not obvious how they can dictate duties to the *res cogitans* independent of these considerations. And yet, there are strong reasons why we should give the natural law account a careful hearing before we dismiss it.

First of all, one must be clear that to object to physicalism means having a quarrel not only with a few Catholic ethicists, but with the consensus of all mankind. Across ages and cultures, all peoples have believed in natural meanings. If nothing else, they have all agreed on the moral import of filiation and kinship. That one person emerged from the uterus of another is a biological fact. The social state of "motherhood" recognizes not only this fact, but also duties and rights that are supposed to flow necessarily from it. A man has no right to expect love from his neighbors or coworkers. His behavior may warrant their respect, but love can only be an unearned gift. He has no right to ask his secretary "Why don't you love me?" nor would she probably have any answer. Love was never "on the table". A man can expect his mother to love him; the very relationship gives him a rightful expectation. "Mother, why didn't you love me?" is a natural question for an unloved son to ask. There probably is a reason, although no reason could justify so grave a failure of duty. I have special duties to my children and my kin. Partly, this is because they happen to be the people who are closest to me, but this isn't the whole story. I would fail morally if my brother on the other side of the country were homeless and I didn't fly him to me and take him under my roof; yet there are homeless strangers in my very county to whom I am not obliged to make such an offer.

The consequentialist and deontologist can only agree with these intuitions by accident. They will often grant that having children raised by their biological parents is administratively convenient. As a practical matter, it would be hard for the State to find enough caretakers to replace all these parents. But the family is only a matter of practicality, and in fact its ultimate value is open to question. After all, it puts children at the mercy of people with no childcare training and next to no official supervision, all because of a "biological accident"; our bureaucratic age wouldn't tolerate such feudal anarchy in any other area of life. Similarly, they may agree that a particular act of adultery was wrong because it hurt the other spouse's feelings, but they must also admit that this is because that spouse is being irrational. A regime of universal promiscuity, where sex is "just like shaking hands", might well be a happier world, and, consent assumed, wouldn't obviously involve reducing any other person to a "mere means".

Here is the second reason to consider carefully before rejecting the system of natural meanings. As the two examples above indicate, a world without them would be a nightmare. Unchecked by natural law, consent, efficiency, and happiness maximization would replace the love of parents with the expertise of childcare professionals; it would erase the bonds of family, ethnicity, and nation; it would reduce sex to a meaningless pastime. Our desires would be satisfied. We would all be happier. Or would we? For me, one of the most important aspects of happiness is the knowledge that I personally matter to some particular other people. Being a man of no great importance, these people are a half-dozen family members. What I do matters because they depend on me and they care about me. In the post-natural bureaucratic utopia, there will be nothing like this. What I do won't matter much to anyone else–this will be true by construction. If anyone really depended on me, that would limit both our freedoms. It would make my dependent unequal, because if I failed that person would suffer, through no fault of his own, relative to those depending on someone else. There must be supervision, uniform rules, backups and failsafes, so that in the end I can't be allowed to matter to anyone else.

As Hegel pointed out, there is a leap from abstract right and morality to the ethical life. We have no way to put abstract moral rules (e.g. utilitarian or Kantian) into effect–no way to know what they mean–until we are embodied in an "ethical society" where everybody has a specific place and duties. How, though, are we to assign these particular duties? Modern abstract ethical systems can only produce abstract organizations and can never provide this element. In the past, it has always come from relationships like marriage and filiation that rely on natural law for their normative character. After they are wiped out, a utilitarian calculus of the future may register the unhappiness that results, but it could not replace what it had destroyed. Natural law seems to be the only way to lock particular people in duties to each other. There is true happiness from the sense of meaning this provides, and the utilitarian rulers of the future might be forced to reinvent natural law as a "noble lie" to fill this void. Let us then see first if we can defend the theory honestly as truth.

A defense of natural law must establish several points. To fail on any one of them is to fail overall. First, it must defend the claim that there are natural meanings. It must establish that these are not merely projections of our subjective wishes or the mistaking of the customs and assumptions of our own culture for universals of nature. I will address this issue in the next section. Next, it must argue that these natural meanings are morally binding. This step is often skipped over, but I think it's a crucial and underdeveloped part of the theory. Suppose we allow, with Cameron Diaz, that sex has a natural meaning that includes commitment. Why could not the man and woman simply agree that this natural meaning is not the one they intend to give it? That way, no false expectations would be generated; moving on would not be a betrayal. That natural meanings are binding I will argue in this essay's third section. Finally, we must ask how the two meanings, what something naturally means and what we intend, are meant to relate to each other. We must show that natural law does not itself fall back into a different sort of dualism. This will be the subject of the final section.

Desires and goods

Man is an animal, and like all animals is subject to cravings and urges whose satisfaction brings pleasure and whose frustration brings discomfort. It is the mark of a nonrational urge that its aim is a subjective state of satisfaction rather than an objective state of affairs. An irrational animal eats to satisfy hunger, and it congregates with its fellows for the comfort of being part of the herd. An outside observer can identify objective functions served by these urges, how they keep the animal alive and contribute to the excellence proper to its species. The animal itself, if it is irrational, cannot achieve the mental separation from its own immanent compulsions to take this outside view. For small decisions–like the decision to have a snack or watch a television show–humans too are often content to gratify their urges. For important things, though, we demand motives of another sort.

Man is not just an animal, but also a person. To be a person means that one is not locked in immanence; one can take an outside view even when one's own impulses are in play. In addition to being driven by urges, we can be motivated by reasons. For rational actions, the ultimate end is not subjective satisfaction, but some objective state of affairs regarded as good. Let us call these ends–objective states of affairs regarded as valuable in themselves–as "goods". Because we act to preserve goods, rather than just satisfy urges, we are more than just very clever animals. We hear the claims of objective value; this is our special dignity as persons.

Usually, cravings and goods are not antagonistic motives. Goods serve not to frustrate cravings, but to enoble them by showing how any given craving is ordered to an objective good. Our satisfaction of this desire is "rationalized", not in the common sense of that word as "given a spurious excuse" but in its literal sense. The desire is elevated to rational life; it becomes meaningful as the bodily apprehension of a real good. Mind and body are harmonized. Our natural capabilities as humans also acquire meaning–when we identify what good a capability is ordered toward serving, we say that we have found that capability's function.

Some examples may help. We all know the desire to believe things that comfort us–that we are safe, valued, loved. However, there is also a great good in knowing the truth and comporting oneself to it, even if the truth happens to be distressing. Our sensory organs and our intellect are intrinsically ordered toward truth–it's their function. Notice here that intrinsic function can be something different from adaptive value. No doubt it was the ability to evade predators and capture prey, or something like that, that selected for these abilities. Nevertheless, their function is to truth. No one doubts that truth–at least about important things–is good in itself, and acquiring this good is simply what the senses and intellect do. To know the truth would be for them to be doing their basic activity fully and without hindrance. In the bodily order, there are physical pleasures; they are related to but distinct from the good of health. In the interpersonal order, we crave the feeling of being loved; this is related to but distinct from the good of really being loved and the good of true intimacy. In the social order, there is the comfort of the crowd; this is distinct from but usually related to the good of moral community.

For each good, there is a similacrum whereby one can choose to separate the good from its accompanying pleasures and seek only the latter. To do so is to degrade oneself, to descend into the subpersonal level of immanence, to forsake truth. All forms of self-deception are degrading in this way. So, to a lesser extent, is gluttony, attending to the body as a nexus of pleasures rather than goods. Most pitiable of all are counterfeit interpersonal pleasures. Prostitution is a base substitute for the marital bond, stripping the conjugal embrace of it's personal dimension by paying a woman to pretend to be one's wife. I once saw a news documentary on a service in Japan whereby lonely old men could hire a group of actors to pretend to be their family for a day. I thought it was the saddest thing I'd ever seen. What a great failure it is of that society that there seem to be so many people living without the genuine good of family love.

The list of natural goods doesn't itself provide us with the first principles of practical reasoning. These are given by the two great commandments: to love God with all one's heart, mind and soul, and to love one's neighbor as oneself. What natural goods do is to tell us what it means to love one's neighbor and what it means to love oneself. We love them by promoting what is good for them. Of all the natural functions identified by natural lawyers, the most noble are those identified as serving the good of other people. These functions identify humanity as being "designed" for love. Hence the special attention natural law gives to man's reproductive capacities. Most of our bodily features are ordered to our own good, but masculinity and femininity are ordered to serving another. Every difference between men and women points to a way that each is called to promote the good of child or spouse. It is obviously not for their own good, individualistically conceived, that women have breasts, but for their childrens'. (We natural law advocates really like tits. They're such obvious examples of this kind of thing.)

One might object that this perception of natural goods is really just a projection of the human mind, rather than a real feature of nature. This objection fails to recognize that the human mind is itself a part of human nature, so that if our intellects are apt to assign a particular meaning to certain biological facts, this is itself a fact of human nature. The accusation of projection is only meaningful when the subject and object are different. It makes sense to say that "humans find worms disgusting" is a fact about human nature rather than worm nature and should be considered irrelevant to the study of worms. That human reason discerns gender differences as being ordered to family and reproduction is not extraneous in this way.

A more serious objection is that our understanding of human goods and functions might just be cultural artifacts. After all, we do see nontrivial differences in mores and ethical beliefs between cultures. The response to this objection must be more subtle, because it does point to an important aspect of social life. Our recognition of human nature is mediated by our culture. It's not simply that some parts of morality (the natural law part) are given directly by nature while some other unrelated parts ("mere" custom) are set by the culture. If it were that simple, natural lawyers wouldn't have to care about the culture. Nor can we settle for the cultural relativism of many anthropologists, according to which there are certain universal tasks that any collection of humans must perform to survive multiple generations (this being the "natural" part) but that how these tasks are fulfilled (e.g. children raised by parents or by the tribe as a whole) are cultural/historical fabrications about which nothing else can be said, at least on the level of universal human nature. An advocate of natural law reads a thick account of human flourishing from the data of human nature, and not every arrangement that enables social survival will also be found to promote integral personal excellence.

I wish to avoid the error, common among natural law ethicists, of trying to prove too much at an overly abstract level. There's no need to claim that my culture has a complete list of human goods or that it has a fully adequate understanding of any of them. In fact, I will be arguing later (in the final part of this series) we usually don't understand the natural meanings of our acts in their full depth, and that this is an important part of the natural law understanding of the human condition. Nor is it true that humanity has never posited false goods. Liberalism itself could be said to be positing a new fundamental human good, one unrecognized as such by all past civilizations, namely personal autonomy–a sort of super-good that overrides all others. Since I reject this elevation of autonomy, I cannot argue in general that anything ever believed to be a human good must really be one.

How does one tell true goods from false ones. I believe that children are a true good and autonomy a false good, but how can I be sure of this? There are several clear indicators. First, there is the consensus of all mankind; every people except our own has always regarded descendants as a blessing, and everyone but the perverse West has regarded individualism as a social disease. Second, there is consistency with the great commandments. True human goods give us ways of loving God, self, and neighbor, and while it is always possible to pursue a genuine good illicitly, i.e. in a way incompatible with these loves, no genuine good involves rejecting the commandment by its very nature. Having children with one's spouse is an expression of and opportunity for love of neighbor. Autonomy, on the other hand, involves by its very nature a rejection of God's rightful sovereignty. Third, there is the consistency between goods. Since human nature is presumed to be intelligible, no true good should intrinsically contradict another one, although, again, accidents of circumstance may force us to choose between them. So, for example, a man must in practice often sacrifice many true goods for his children, but having children doesn't intrinsically preclude any other good. Autonomy, on the other hand, intrinsically requires an at least partial rejection of the good of knowing the truth and the good of living in community. Both truth and community limit one's ability to posit one's own conception of the Good in complete independence of an objective order of being and of other people. Fourth, there is objectivity; as we have said, the point of natural goods is that they emancipate us from our own point of view. The claim of autonomous man to dictate all value from his own will makes it impossible for him to escape from himself, just as an emperor who conquered the whole world would have no way to visit a foreign country. Finally, there is the consideration of function: a true good involves the perfect activity of some natural human function. Begetting and raising children is the execution of many natural functions (functions that would otherwise have no natural meaning at all). Here the defender of autonomy might seem to have a leg to stand on. Surely the autonomous positing of meaning is the highest execution of our faculty of choice? In fact it is not. Conversion and martyrdom are the highest examples of free choice, and these are authentic but not autonomous. In them, a person freely affirms what is recognized as an objective supreme Good. All other rational choices do this same thing, if to a lesser degree. Positing a meaning of life as a naked act of will would be something much different—a perverse form of choice detached from the larger context of human goods. (In fact, most such attempts to define the good for oneself just involve delivering oneself over to subrational impulses. It could hardly be any other way. Man cannot really posit goods; he can only recognize them. If he discards these preexisting goods and looks inside himself for another principle of action, he will find nothing but his pre-rational cravings.)

From the above, one can see that there are rational criteria for distinguishing true from false natural goods. One can easily convince oneself that the traditionally recognized ones show all the marks of being genuine.

What my body means, what I mean

Suppose it is true that there are natural meanings to our corporeal acts, independent of and prior to any additional meanings we choose to confer upon them. To what degree am I accountable for the natural meaning of my acts? To take a common example, let us admit that sexual intercourse has a natural meaning and purpose, that it is about procreation via family, binding generation to generation and husband to wife, and expressing a radical donation of self to one's spouse. Are men and women always obliged to mean all this whenever they engage in the conjugal act? Must I mean what my body means?

One position would be that natural meanings have, of themselves, no moral import. This would salvage the liberal position, even after admitting natural significations. Most liberals would frown on a man deliberately promising lifelong fidelity to a woman without meaning it. On the other hand, they would insist that what the two parties understand by the conjugal act is the only morally relevant data. A man and a woman who wanted the incidental pleasures of sex without the commitment the act implies could just agree not to mean by intercourse what intercourse naturally means.

This position has the advantage of allowing all sorts of indulgences while attempting to maintain some moral standards. As a way of relating to one's body and its given "language" for expressing love and intimacy, though, this is very unsatisfactory. It implies a practical Cartesianism. My ego or self is conceived as an entirely separate thing from my body, a thing that I am said to "own" the way I own my furniture. But my body is my interface with the world and my fellows; in separating myself from it, I separate myself from them. A lover doesn't see me, doesn't touch me, isn't close to me; she only sees, feels, and embraces my body, an automaton I control but that is too separate from my "self" to be a true locus of intimacy. What's more, the choice of whether or not to endorse natural meanings is one that we never approach in a contextual vacuum. The natural meanings are always given. They provide a context that conditions any other meanings we choose to affirm. If I have sex with a woman without marrying her, I am rejecting her as my wife and treating her as unworthy of that commitment. I can't object that marriage was a proposition never brought up, and therefore never rejected. The act of intercourse itself brought it up by natural signification. At that point, the only choices are to consciously endorse the body's promise or to repudiate it. If you want to not marry a woman and not reject her, there is only one way: don't sleep with her.

The most obvious alternative would be to acknowledge a duty to always consciously mean by an act whatever that act naturally means. This is closer to the natural law view. It would mean that, before I perform an action, I should consider the natural meaning, translate it into a series of propositions of the kind I can mentally affirm or deny, and then affirm them all while performing the action with a clear conscience. This view certainly respects the language of the body; in fact, it errors in being too conscientious. Must we really expect every young bride and groom to enumerate in a set of clear propositions the whole meaning of marital love, in all its depth and force and subtlety, before they are allowed to consummate their marriage? I have certainly never done such a thing, nor do I believe that any philosopher or saint has ever done it; I doubt the thing could be done at all.

One important problem is that natural acts and relations like marriage are only really understood from the inside by engaging in them and being mentally shaped by the experience: "conatural knowledged", as the Thomists call it. No doubt the bride and groom must have some idea what marital love means, or they couldn't meaningfully promise it, but their understanding of it is expected to grow as they live it. Living marital love forms the mind and the imagination, so that one can more fully understand what it is that one initially promised. To expect full understanding from the start would have things backwards.

More fundamentally, the second approach falls into the same rationalist error as the opposite, liberal, position. It assumes that the only kind of meanings are the kind that can be reduced to finite sets of propositions. This, however, is not true, as we know from the philosophical investigation of art. A work of art is certainly meaningful, and may even have a "message", but the meaning can never be completely captured by a verbal explanation; explanations of what the artwork "*says*" never really capture what it *shows*. Natural meanings are another case of showing rather than saying. They contain propositions, but they are not exhausted by them. They are in a sense larger than our minds. What's more, the fact that something is expressed naturally rather than verbally/intellectually is itself significant. If a couple were to read off to each other all of my statements about the meaning of sex, this would not be identical to actually performing the marital embrace.

The body's promise, the mind's amen

Is there then no way around rationalism and the dualist's alienation from the body? In fact, there is another possibility, one that doesn't cut the person off from the suprarational capacities of his body to express meaning. Rather than saying, "This act means X, Y, and Z; therefore I affirm X, Y, and Z", he can say "I affirm the totality of what this act means." If he knows that the act naturally means X, Y, and Z, then he must indeed accept those propositions, but he doesn't truncate the act's meaning to his partial understanding of it, nor to his intellectual, linguistic mode of signification. He accepts that his actions have dimensions of meaning that he may not entirely understand, and yet he commits himself to the whole meaning. He may not realize all that he has promised his wife, but even what he doesn't yet understand he acknowledges as already promised.

It is this third way that natural law proposes as man's proper way of being in the world. One can see why, despite being the true and only way to overcome alienation from one's body, natural law has been embraced more readily by the less intelligent sectors of society. Those with high IQ are more confident in their ability to give meaning to their lives through shear intellectual exertion. They think it fitting that a smarter man can think up a more comprehensive statement of love than a duller man, and they are less eager to imagine that God Himself has given to every man, regardless of intellect, a way of "speaking" his love for his wife with a profundity that no human intellect can match. Those of us who lack the elite's mental gifts also lack some of their hubris. We would not wish for the depth of meaning in our lives to be limited to what our own imaginations could provide.

We Christians believe that God Himself uses natural significations, the "language of the body", to make Himself present to us in the sacraments. God doesn't overwrite the natural meaning, but uses it to express His relationship to us. It is precisely the natural meaning of marriage as total self-donation between husband and wife that lets it serve as the living image of Christ and His Church. And it is fitting that a suprarational mode of signification should serve as the channel for the superhuman gift of grace. When I receive the Blessed Sacrament, the priest holds the host before me saying "the body of Christ", and I say "Amen". What does the "amen" mean? Not that I can really fathom what it means that the thing before me is the body of the Incarnate God, or that I could fully say what it means–what I'm "getting myself into"–for me to consume it. I have some idea, based on the natural symbolism of consumption, but my "amen" means "I mean what this act means". Because I can say this, I can say more than it is possible for a human mind to say; I can perform a supernatural act.

Even more important is the mode of expression natural meanings provide. Natural meanings are given, rather than being products of one's private intellect. They allow us to step outside the limits of our imaginations, of our personal fixations and eccentricities, of the personality and style that we craft for ourselves. What I say about marriage, fatherhood, and filiation is always colored by my self-image, my idea of what "a person like me" would say. Natural meanings, by their impersonal–let us instead say "suprapersonal"–nature, allow me to step outside myself and make a completely authentic response to the thing itself. Being a husband and father means taking on a universal role, a role not of my making but one that lets me participate in the mystery of creation. The ephemera of my personality fall away, and I engage this mystery, not as "bonald" (35 year old, assistant professor, Star Trek fan, etc) but simply as Man. By my imagination, I have my own private world, but by natural meanings, I am one with every human being who ever lived. Fatherhood means the same thing for every father; it's bigger than any one of us, and yet it is at the core of each of us. Reflecting on these matters helps us see the real unity of the human race, the unity alluded to in the expression "Man" ("Adam" in Hebrew). Man is the whole race considered together as one, but Man is also the essence of each individual, what we find when we look deeply into ourselves. This escape from oneself and into Man is so important that cultures create formalized rituals–at weddings, funerals, etc–to provide more of it. Here again, part of the act's meaning is its universality, that I speak the same wedding vows my father said and my son will say.

In this matter the Christian has an advantage. What is abstract for natural reason becomes concrete and vivid in the light of the Faith. God's substance and essence are one, so He alone can bridge complete universality and concreteness. We believe that Man was made in His image, and at the appointed time, God Himself became Man, a new Adam, making Himself the core of humanity. So when he acts "as Man", the Christian realizes a sense in which he is acting "as Christ". When the body makes a promise (through sex, childbirth, etc), it is ultimately God Himself making the promise. If we would not be so mean as to break our own word, how much more should we take care not to break His!

So we find our corporeal existence charged with meaning; God Himself has lent it His own voice. Will you protest against this aspect of human nature because you didn't choose it? But this is what you are! This is your inmost nature. Surely the proper response to so great and holy a thing is reverence. Reverence and gratitude. Let us embrace our place in the order of nature, the place chosen for us by the Creator. Let us respect the language of the body, with its suprarational, suprapersonal mode of signification. Let us follow its calling to grow out of ourselves by putting on Man.

The Conservative Vision of Authority

I. The moralization of society

For classical liberals, the problem of politics was to find a way of restraining power; for modern liberals, it is how to maximize autonomy; for socialists, how to distribute the benefits of society fairly. For conservatives, the basic problem is the moralization of society, that is, the attribution of moral significance to the relations of people in community. For the citizens of a "moralized" society, all the major aspects of existence are colored by ideas of duty, loyalty, and status. For example, being a man or a woman isn't just a piece of biological data; it is a calling to the station of mother or father. Thus people read in their very bodies a summons to socially useful self-giving. The fact that someone is my parent or mate or child confers automatic rights and duties. Neighbors become countrymen; power becomes authority; work becomes cooperation in the divine act of creation. Moralized society secures each man's dignity in the most profound sense of assuring him that his actions really matter. As Hegel explained, only a moral (ethical, in his terminology) society can reconcile the limited scope of man's individual concerns with the universal scope of his reason. According to the former, the scope of the average man's actions is necessarily small, and these primarily affect a small number of people close to him. According to the latter, man is able to formulate general moral principles. These, however, will be either global or abstract. The former, such as "pursue the overall happiness or progress of mankind", give only a small significance to a man's daily actions, and that in an always indirect and often unclear way. The latter, such as "love your neighbor" do grant a man's actions direct significance, but they are too abstract to tell him what he owes to his wife as opposed to his coworkers as opposed to visiting foreigners, etc. What we need to bridge this gap is a social context which makes it clear what love of a person implies for each recognized relationship. Ethical society is the conservative, Hegelian solution to the problem of reconciling the universal and the particular sides of man, so that he achieves his full dignity.

Liberalism has sought to free man from these preset roles and duties. Everywhere we hear the cry that people should not be "restricted" by gender roles, kinship ties, or national loyalties. People must be free to choose their own meanings. But to say that a thing can have any meaning we choose to give it is to say that that thing is meaningless in itself. All of Nature, including our own bodies, has been recast as intrinsically meaningless raw material, to be exploited as we (either individually or collectively) see fit. This has undoubtedly expanded the realm of human freedom, but at the cost of alienating us from the natural and social world. We are given more choices, but at the price that our choices lose all real significance. For conservatives, this is too great a price to pay for freedom.

II. The network of dependencies

The most fundamental fact of life, from which all serious social relations proceed, is man's dependence. He relies for his needs on others, and they rely on him. People have never been independent, nor can they be, nor is independence a healthy ideal. Nor are most relationships of dependency arbitrary.

Many are natural in the sense that they "suggest themselves" to the minds of most people, and they could only be replaced through some sort of totalitarian government organization. The dependences between generations (young children on parents, elderly parents on children) for basic needs are of this kind. So too are territorial relations: the mutual dependence of those living close together to maintain those common goods—such as public order or shared language, customs, and currency—that make the good life in common possible. Through constant intrusion, the government could break the dependence between generations and between neighbors; it could insist all dependence be on the state itself, but most of us realize that this would constitute a continual act of violence against the natural development of personal relationships.

A key difference between the liberal and the conservative is their attitude to natural dependency networks. A liberal judges these relations according to an independent, abstract standard ideal of freedom or equality; then he demands government act to rectify the "injustices" he finds. The conservative, on the contrary, has no abstract, "outside" standard with which to judge his society; rather, he builds his ideas of equality and justice around existing dependency networks. To the liberal, this is acquiescence to injustice. To the conservative, the liberal is a menace to the social order.

From dependencies, we derive duties. To those who rely on me, I have duties. From those upon whom I rely, I have rights coupled with the duty of gratitude. With duty, we have entered the moral universe. Duty is the mark of citizenship in a moral community. Without it, one is not yet a true partaker in the spiritual good offered by this sort of community. So, for example, as long as the products of a culture are simply available for my optional enrichment, I am not a member of that culture, but only a consumer. Only when that culture's traditions become a trust which I am charged with handing down have I truly entered into the stream of that culture's life and made it my own.

III. Loyalty and Love: the horizontal completion of moral community

There's a tendency today to see duty and love as opposing motives. Duty is what we do against our wills out of obligation. Love moves us willingly and spontaneously. An act may be done out of duty or out of love, but not both. Hence the romantic objection to marital commitment—that it adds to a love relationship the alien and antagonistic element of duty.

In fact, this alleged conflict between duty and love is contradicted by all of our experience, in which we find the two to be organically connected. Self-donation belongs to the nature of love. I can't give myself totally to someone today while planning that I might abandon that person later. Thus, love's own inner dynamism drives the lover to promise lifelong fidelity to his beloved. In romance, parenthood, and friendship, commitment is the fulfillment of love. Conversely, commitment and mutual dependence naturally foster love and loyalty. A platoon of soldiers will generally be more devoted to each other than the members of a bowling club. Commitment is organically linked, not only to devotion to individuals, but also to devotion to groups: loyalty to the family itself, the tribe, the guild, the army, the country, whatever group that relies on me and on which I rely.

IV. Authority: the vertical completion of moral community

The interconnection of dependence, duty, and loyalty raises a community to the moral sphere. Of themselves, however, these are not sufficient to satisfy the universal aspect of man's reason. Each group to which a man belongs is necessarily particular and limited. He can look beyond the group; he can recognize objective goods outside the group and feel the potential call of duty to them. Each man will naturally be a member of several such groups. He will be aware of individuals and groups to whom he is not connected, but whose rights he knows he should respect. He will recognize duties toward things—like truth or nature—that transcend human interest altogether. Therefore, men will not be satisfied with a community that stands for nothing beyond its own collective self-interest. Such a community has not yet recognized and addressed them at their highest level.

A man forms his self-identity largely around his loyalties. To be fully integrated, he needs an ultimate loyalty that defines who he ultimately is. However, none of his particular communities has the right to make such a claim on him. To attempt to do so would be tyrannical; it would mean telling him to disregard some valid loyalties while giving to one an ultimacy it doesn't legitimately possess. Man is ordered to the entirety of the moral order. Therefore, the way for a community to legitimate itself is to present itself as a collective commitment to the moral order as a whole. A family or a state then sees itself as a group built on a common dedication to Goodness itself and Justice itself.

This idea completely reshapes the individual's understanding of the community's claims on him. The community is no longer completely self-interested, but points to a good outside itself. Nevertheless, the community is not thereby reduced to a means to an external end. The end is an affirmation of the moral order, and the community precisely is this affirmation. What has been introduced is the element of *authority*. So the difference between a community with authority and one without it is not that the former is more restrictive or "bossier". The Soviet Union was totalitarian but anti-authoritarian. The difference is that a ruler with authority speaks not only in the name of the people's good or the people's desires; rather, he speaks primarily for Justice. In doing so, the ruler addresses his subjects at their highest level of morality.

It would, however, be a misunderstanding to think that, because a ruler with authority (a king or paterfamilias, say) represents universal justice, that his jurisdiction is therefore universal and unlimited. On the contrary, authority is naturally plural—in that each person is subjected to more than one of them—and limited—in that the ruler is only entitled to speak for Justice to a limited group of people under his authority. Recall that authority is the solution to the problem of multiple loyalties. By seeing his obedience to multiple authorities as all rooted in an allegiance to a single moral order, the subject secures a unitary identity. He has an ultimate allegiance, not by picking one authority and placing it over all the others, but by identifying a transcendent source that directly legitimates them all.

Authority does mean that the ruler's commitment to justice is not a merely partial thing. Fathers and kings encourage all of the virtues and discourage all of the vices in their charges, not just those that directly affect the group. Authority figures must even constrain their own subjects if needed to protect the legitimate rights of outsiders. Here is a striking difference between an authoritative ruler and a mere agent of the people's will. Authority is the answer to the cosmopolitan's claim that loyalty to particular groups bespeaks a limited moral vision, that it is merely a form of collective selfishness.

A fully developed moral community will have institutional symbols of both aspects: the horizontal completion of loyalty and the vertical completion of authority. The former institution expresses the unity-in-mutual-dependence of the group, its bonds of loyalty and compassion. The latter institution expresses the unity-under-judgment of the group and rebukes the group, if necessary, for its moral failings. The two symbols are made clear by keeping the two institutions distinct. In the family, the mother is associated more with the horizontal symbol, the father more with the vertical. In the State, the deliberative body (e.g. Parliament) expresses horizontal unity—the community united in discussion of the common good. Parliament claims to speak for the people. The vertical symbol is borne by the king or (in the United States) by the Supreme Court. These speak to the people in the name of higher authorities: God, past and future generations, and the fundamental laws or Constitution.

V. The transcendent ground of authority

Authority claims to speak for the moral order as if this were a unitary thing, like Plato's conception of the Good. In evaluating the reasonableness of authority, one must ask if it really is meaningful to invoke a coherently unitary and ultimate Good. It would seem that authority is basing itself on some very strong, and very questionable, metaphysical premises. Does one really need to accept these premises to appreciate the claims of authority?

Yes, for authority in the full sense that I'm describing it, I believe one does. Therefore, although this is an essay in politics rather than metaphysics, it is necessary to briefly describe the worldview in which authority ultimately makes sense. One who considers the nature of goodness or value confronts a problem of the One and the Many that is precisely analogous to the problem of multiple authorities described above. Goodness in this world is irreducibly plural: there is no univocal quality that accounts for the goodness of an ecosystem, a person, friendship, courage, knowledge, music, etc. Furthermore, some goods are not only distinct but seem unable to coexist with other goods: a human can't have both masculine and feminine virtues; a community can't have the intimacy of a family, the freedom of the market, and the impartiality of the state. To choose only one quality in this world and assign it absolute value would be a sort of mental tyranny. Nevertheless, goods must have something in common if the word "good" is to have any meaning at all, above the subjective meaning of "whatever I happen to like". Although not every virtue and perfection can coexist in every subject, to claim that purely good qualities themselves contradict each other would make goodness incoherent; morality would then be the futile attempt to reconcile contradictory values.

Against this monstrous possibility, most men have asserted that goods and perfections do not contradict each other. The purely positive elements of masculinity and femininity, of being a dog and being an angel—that which makes these things good— do not contradict each other. They could in principle coexist. It's only the limited natures of humans, dogs, and angels that make this coexistence impossible for these subjects. All good could coexist in perfect unity and harmony in a being with no limiting nature, that is, in God. God is the answer to the unity-in-plurality of the world's goodness, as He is of the world's being. To Him is the ultimate allegiance that gives one's life unity and integration. God is, in a sense, the mirror of the soul—the ultimate unitary object to complement the unity of each subject. However, positing devotion to God as the ultimate ground of morality doesn't reduce finite goods to mere means any more than grounding communities on a devotion to Justice reduces them to means. The analogy between the two cases is particularly strong. To the authoritarian mind, moral communities simply are collective affirmations of Justice—serving this end is their inmost essence. To the religious mind, finite beings simply are glorifications of

God—serving this end by their inmost actualities and perfections through which they participate in Him.

The actual existence of God is a topic beyond the scope of this essay. It is important, though, to appreciate how closely the idea of authority is connected to the idea of God. We can connect the two yet more closely and summarize all that was said above in the following formula: to be in authority is to be God's representative. I believe that the modern insistence on carrying out political science in entirely secular terms is the reason that authority's true nature is usually misunderstood or ignored. Also, I think it fairly certain that authority in its full sense can only exist among a religious people.

VI. Collective response to God in its contemplative and practical respects

One might object that the above description confuses the state with the Church, authority with religion, the ruler with the priest. Surely it is the latter that has always been charged with the intercourse between God and society. In fact, both ruler and priest mediate God's presence socially, but in very different ways.

Authority in the state and the family address in God's name the practical reason. Authority always speaks in the imperative. "Do this. Don't do that." Authority *qua* authority never speaks in the declarative. It would be meaningless, for example, for the ruler to command that gambling is wrong. He may, however, command that the wrongness of gambling be taught in schools, or that gambling shall be punished in some particular way. Because it speaks in the imperative, the statements of authority are particular rather than universal. A meaningful command is always limited to its intended recipient. A ruler can order one subject to stand up and another to sit down without contradicting himself.

The social experience of God has a theoretical or contemplative aspect, as well as a practical one, and this contemplative encounter with God is the realm of the Church. It consists, first of all, in dogmas—declarative statements about God, His relationship to man, and morality. Unlike orders, dogmas are by their nature universal; if one is true at all, it is true for everyone, everywhere. While diversity of authorities, customs, and cultures is natural and good, diversity in dogmatic belief is bad because it means that at least some people are ignorant of the truth. Ideally, there should be one Church.

Most of the contemplative religious life involves communication with God: statements *to* or *from* Him rather than statements *about* Him, *I-Thou* discourse rather than *I-It*. In recent centuries, this part of religion, at least, has seemed to be a necessarily private affair. In the confines of my own heart, I can offer love and praise to God, but how can a group do this? Groups may take collective actions, but surely they don't have collective beliefs or feelings?

No prior age would have agreed with this religious individualism. A group can indeed collectively express a belief or feeling; this is what is accomplished through ritual. Consider a group of Americans standing for a recording of the national anthem before the start of a baseball game. Every one of them might have his mind elsewhere—on the coming game, for example—yet an expression of patriotism has certainly taken place. Who precisely made this expression? Not the individual: he might not be thinking of his country at all, and the fact that he's standing with his hand on his heart only has a certain meaning because the group gives it a meaning. No, in rituals, it is the group itself that speaks. Of course, the above example is a sort of worst-case scenario where only the group speaks. To be fully meaningful, each individual should consciously affirm what the ritual expresses. Even so, it is the collective making the statement, not each individual separately. Performance of the ritual unites all who have participated in it into a single voice, even those separated by distance or death. This is a key part of its meaning. In our public relationship to God, the Church is the "we" who speak to God and the "us" to whom He speaks.

Finally, the Church is charged with symbolizing both God's presence in the world and His transcendence of the world, so that these intuitions are woven into the common life of the community. This is accomplished by the setting aside of a sacred realm in which the presence of God is especially attributed. Sacred places like temples, sacred objects like icons and relics, and sacred times like holy days assure the community of God's nearness while simultaneously focusing this presence to distinguish God from the profane world.

The roles of the Church are, then, dogma, ritual, and consecration. The roles of authority are to establish justice and defend the common good. In the family, the two roles are combined: parents both teach and govern; the family is both a domestic church and a domestic kingdom. In the wider society, the roles are divided, with the Church taking on one, and the State the other. The two are always distinct, but not separate. The State relies on the Church to consecrate its authority, since authority is itself a primary example of a sacred thing. The Church consecrates the rituals that bind the community together, fostering a unity on which the State relies. The State's commands base themselves on dogmas. ("Don't gamble," is based on "Gambling is wrong.") Both Church and State are sovereign in their own sphere, and they stand or fall together.

Today, the Church has been effectively marginalized, and authority has lost its religious aura. The State has lost none of its will to power, though. With the eclipse of the idea of authority, the State is no longer restrained either by respect for a Higher Power or by respect for the equally legitimate authority of the family. The fall of authority is the rise of administration. Rather than the agent of Justice, the State makes itself the enabler of personal indulgences, the champion of our vices. As the realm of meaningless consumption expands, the sacred realm contracts, and our imaginations with it. Are we even capable of realizing, I wonder, how much we have already lost?

Evolution and Aristotle

Evolution and Divine causality

From time to time, I've seen newspaper articles reporting surveys on the relative popularity of "evolution" and "creationism". The survey will have questions which ask whether one believes that life or humanity A) was created by God or B) evolved from lower forms through natural processes. These articles always end with reporters lamenting the "unscientific" attitudes of Americans, because some people checked "A". The real scandal, though, is the philosophical ignorance of reporters who think A and B are mutually exclusive.

Let's take a simpler case. Suppose there were this survey question: "I exist because A) God created me, or B) my parents produced me through the natural process of procreation." Religious people are always thanking God for creating them, right? So they must believe A. On the other hand, they surely know about the birds and the bees, right? So they must believe B. This must be a great mystery, I suppose, but this example should show that modern science doesn't have anything in particular to do with it.

The mistake in both these survey questions is that it mistakes God's activity for being like that of other actors, as if God were one cause among many. It's as if we were to regard Him as a fifth Force, on an ontological level with the other four, so that what's caused by God is not caused by natural forces, and vice versa. That's not how theists understand divine causality. As theists understand it, God is the cause of everything, including natural events. When a stone rolls down a mountain, it is God who creates the stone and holds it in being from instant to instant, God who creates and maintains the mountain in existence, God who maintains the gravitational field driving the motion, God who gives these things their specific natures, and God who causes them to interact with each other the way they do. A theist can simultaneously believe that he is created by God and that he was produced by his parents precisely because the two forms of causality operate on different orders. Rather, God caused my parents to give me life. Without God's creative action, my parents couldn't exist for an instant. In scholastic language, God is my *primary* cause, and my parents are my *secondary* cause. So it is with every natural event. When a theist hears that X did something to Y, he understands that God created X and Y, and He caused X to do whatever it did to Y. The relationship is sometimes compared to that of a playwright and his play. Who caused Desdemona to die, Othello or Shakespeare? Either or both, depending on your point of view. Note, though, that if one says that she died because that's how Shakespeare wrote the play, it would not follow that Othello was actually innocent, and that his hands were guided by some magical force. No, Othello freely killed her in a jealous rage, *because* that's how Shakespeare wrote it.

If these events have natural causes, why invoke God at all, then? Why not say that some things just happen to exist, without anything causing them to exist? Why not just say that the universe and the stuff in it is just there? The reason is that everything in the universe is finite and contingent. Pick any object in the universe. Suppose you know everything about that thing—its essential nature and all its intrinsic properties. That information can't tell you why that thing should actually exist at all, why it should have that particular nature, or how many instantiations of that thing there actually are. There's no logical reason why there might have been a universe without that thing at all. If there is a reason for the thing's existence, it must come from outside. Suppose a thing X can exist for no reason at all. Then, one might wonder, why don't instances of X just pop into existence out of nothing all the time? What's to stop it? But if such a thing was possible, there could be no order to the universe, because imaginary objects would always be randomly popping into being. Therefore, contingent beings can only exist if they're caused. Since a collection of contingent beings is still contingent, the only way contingent beings can exist is if something non-contingent exists. Such a thing would have to be inherently single and totally self-complete and self-sufficient. One can argue that the only conceivable such being is God.

The above is a version of the so-called "cosmological argument", which goes back, in its essentials, to Aristotle. I present a fuller version of the argument in my Defense of Religion. Philosophers have argued for and against it for millennia. The important point is that neither evolution by natural selection nor the big bang theory affects the arguments one way or the other. The cosmological argument is as good as it ever was. (Conversely, one could say that the argument is as bad as it ever was, since the major objections to it were formulated by Hume and Kant long before *The Origin of Species*.)

People who think that evolution threatens belief in God tend to have an idea that some kinds of universe could "just exist" without a cause, while others couldn't. They see the current world, with all its beauty and order, and they think that surely this world requires an intelligent cause. When they think of the mess of subatomic particles created by the big bang, though, they think that probably that's the sort of thing that could "just exist". Now, since modern astronomy, geology, and biology tell us how the latter state can naturally give rise to the former, such people will tend to think that their original intuition of a divine providence must have been mistaken. But in fact, the error was in seeing the primordial "mess of particles" as a random chaos. In fact, the universe at this time was, in a way, highly ordered and intelligible. It consisted of a fixed set of particles that obeyed a very precise set of mathematical laws. It's only because of this order that the more visible order of our world has come into being. If the universe had been a true chaos, with no law or regularity, nothing could have come out of it. So the mess of particles has the same combination of order and contingency that leads one to infer a divine Creator.

All the most philosophically grandiose claims made for the theory of evolution rest on the idea that natural selection is a mechanism that allows order to come into being out of chaos. In fact, this is not true. For natural selection to work, there has to be fixed regularity in the environment and in the laws of nature. If the "rules of the game" changed from generation to generation, so that what helped one generation to survive hurt the next, natural selection would never be able to operate. So the correct way to understand Darwin's mechanism is not that it creates order out of chaos, but that it explains how order in one order can spill over to order in another order. This is still a remarkable achievement, but one that can't possibly explain why there should be order at all. Nor can physics or chemistry explain this. Science is fundamentally a description of the cosmos, not an explanation. It tries to determine what the order of the world actually is. It can't explain the order itself, however, because it must presuppose this in all its explanations.

Human distinctiveness

The problem of species

Traditionally, people have believed that the world is full of qualitatively different kinds of things; that is, there are a multitude of distinct species. In the realm of living things, there was seen to be a vast gulf between plants and animals, and between irrational animals and humans. These categories were based on what were seen as the characteristic activities of each type of organism. Plants do things like absorb nutrients and grow. Animals do "vegetative" things like this too, but they also sense their environment and move. Humans do both vegetative and animal activities, but we also engage in abstract thought. Of course, it was also generally believed that there are many different species within the plant and animal kingdoms as well.

Since Linnaeus, modern biologists have put far more thought and precision into taxonomy than the ancients ever did. Ironically, the farther these efforts have gone, the more skeptical moderns have become over whether the thing can really be done in a non-arbitrary way at all. First, as more species become known, the separation between them gets smaller. It becomes more difficult to say exactly where one species ends and another begins. Two equally reasonable definitions might give slightly different answers. Even if intermediates between clearly distinct species don't exist now, oftentimes they did in the past, and we have fossils to prove it. This leads one to ask, "Isn't this whole exercise arbitrary to begin with? Shouldn't we just think of a continuum of animal properties, with no qualitative jumps?" At the same time, some biologists seem to take a postmodernist's delight in "problemetizing" the old categories, e.g. showing how plants can—in some sense—move or sense, or showing how animals can—in some sense—reason. I often see articles written for a popular audience making great claims for animal intelligence. Dogs use logic, apes communicate, etc. One very popular claim now is that animals have morality, by which is usually meant empathy and self-sacrifice, but sometimes also a sense of fairness. The implication of all this is clear, but in case you're not clever enough to see it, these ardent biologists never miss a chance to point it out for you: human beings are qualitatively no different from animals. It's not that we have some quality that other animals lack entirely; the differences are all just quantitative. Your capacity for abstract reason is, say, 40% higher than that of your pet dog; your moral sense is perhaps 20% more developed. What would it mean to accept that humans are not different from other animals? The conclusions we're usually asked to draw are these: we should treat animals more like we treat humans, and we should think of humans more like the way we think of animals. The first consequence, of giving animals what we think of as "human" rights, would at worst be an inconvenience. The second consequence, however, would be devastating, as it would invalidate the idea that human beings have a unique calling, a qualitatively higher state of perfection, and therefore a unique dignity.

In this case, evolutionary history does seem to give some real ammunition to one side of a philosophical debate. Even if it seems clear today that humans are really different from lower primates, this distinction will grow less and less pronounced as we look farther and farther back on our hominid ancestors. Where can we draw a line, saying "this form is human" while "this only infinitesimally different form is irrational animal"? But if we can't draw a line, then how can we maintain the idea of a species—in its ontological sense—at all? A crucial feature about species is that an individual either belongs, or it doesn't. Therefore, it must be transitive. That is, if A and B are the same species, and B and C are the same species, it must be true that A and C are the same species. From this, you'll immediately see that evolution has blown out of the water one possible way of identifying species: that of reproduction. When I was in grade school, I learned essentially that A and B belong to the same species if they can successfully procreate with each other, or if A can give birth to B, or vice versa. Now, according to the (well substantiated) claims of evolutionary biology, there's an unbroken reproductive chain connecting humans to lower animals, and eventually to single-celled organisms. So, if we are to defend the existence of species, we must admit that procreation can cross from one to another. We must also be able to defend the claim that two empirically very similar animals can belong to completely different ontological species. We are thus in a more difficult situation than the ancients. While they could imagine as well as we various intermediate forms between the observed species, they weren't forced to take these imaginations seriously. They could always say "Sure, it seems like you could have something half-way between a man and a beast, but this could just be because of our ignorance. If we understood human and beastly natures better, we would see that such intermediates couldn't really exist. After all, we don't actually see them, do we?" Now we know they can exist, because they did exist, so the problem has become critical.

It might seem that defenders of human uniqueness are in a desperate situation. Nearly all of biologists and philosophers are against us, and they have an impressive amount of data to support their position. Should we be panicking? No, in fact we should not even be worried, because in spite of all the above, we defenders of human distinctiveness can be sure that we're right. The anti-distinctiveness arguments, when carried to their logical conclusions, result in absurdity. They forbid us to draw species lines anywhere; they forbid us to assert a qualitative difference anywhere. The ultimate consequence of this is that there is no qualitative difference between a human being and a plant, or between absorbing light from the sun and writing this essay. That's just crazy, and arguments that give crazy conclusions must be flawed. To reclaim our Aristotelian heritage, however, we must understand why these arguments are wrong.

Essential acts

The key is Aristotle's idea that there can be objective purposes in nature. For example, one can hardly deny that it is meaningful to make statements like "the heart is for pumping blood", and that these statements make no reference to any conscious mind, i.e. the above does not mean the same thing as "I like for my heart to pump blood". It means that there's an idea, "blood-pump", that is unique in allowing us to make sense of the heart. In the same way, "reasoning animal" is an idea that allows us to make sense of the various facets of human nature. The important thing here is that there's a distinction between a thing's precise state, on the one hand, and the essential idea it embodies, on the other. A heart doesn't have to pump blood very efficiently to be a heart, and a man doesn't have to think very well to be human. They just have to be structured to do these things to such an extent that one could say that these purposes are what they're objectively "made for". In fact, we expect essential ideas to be much clearer in the more fully developed organisms or organs, rather than in the transitional types. What a thing is essentially, though, depends on what we're calling its essential idea, rather than its precise state. Here is the crucial point: *the former can change discontinuously even if the latter changes continuously.* Two organisms might be physiologically very similar. One is designed for activity X but does it in a very rudimentary way; the other is not designed for X, but has organs that perform something very similar to X while in the process of doing something else. These organisms may be so similar that a single mutation can account for the transition from one to the other. They would nevertheless be essentially different beings; they would belong to different species.

The transition point between doing something poorly and not doing it can be very difficult to determine. This does not necessarily mean that it isn't there, though. It may be just an indication of our lack of perceptiveness. For example, just about anybody could tell the difference between how a professional swimmer swims and how someone who can't swims will just flail around in the water. That's because the professional swimmer executes the ideal form of swimming very completely and precisely, so it's easy to make out what he's doing. The movements of the non-swimmer have no guiding reason at all. We can, however, imagine transitional states of increasingly poor and inefficient swimming. At some point, casual viewers would think that a very poor swimmer is just moving his limbs at random; an expert on human swimming might still be able to make out a degree of organization that's giving the poor swimmer some locomotion. As we get closer and closer to the transition point, one would have to be more and more perceptive to make this out. For sufficiently special cases, perhaps no one alive could tell whether or not swimming was going on. This may only reflect our mental limitations, however. It doesn't mean that there's no sharp transition in essences, still less that the clearly different behaviors of the professional swimmer and the non-swimmer are really the same, after all.

The human quality

What about humanity, the really important case? Is it plausible that there's a difference in essential idea between human beings and other animals? We generally think that our intellects set us off from the lower animals. The biologists, however, have been gleefully pointing out to us evidence of animal intelligence. They claim that our mental superiority is only a matter of degree, not one of kind. If this were true, it would prove that there is no distinct human essence. If human beings are a distinct kind of thing, there must be something qualitatively different in how we think. A greater degree of animal intelligence wouldn't matter for philosophical purposes. Aristotle claimed that the distinctive human activity was abstract thought, i.e. the ability to apprehend universal ideas. He believed that this activity was essential to humans, i.e. that a human being as a whole is manifestly made for contemplating abstract ideas. He also thought this type of thinking is qualitatively different from what animals do when they think.

A man and a dog are walking in the woods, when a bear appears. The dog associates the bear with danger, and it runs. The man associates the bear with danger, and he runs. Where's the difference? The difference is that the man can think to himself not just "This bear wants to eat me!" but also "bears sometimes eat people". The former is a statement about this particular situation. The latter is an abstract statement about the nature of bears. The statement "it's the nature of bears to eat people" doesn't refer to any bear in particular, or even to anything in the world that we can see or hear. Its subject is a universal idea—"bear". This is the qualitative difference. But doesn't the dog also act on this abstraction? Doesn't the fact that it run from the bear mean that it also grasps that bears in general tend to eat dogs in general? No, it doesn't imply this at all. All we know is that the dog associates this bear with danger, not that it has consciously formulated an abstraction that would explain the association. There are, in fact, good reasons to doubt that dogs do so. It is anthropomorphism to assume that when a human and an animal do the same thing, they understand it the same way.

The sign and instrument of man's capacity for abstract thought is language. Without language, it would be impossible for us to mentally manipulate abstractions. Conversely, an animal with the capacity for abstract thought will almost certainly develop language very quickly. Again, we must not be misled by analogous behavior in animals. A pack of animals may have a set of calls—one indicates danger, one is an invitation to mating, etc. This is communication of a sort, but it's not language; it's more just an attempt to elicit certain behaviors. Only human languages have both signs that signify abstractions as well as syntax rules that allow us to combine abstractions in infinite combinations.

It also seems that abstraction is the only qualitative difference in human thought. Once a species has this difference, it will quickly be led to some form of art, history, science, religion, and group authority. A cascade of abstract questions will inevitably carry such beings to develop all these essential elements of a complete worldview. The statement "bears eat people" is already rudimentary science. It also contains in itself the ideas of distinct subjects, of essential natures, and of causality; further abstraction will extract these elements, making a rudimentary philosophy. From the idea of causality will eventually come the idea of God, the Creator of the world. Of course, it may take many generations to formulate these ideas, but they involve no new activity, only the process of following abstract thought where it leads. The first men might not have been very good theorists. They might have been quite frustrated that they lacked the mental equipment to deal with the questions that they kept coming up with. But this itself would show their essential humanity, which is defined more by the questions we can ask than by the questions we can answer. They couldn't follow the road of abstract all the way—and neither have we—but the crucial thing is that they were on the road at all.

What we've said should also clear up claims that animals have an understanding of morality not qualitatively different from ours. An animal may be distressed by the suffering of others. It may make sacrifices for each other. It may get angry when all the other animals get a treat, and it's passed up. None of this shows that animals have the particularly human type of morality, which consists in the ability to formulate abstract laws of duty and prohibition. When one ape kills another, all the other apes may be horrified, but could any of them formulate the abstract law "it is wrong for one ape to kill another without provocation"? If they could do this, these apes would be ontologically human, because they would have just started dealing with abstractions. The lack of true language, art, religion, and so forth among these other primates leads me to doubt that they have such capabilities. The same would go for the claim that animals have a concept of authority, just because they organize themselves hierarchically. Again, the point is not whether one ape will feel compelled to defer to another; the question is whether it can think to itself: "Subordinates have a duty to obey their superiors. I am a subordinate. Therefore, I must obey."

It's only when we consider what is distinct in human activities that we appreciate their true natures.

What about people who are stupider than animals?

I've just said that it's the capacity for abstract reasoning that makes humanity special. There would seem to be a big problem with this claim: some people don't have this capability. Consider the following:

1. Babies. For at least the first year after birth, human cognitive ability is probably not greater than adult members of other primates. Does this mean that infants should have no more "human" rights than gorillas?

2. Severely brain damaged people.

3. An unconscious person. If he's drugged, it might not even be possible to immediately wake him. Such a person has less cognitive power than an insect. A related case would be a person in a coma—temporary or permanent.

Everyone except lunatic utilitarians recognizes such people as human beings, albeit undeveloped, defective, or inactive in some way. A human baby is a human being. A full-grown chimp that can run mental circles around that baby is not a human being, but an irrational animal. Is this inconsistent with rationality being the distinguishing feature of humanity?

Here it's crucial to recall the Aristotelian distinction between the essential idea of a thing and its particular current actuality. The essential idea of an eye is "seeing organ"; this is the idea that uniquely allows us to make sense of all the details of the eye's structure and function. A particular eye may be damaged so that it doesn't work, but as long as you can make out what its function is supposed to be, the essence hasn't changed. The eyes of a blind man are still essentially seeing organs. If the eye is so smashed up that its function is totally effaced, then it wouldn't even be an eye anymore.

It's the human essence—which is to be a rational animal—that makes someone human, not their present actuality. A baby is essentially human, because the only way to truly understand what a baby is now is to refer to the rational adult it is tending to become. Imagine some alien saw a human infant, but didn't realize it to be an undeveloped human. The alien would not be able to make sense of what he was seeing. How could such a helpless animal survive? Why does it have such a big brain but no control over its environment? Once someone tells the alien "that one's still growing", everything makes sense. It is crucial too that the baby will develop into a rational adult through its own internal process of self-development. Rationality is not a new, foreign structure imposed from outside. One could say "the baby is a potential rational being", and this would be true if we take "potency" in the strict Aristotelian sense of that which is virtually contained in a being's presently-existing essence. There is, of course, another meaning of "potentially rational", namely "can be made rational somehow". So, for example, it may be possible for a sufficiently advanced race to take apart a bag of marbles atom by atom and refashion the matter into a rational being. The case of the human infant is much different. The baby will become rational while keeping the same essence, and thus maintaining its self-identity, and through its own process of natural development. Thus, we should not say that a baby and a gorilla are fundamentally the same now, but we treat them differently because the baby will become rational. The fact that the baby will become rational through its own development, while the gorilla wouldn't in a million years, proves that they are different right now. One possesses the human essence, and the other does not. This essence is present at all stages of development: from zygote to embryo to fetus to infant to child to adult. I myself was once a single cell. The life pattern in that cell has progressed continuously, all the while maintaining its identity, and it will remain a distinctively human pattern until it stops and I die.

The same sort of reasoning goes for the injured and the unconscious man. A human being in a coma is still a rational being, just as the eyes of a blind man are still seeing organs. Although constantly attacked, the idea of a distinct human essence is crucial to moral sanity. Understood correctly, it is as tenable as it ever was.

Ideals and loyalties

Human nature consists of more than just cleverness. Humans are capable of love. They are known to sacrifice themselves for other individuals or for collectives. They have an appreciation of beauty. They acknowledge the holiness of God and arrange their lives around their access to the sacred. These four activities—love, self-sacrifice, aesthetics, and religion—all involve value-responses. Each treats an object as something valuable in itself, rather than a mere means for satisfying some pre-existent desire. Love for family, tribe, country, and God obviously have a great deal to do with how we justify our social relations.

How did humans come to experience such powerful motivations? Evolutionary psychology has appealed to natural selection for explanations. The precise form of the theory depends on what is regarded as the subject of evolution. Anything that propagates itself through individuals can experience selection pressure. One could appeal to the selection pressure on genes. So, for example, it is a well-known theory that humans became altruistic through being willing to sacrifice themselves to save their kinsmen; through kin-altruism, the gene effectively sacrifices one copy of itself to save other copies. Others have considered how natural selection will affect the evolution of group life. Groups that encourage individuals to sacrifice themselves for the group—through either patriotism or religion—will be better able to survive and prosper than groups without these means of social control. Finally, it has been suggested that ideas themselves (what Richard Dawkins calls "memes") are what have adapted to preserve themselves. Memes that find was to make themselves plausible and stifle dissent will propagate further than memes without such defenses. This analysis has been applied most famously to religion. Also, these theories are not mutually exclusive; there's no reason to think that natural selection hasn't been working on genes, groups, and ideas simultaneously.

The above theories help explain why whatever it is that makes humans capable of love and religion has become such a big part of us. Their proponents, however, are apt to claim more. It is sometimes claimed, and very often silently implied, that evolutionary psychology has revealed the true nature of love, beauty, etc. So, for example, love may seem to be a response to the value of another person, but really it's just an impulse directed towards preserving or propagating one's genes. One may seem to be admiring the beauty of a landscape or a woman, but really one is subconsciously responding to signs of a hospitable climate or a fertile mate. Religion may seem like a response to God's majesty, but really it's just an idea using individuals to spread itself like a virus. If these claims were true, they would be devastating for love, aesthetics, patriotism, etc.

An essential aspect of each of these things is that they present themselves to the subject as objective responses, as giving an object "its due". If this aspect is an illusion, then love, beauty, and religion are lies. Rather, they don't really exist at all.

Before we accept these distressing conclusions, we should ask ourselves if they have really been proved. Is it necessarily true that because X is useful for Y that the use for Y is X's true nature? No. In fact, there is no logical connection between the two statements at all. Proving, for example, that religion fosters social cohesion does not prove that the true nature of religion is social cohesion. Nor does it prove that religion has no essence except to be whatever it is that fosters social cohesion. Evolutionary psychology cannot establish this connection any more than anything else can.

Let's try to understand better why it is that people tend to think otherwise. First, an explanation is proposed for why humans have value response X. This is presented as an explanation for X. The explanation offered for why I experience X has to do with things internal to me: my genes, my memes, etc. So X is really determined by the subject (me) rather than by the object (God, my country, a woman, little children, etc). Therefore, X is not really a value response at all; it must be something more like an urge. This is what people are thinking when they say that evolution has revealed what love, altruism, or religion really is. However, it's not true. It's also possible that a better analogy for these things than urges would be sense perceptions. Evolution certainly does explain how it is that animals have come to have eyes and ears for seeing and hearing. The explanations, of course, depend on promoting reproductive success. This does not mean, however, that sight and hearing are really illusions, that they aren't real perceptions of the world. Nothing prevents us from imagining value responses from the analogy with sight. We may imagine that there really is something objectively precious about individual people or communities, or that beauty and holiness are real qualities in the world. We may further suppose that there is some sort of faculty for perceiving these qualities that could be developed by rational creatures. Next, we may grant the evolutionary psychologist's arguments for why love, patriotism, and the rest promote genetic or group survival. Then this would explain why natural selection would tend to favor a more and more refined sensibility to these qualities, so that men would become more loving, patriotic, religious, and the rest. Just as the usefulness of sight presupposes the existence of light rather than calling it into question, so this explanation presumes that our value responses are what they manifestly seem to be. Scientifically, the urge theory and the perception theory are identical. The difference is that the latter is a philosophically more satisfactory explanation.

The theory of meme propagation requires further comment. The correct way to understand this theory is to see it as a contribution to the sociology of knowledge. It looks at the way ideas propagate and persist in a society while abstracting from the question of whether or not these ideas are true. From some basic assumptions about how ideas spread, one could put together a mathematical model which would apply equally well to the spread of Christianity through the Roman Empire, the spread of Newtonian physics through seventeenth-century England, or the spread of people quoting Monty Python movies through the contemporary English-speaking world. The differential equation might be pretty much the same as one describing how a virus spreads through an organism or a society, so one could say, if one wanted to be insulting, that Christianity or Monty Python "spread like a virus". This would tell you nothing, though, about the truth or value of the memes in question. Nor does the fact that people who hold memes like Christianity or Marxism tend to be psychologically invested in their beliefs, or that they discourage disbelief, in itself argue against the truth of these ideas. Such properties can be expected in any socially relevant belief system, as more adequate sociologies of knowledge recognize.

Original sin

Although the doctrine is most central and most fully developed in Christianity, many theistic religions have some notion of a Fall and of original sin—the idea that people are sinful and the world is messed up because of some transgression by the first humans. To unbelievers, this idea sounds crazy. First, it seems unnecessary: we know perfectly well why people are bad already. Natural selection explains why humans feel hunger, sexual desire, and desire for status; it's inevitable that some people will sometimes use illicit means to satisfy these natural cravings. So, for example, evolution explains lust, and lust explains adultery. What more is to be said? Second, it's not clear how sins of one or two people could have such an influence on all the rest of us, even if we all are descendents of these two.

Such skepticism is only reinforced by the fact that Christians have generally done such a poor job explaining the doctrine. Often, those who take it upon themselves to explain original sin have ended up replacing the idea with some other one. For example, original sin is sometimes recast, not as an explanation of sin, but as simply the statement that people are sinful. For many, it has come to mean only a pessimistic attitude towards schemes for the perfection of man, or else it's a general acknowledgment that one's own motives (as well as others') are tainted with selfishness. Sometimes, the doctrine is taken as a metaphor for the loss of childhood innocence or, for those of a more Hegelian disposition, for the alienating effects of the subject-object distinction. Let us, rather, be fully honest and consider the doctrine in full: the Fall refers to a purportedly actual, historical event that has had vast repercussions for all future generations. We shall see that there are good reasons for theists to believe that such an event actually took place.

The nature of sin

What is it about human sinfulness that Christians think requires a supernatural explanation? Let's return to the above example of an adulterer. His motivation is obviously sexual desire for a woman not his wife—what else is there to explain? First of all, a man is not just a machine that automatically responds to his strongest current drive. We are not mere slaves to our desires. If we were, we would be no more capable of sin than are animals, washing machines, or rocks. Each man is also self-consciously immersed in a world of value and disvalue, good and evil, duty and prescription. The adulterer has some idea that the wife he betrays and the mistress he exploits are not just raw material for his gratification. They are people, human beings, each one precious for her own sake, each one deserving to be treated as an end, not just a means. He also has some idea of the holiness of the conjugal bond and the viciousness of its desecration. He must have at least some sense of these truths, or else he would not be culpable for his evil. The sin does not consist in the desire that motivates it. The sex drive is, in itself, good and natural, and it has a necessary function. It's not sinful to be attracted to a woman; what's sinful is to ignore the fact that she is also a person entitled to respect and concern. What makes the sin is the negative act of ignoring objective values, of ignoring their claims on us. A man who felt a powerful desire for a woman but suppressed it out of devotion to his wife would not be sinning at all. In fact, we regard the refusal to give in to temptation as particularly meritorious, precisely because the positive act of recognition or love needed to persevere must be particularly strong, and this positive act is what we praise.

Sin, therefore, can only take place where there is some recognition of true values. On the other hand, men are prone to sin because this recognition is so dim in us, so easily put out of mind. Consider another case. Suppose a man who loves his wife at least somewhat receives news that she has been killed in an airplane crash. Then he finds out that the report is wrong—his wife is waiting safely for him at the airport. In his intense relief, the husband is at that moment acutely conscious of his wife as a unique, precious, and irreplaceable person. The special intuition provided by love of the incommensurable value of this particular person—his wife—is fully active in him. At this moment, it is inconceivable to the husband that he would ever be unfaithful to his wife. If Aphrodite herself were to appear naked and throw herself upon him, he would not be stirred in the least. At least for a moment, he has lost the ability to sin in one particular way. Is it because love has somehow sapped away his freedom? Quite the contrary—love has rather awakened him to see things as they really are. One thus awakened to the preciousness of his wife would never be unfaithful, just as a man without a blindfold would never walk off a cliff. A man deadened to love may stray, just as a blindfolded man may fall off a cliff, but this hardly makes such pitiful men more free. One should rather say the reverse, because the latter men only act as they do because they don't fully know what they're doing.

Each of us lives in a moral stupor, a state of being only half-aware. Even though we have flashes of insight into the preciousness of our loved ones, they don't last. We fall back into insensibility and petty selfishness. As for those outside our small circle of intimates, we never truly appreciate their value and beauty at all, because only love makes such perception possible. Most of us don't perform spectacular evils like adultery, but we behave selfishly in smaller ways, in our words and our thoughts. Most often, our sins are sins of omission—like Dives we fail to even take notice of the suffering we might easily assuage. Dives was a man who sleepwalked through life; every day he saw Lazarus, but he never really registered him in his mind. He never saw that Lazarus as someone who it was his responsibility to help. He never consciously chose to ignore a duty, and he was genuinely surprised to find himself one day in hell. Sin he did, though, and so do we all. We too sleepwalk through life, using and ignoring our fellow men, sinning dozens of times each day without even realizing it. Indeed, one might almost say that we are in the worst possible state—with only enough awareness to be culpable and not enough to be good. Unlike any other animal, human nature seems to condemn itself: we naturally make demands on ourselves that it's naturally impossible for us to fulfill.

Man's alienation from God

In religion, too, human nature seems to overstep itself. The existence of a perfect, self-subsistent Creator is implied by creation, and no culture has failed to attain the idea of God. But although we can infer God's existence, we cannot truly comprehend the divine nature—what it means to be atemporal, utterly simple, pure act, etc. Of course, the other animals don't comprehend God's nature either, but they have no sense of this gap in their knowledge. Unlike them, man *knows* that he doesn't comprehend the most basic principle of the universe. As Pascal put it:

> *What can be seen on earth indicates neither the total absence, nor the manifest presence of divinity, but the presence of a hidden God. Everything bears this stamp...*

> *He must not see nothing at all, nor must he see enough to think that he possesses God, but he must see enough to know that he has lost him. For, to know that one has lost something one must see and not see: such precisely is the state of nature.*

> *–Pensee 449*

God is also a personal Being, Someone who I could befriend and love. Indeed, it seems that I owe Him that much. I don't love God though, because I don't know Him, as one person can know another. I can't love a stranger, no matter how much I owe that stranger and no matter how much I've been told about what a great guy he is. Unless He reveals Himself in a personal way, God is a stranger to me.

The fulfillment of the aspirations of human nature is naturally impossible. This is the dilemma. To quote Pascal again,

Man's greatness is so obvious that it can even be deduced from his wretchedness, for what is nature in animals we call wretchedness in man, thus recognizing that, if his nature is today like that of the animals, he must have fallen from some better state which was once his own.

Who indeed would think himself unhappy not to be king except one who had been dispossessed?...Who would think himself unhappy if he had only one mouth, and who would not if he had only one eye?

–Pensee 117

Why doesn't God show Himself? He does, all the time and everywhere. In fact, none of us has ever seen anything what wasn't an act of God showing Himself. Every created thing is a manifestation of God. Everything and everyone is animated by His existence, and all symbolize Him, each in its own way. The real question is not why God fails to show Himself, but why we lack the perception to notice how He's revealing Himself all the time. Our state is rather like someone who stares at a painting, takes note of each bit of paint, but is too dull to notice that the gobs of paint together form a picture. Or imagine watching a girl walk across the street and thinking of her as just a collection of molecules, without noticing that these molecules together constitute a unitary living being. Of course, God is more than the animating, unifying principle of the universe, but He's not less than this.

Christians regard these two issues—the inability to truly appreciate and love other people as they deserve, and the inability to see God in all things—as two parts of the same infirmity. If we could see how each person is an image of God and is designed to share in the perfect love of the Trinity, the Christian believes, than we could really appreciate each person in his or her full glory.

The meaning of grace

Why do we lack the perceptiveness to see God? Again, there seems to be a straightforward answer: it's simply beyond human mental capacity. This is true enough, but someone who believes in God has no reason to accept the assumption that man should be left to his own devices. There's a benevolent God out there who knows what we need. Why doesn't He help? Wouldn't it be possible for God to use His powers to augment our natural capabilities? He could share with us His vision of things as they really are. To return to the earlier analogy of sleepwalking, He would "wake us up" by sharing His "God's-eye" view of the universe and each other. In his speculations on heaven, St. Augustine has beautifully described this possibility:

> *Wherefore it may very well be...that we shall in the future world see the material forms of the new heavens and the new earth in such a way that we shall most distinctly recognize God everywhere present and governing all things, material as well as spiritual...As we do not believe, but see that the living men around us who are exercising vital functions are alive, although we cannot see their life without their bodies, but see it most distinctly by means of their bodies, so, wherever we shall look with those spiritual eyes of our future bodies, we shall then, too, by means of bodily substances behold God, though a spirit, ruling all things...God will be so known by us, and shall be so much before us, that we shall see Him by the spirit in ourselves, in one another, in Himself...in every created thing which shall then exist.*

–City of God XXII

This augmentation of human nature is called "grace" in Christian theology. (In the quote above, Augustine describes it in its full form, the beatific vision.) The Eastern Churches often use the bolder term "theosis" or "deification", because it involves a sharing in the divine nature or "energies". We can now state with precision the question which the story of the Fall is meant to answer: why is mankind not now in a state of grace? However well or poorly Augustine's quote describes the future life, we can all agree that it doesn't describe this life at all.

The possibility of grace

There are two possibilities: either it had to be the case that humanity lacks grace, or it didn't have to be the case, i.e. original sin is either necessary or contingent. Let's consider the first possibility first: why might it necessarily be the case that men lack grace? There are three possible answers. The first is that God doesn't exist. This would certainly explain the lack of divine assistance. I will assume that the reader is already persuaded of God's existence, either for the reasons given in my Defense of Religion or for some others, so I will not consider this possibility further. The second possibility is that our moral and intellectual limitations are integral parts of what we are. This is a very depressing thought, as it implies that my selfishness and ignorance at least partly define me, so that I can't rise above them without ceasing to exist. In this case, we could hardly even condemn the evil inside us, because the good couldn't exist without it. This, however, contradicts our intuition. Consider the example of above of the husband awakened to love. If he could permanently in this awakened state, he certainly wouldn't cease to be himself.

The third possibility, which is related to the second, is that grace—the partaking of divine nature—is a contradiction, because no being can act except through its own nature. This is the most powerful objection to the doctrine of grace, because its premise is actually true of most objects. Suppose God wished to give intelligence to a stone, and to do this He caused thoughts to take place inside that stone. Perhaps He could do this, but one should seriously doubt that God had thereby given the rock a mental life. What would make the thoughts God creates belong to the stone, as opposed to belonging to some kind of ghost that God has put in the same spot? One could say that the rock's nature is its one principle of unity, so we only count those acts that take place inside the rock as "rock acts" if they are acts of rock nature. I myself think this reasoning is valid, so it follows that even God could not make a rock think. Nor could God make a rock fly, even though He could cause it to move through the air, because "flying" means "moving through the air through one's own natural act". Couldn't we say the same thing about grace, namely that although God can create divine thoughts, He can't make them our thoughts? Here we come to a crucial distinction between things and persons. A thing has only one principle of unity: its mode of operation specified by its nature. A person has two such principles: his natural mode of operation and his subjective unity of experience. The latter principle, called by Kant the "transcendental unity of apperception" is entirely different from essential unity. It comes from the fact that I can premise every piece of knowledge that I have with the phrase "I know that..." and refer to the same "I" in each case. From the point of view of transcendental unity, some of my knowledge might come from naturally human modes of knowing, and some of it might come from supernatural modes of knowing. This distinction between nature and person, introduced by the Cappadocian Fathers, is crucial to Christian theology. It allows Christians to state the mysteries of the Incarnation (one person with two natures) and the Trinity (three persons in one nature) precisely. It also shows why grace is a real, logical possibility.

If men don't have to lack grace, then the reason for its lack must be contingent, i.e. historical. Either God just decided not to offer His divine assistance to us, or He did offer it, and we refused. Pure reason can't tell us which it is. The doctrine of the Fall, of course, is simply the assertion of the latter possibility. Adam and Eve were given primordial grace but rejected it through sin, and we're all paying the price. Because the doctrine of original sin regards evil as non-necessary, it should arguably be regarded as an optimistic idea.

The Fall and natural history

There are two major objections to this claim. The first objection is that it is contradicted by the evidence of evolutionary biology, which suggests that there was no original human pair, but rather a slow evolution through imperceptible changes between lower primate and modern man. However, if one accepts my argument given earlier that ontological species distinctions are meaningful and exist, than during this empirically continuous progression, there must have been an actual first human—the first one to cross the threshold. Of course, the first two may not have been the Y-chromosome Adam or the mitochondrial Eve identified by geneticists. Genetics has, however, definitively established one piece of the Biblical narrative—namely, that the present human race all descends from one small group. This group lived in Africa some 50,000 years ago. True, the genetic diversity of the human race indicates that we descend from a group of a few thousand, not two. Remember, though, that the first true humans (e.g. "Cain" and "Seth") were surrounded by humanoids with whom they could successfully mate. In any event, the claims "there was a first man", "there is a man from whom all humans are descended", and "there is a woman from whom all humans are descended" are all true, and no version of the doctrine of the Fall requires anything more.

In Adam all sinned: the spiritual unity of mankind

The other, more interesting objection is that original sin is unfair: why should the rest of us be punished for what Adam and Eve did or failed to do? Within the Christian belief system (the one in which the doctrine of the Fall plays the largest role), this can be naturally understood by seeing salvation as primarily a corporate rather than individual affair. God draws all human beings in a state of grace together into a sort of spiritual organism in which each individual is a distinct organ; we were to see and love Him not separately, but together. The attraction of this picture is that it gives God a way to connect people not only to Himself, but also to each other. The drawback is that, by connecting all people in their assent toward God, when one person falls, he can pull others down with him. We can sabotage each other not just naturally, e.g. through bad example, but also supernaturally through abdicating our roles in the operation of grace. In this picture, Adam and Eve must have been essential "organs", because the spiritual union of mankind couldn't function without them. Indeed, to fix up the situation, Christians believe that God had to create a new Adam (Jesus) and a new Eve (Mary).

Christianity (and, to a lesser extent, other theistic religions) has built up an impressive body of doctrine, mysticism, and speculation around the ideas of grace, deification, and the spiritual union of mankind. It's not the purpose of this essay to go into all that. We can't prove from pure reason that anybody has ever actually been in a state of grace. (If we could, God's gift of it would not be free.) We can't even take all the mystery out of the idea—nor should we expect to be able to do so. It's important to understand, though, that these doctrines are as rationally defensible as they ever were.

The Defenses

In Defense of Censorship

We Westerners are used to hearing about the need for laws to protect the rights of the individual. No doubt it seems strange to our ears to hear that there must also be laws to protect the community, and yet it is true. The community has its own character, by which I mean something different than the sum or the average of qualities of the people who make it up. One obnoxious person can spoil the atmosphere of a party; a company of men is often braver as a group than any of them would be as individuals; a religious congregation can be said to collectively accept articles of faith about which many of its members harbor private doubts. In each case, it's a question of what belief sets the tone of the group, not the secret thoughts of individuals. A set of shared beliefs, customs, and authority is the very stuff of which a community is made. Its members have a strong interest in making sure that the beliefs are true, the customs good, and the authority respected. The communal atmosphere has a powerful influence (for good or ill) on the conscience of each individual; a strong collective sense of justice and piety is also a good thing in itself. An attack on a group's beliefs and customs is an attack on the group itself, a call for it to be reconstituted along different principles. On vital matters, the community will always have an opinion, and those who disagree will find their voices less welcome in the public sphere than will those who agree. Censorship is a community defending itself against attack. No society ever has or ever could survive without it. Censorship is the basis of civilization.

Are there really collective beliefs?

Why then does censorship have such a bad name in our society, so much so that when we do censor (as every society must) we always feel the need to call it something else? There are two main arguments against censorship. The first is to deny that there really are such things as collective beliefs or collective morals in the sense I described above. Only individuals have beliefs. Individual beliefs can't be legislated, and to attempt to do so would be tyrannical. Therefore, censorship is both tyrannical and futile. This argument would be very strong if there were indeed no real collective beliefs and if censorship really did therefore aim to control private beliefs. However, I think it's pretty clear that something like what I've called the collective "tone" does exist. Consider an example. Sixty years ago in the United States, when someone publicly defended extramarital sex, he was accused of being a "pervert" or being "immoral", and he would certainly not be regarded as respectable. The collective belief and expectation was that sex only belongs in marriage. Unmarried couples knew better than to openly flaunt this expectation. Of course, many privately dissented from this view and acted on their dissention, and many more accepted the belief in theory but acted against it anyway, but the public line was clear. Today, by contrast, when someone publicly criticizes extramarital sex, he is accused of being a "prude" or a "religious fanatic", and he is liable to be ridiculed in university classrooms and late-night talk shows. Unmarried couples openly cohabit, and it would destroy a person's reputation if he publicly criticized them. The collective opinion has definitely turned from chastity to licentiousness. Once again, many people dissent from the collective view, but they are keenly aware of holding a disapproved opinion. I think it would be difficult to argue that this change has not occurred or that it hasn't had significant effects on teenage pregnancy rates, divorce rates, and many other matters of public importance.

Will the truth win out on its own?

The strongest and most popular argument against censorship is that the free exchange of ideas does a better job of promoting true beliefs and good customs. The idea is that if every side is allowed to make its case without obstruction, the truth will naturally win out. After all, true beliefs are guaranteed to be logically self-consistent and consistent with all accurately-determined facts, while false opinions will often fail one or both of these tests. This is the argument made by J. S. Mill in his celebrated liberal tract *On Liberty*. Mill goes so far as to say that beliefs which are supported by tradition or authority should be regarded as especially suspect, because they haven't yet shown their mettle in the test of free debate.

What can the defender of censorship say to this claim? Only that it is simply not true. For a race of purely logical intelligences, free debate might work like this, but not for real human beings. For a human being, there are aspects of a proposition which attract him and which are uncorrelated or even negatively correlated with the probability of it being true: how well it flatters his pride or helps to rationalize his vices, how much it relies on apparently simple concepts and avoids challenging his imagination, how well it is able to discredit its opponents and shut down debate in its favor. One need only consider Richard Dawkins' theory of the spread of "memes" to imagine the possibilities. If, then, free debate will generally not lead to the truth, then this gives us one means of deciding when censorship is necessary. What ideas, or more importantly, what rhetorical tricks must a debating community disallow in order to keep the search for truth on track?

In this context, one often hears appeals to the example of science. Here, we are told, complete freedom to criticize old theories and suggest new ones has undoubtedly led to an advance in knowledge. In fact, the equation of science with free debate reflects a misunderstanding of the scientific enterprise. The scientific community has rules—rigidly enforced—regarding what may and may not be said while engaging in scientific discourse. One may not fabricate or misrepresent data. One may not attack the character of a fellow researcher in order to discredit his theory. One may not accuse him of forging or plagiarizing data without strong evidence. One may not criticize a theory by asserting that negative social or political consequences would follow from its acceptance. One may not criticize a theory for its disagreement or agreement with a religious or political authority. One may not draw philosophical conclusions from empirical data, or vice versa. If a scientist violates any of these rules, his professional reputation, and usually his career, will be destroyed. Science owes its success not only to the freedom it does allow, but also to the freedoms it doesn't. The community knows that, if personal aspersion or political passion were allowed into scientific debate, they could quickly destroy it or render it fruitless.

As a second case, let us consider public debates over morality. Here the dynamic is quite different than in the case of the sciences. Concern over the public consequences of accepting some ethical position is obviously legitimate, and therefore they should be heard. On the other hand, moral debates have their own illegitimate temptations. When I am trying to decide whether or not an act is morally licit, it can certainly affect my judgment if I have a strong desire (or a desire that can be made strong by enticement) to engage in that act. This desire has no relevance to the act's morality—its influence is illegitimate, but it is there nonetheless. To take an extreme example, suppose an enlightened high school decides to host a debate on the morality of premarital sex, in order to help students "make up their own minds". First a Catholic priest admonishes the students to chastity, then a utilitarian bioethicist encourages them to satisfy all their carnal desires—just put on a condom first! Is it really credible that the teenage boys will make a decision based entirely on the logical merits of each side? In the same way, is it credible that utilitarianism/consequentialism holds the place it does in our public debates entirely because of its philosophical merits? Is it really so demonstrably superior to teleological and deontological ethical systems? Only in the sense that it makes the fewest inconvenient demands on its followers, it seems to me. So it would seem that free debate on ethical matters does not lead to moral truth. In fact, what it seems to lead to is a race to the bottom to whatever position is most permissive. Hardly surprising, then, are the efforts by authorities in most times and places to suppress threats to "public morality". A moral consensus seems to be something that doesn't take care of itself.

Another concern of censors has always been to safeguard what we may call "the sacred", that is, whatever the community believes should be regarded with reverence. Governments have therefore prohibited public displays of blasphemy, obscenity, the desecration of revered symbols, and the large-scale promotion of irreverence among the young. Again, the intention is not to regulate private feelings—which would be impossible—but to safeguard the communal norm. The question is whether the public will be dominated by those who revere the symbol or by those who ridicule it. Whose sentiments will be the default, the taken-for-granted, position in the public sphere? As in the case of moral debate, it would be foolish to think that the best positions on these matters would naturally win out in an unregulated debate. The two sides do not fight from symmetric positions. Reverence requires a profound spiritual concentration, whereas any fool can adopt an attitude of cynicism. One snickering guest can destroy the atmosphere of solemnity at a wedding or a funeral. The impious can always seize the public space away from a religion by ridicule. Even if their jokes, slanders, and innuendos don't add up to an actual argument against the religion's claims, these stunts often succeed in fostering attitudes of suspicion and cynicism that are incompatible with faith.

The false ideal of neutrality

Here we come to the crucial issue—the liberal ideal of neutrality. Recall that the central tenet of liberalism is that the state should be neutral between competing comprehensive theories of the good. Each of us has our own conception of the good life, but, it is said, we can step outside of our own beliefs to adopt an "original position" above them all, and from this position make decisions which favor each view equally. It is not surprising that liberals should embrace the ideal of free exchange of ideas; it bears a great similarity to their political ideal. On any given issue, the liberal would recommend that we initially adopt a neutral and unprejudiced view, listen attentively to all of the arguments that anyone can think of, and then make an informed and rational decision. The conservative, however, realizes that there is no such neutral position above every idea of the good (or, if there is such a position, it would not be possible to draw any normative conclusions within it). He asserts that the neutral position advocated by liberals is really just utilitarianism/consequentialism/individualism in disguise. The calls for open debate based on "public reason" are really attempts to preempt the debate by excluding all non-liberal points of view.

Something similar is the case for debates over morality and the sacred. The liberal demands that we, or at least the public as a collective, adopt a neutral position between the two sides. We must be skeptical of all claims, they say, and not prejudice the issue by allowing authority to weigh in on one side. But this "neutral position" turns out to be identical to one of the sides of the dispute. Consider moral debates. To neutrally judge between two competing moral systems, one would have to disregard each system's claim that adherence to it is intrinsically good—otherwise, one would be judging from the "inside" and not from a neutral position at all. But if a morality can't be an end, it must be a means to an amoral end (e.g. maximum or equal preference satisfaction). However, to look at morality this way is already to embrace consequentialsim. It is not surprising, then, that free debate on moral issues always results in a race to the bottom, i.e. to utilitarianism. It would do so even in the absence of self-interest. The case is even clearer for sacred matters. No one would suggest that, in order for me to be a rational person, I should be neutral between the options of trusting or mistrusting my wife until a careful investigation proves her honesty and faithfulness. Even to undertake such an investigation means choosing not to trust her, and this means ruining my relationship with her (even if she doesn't know it). Surely it is more reasonable to trust those with whom we have valued relationships until we have good reasons to doubt them. So it is also with religion and tradition, which are our relationships with God and with our ancestors. There is no neutral ground between trust and suspicion, between faith and doubt. To demand investigation on these terms is to prejudge the issue.

Free speech and accountability

There is one final argument against censorship—that it is a necessary check on the abuse of power by the government. Allow magistrates to suppress reports of their misdeeds, and they will be completely unaccountable. This is a strong argument, but it only applies to a minority of censorship cases. It is a fundamental rule of justice that no one should be the judge of his own case. Thus it does seem that government officials should not be allowed to censor criticism of their policies or allegations of abuse of office. However, their inability to defend themselves doesn't mean they can't discourage attacks on other authorities, such as parents or the established church. Nor does it mean that they should tolerate attacks on articles of natural law, which are not matters of personal policy. People should be allowed to criticize a change in the tax or interest rate, but calls for easy divorce are a short road to the moral sewer.

The inevitability of censorship

At the beginning of this essay, I claimed that censorship is both beneficial and inevitable. So far, I have only defended the first claim. From what I have said so far, it will be clear that censorship is necessary if a society is to keep from falling into utilitarianism and atheism. However, suppose one were to embrace, or at least resign oneself to, these positions. Couldn't an atheist, utilitarian community survive without censorship? At one time, such a question would be theoretical, but today there are a number of such communities embracing the entire populations of Europe and Canada. When we examine these societies we find, rather than utopias of free expression, regimes which police public expression to a degree that would have been inconceivable in the Middle Ages. These countries have draconian laws against "racism" and "hate speech" which in practice forbid practically any expression of disapproval for wedge minority groups or any expression of cultural or ethnic pride by the majority group. Some have outlawed criticism of Islam or homosexuality. Most bizarrely of all, it is a crime in some European countries to deny that the Nazi Holocaust ever happened. This certainly seems peculiar. Why should censorship be necessary at all? After all, the social dynamics I described above would all seem to favor the established positions, so these governments needn't fear free debate for any reason I've given so far. Also, the governments in Europe and Canada largely control the schools and the media, so this would give them an enormous advantage in any public debate.

It would seem that human beings have some inclinations which can't be satisfied in the atheist/utilitarian/cosmopolitan/androgynist framework of contemporary Europe. The most relevant in this case is the tendency to love and favor one's own group, be it religious, cultural, geographical, or ethnic. For half a century, Europeans have been brainwashed to believe that all races and cultures are identically good (except for their own race and culture, which are worthless), and that the most evil thing that anyone can do is to show preference for one's own kind and their ways. In spite of this, the tendency to love and loyalty for one's own group is so strong that it keeps popping up even against the wishes of the ruling class. We see this above all in clashes between the ruling class and lower-class whites over the issues of mass immigration and the Islamization of the European continent.

As a conservative, I might be expected to object to the European form of censorship, or at least use it to gloat over liberalism's hypocrisy. On the contrary, I realize that European governments have the same imperative as all governments: to maintain their own legitimacy. If a state can't do this, all is lost. This is why every state regards it as a crime to publicly challenge the government's authority and to incite insurrection. This would be an attack on what Eric Voegelin called the "existential representation" of the people. However, most societies also have what Voegelin called a "cosmological representation" and a "transcendental representation", i.e. the state is legitimated in the eyes of the people by reference to an alleged order of nature or of morality. In such societies, an attack on this idea of natural law or divine order or whatever is an attack on the authorities that these beliefs legitimate. In medieval Europe, one could not publicly deny that Jesus Christ rose from the dead. In contemporary Europe, one cannot publically deny that Hitler killed six million Jews. In both cases, we are dealing with civic myths. By "myth", I don't mean to say that these events didn't take place (in fact, I think they both did); I mean that they both serve the purpose of legitimating the social order. In the Middle Ages, kings held their authority from God, the same God that was revealed through His Son. Remove the revelation, and you remove the Divinity. Remove the Divinity, and the king's authority is reduced to raw power. The European Union, on the other hand, claims its reason for existence in the viciousness of the European nationalism which it is meant to fight. Just as Christ's passion and resurrection disclosed the true nature of God and our relationship to Him, so the Holocaust supposedly disclosed the true hateful nature of every form of European group loyalty. In the official view of European history, Nazism is read backwards into the entire history of the West: from Roman patriotism, to Catholic universalism, to French absolutism and Prussian militarism. All of it is pure evil. Therefore, the EU must destroy the peoples of Europe and fashion a homogeneous race of impeccably tolerant liberal cosmopolitans. If anyone questions this narrative, say by praising some aspect of the European past, he is implicitly questioning the European Union's claim to authority. This is the one thing that no state, whatever its stated beliefs, can tolerate.

In Defense of Regional Cultures

Conservatives generally oppose large-scale mixing between cultures. People often find this hard to understand. Do we regard other cultures as inferior? Do we actually hate them? Multiculturalists think so. They claim that cultural loyalties are actually constituted by their hatred of a posited "other". They use their control of the schools and media to discourage attachment to one's own people—which they call "racism"—and piety towards one's fatherland—which they call "nationalism". In the western world, school history lessons consist almost entirely of the demonization of our own ancestors.

In fact, this suspicion of natural loyalties is quite unfounded; my love for my own country is no more based on hatred of other countries than my love for my own wife is based on antipathy towards other women. Nor is patriotism based on an idea that one's country is "superior" in some way to others, any more than my piety towards my parents is based on a belief that they are superior to other people by some objective standard. So, if other cultures are just as good as ours, why doesn't a conservative want to "enrich" his society by filling it with many different cultures? The short answer is that that's not how culture works. If you mix two cultures, you don't get twice as much culture; you destroy both of them.

The function of shared culture

A culture consists of a people's shared customs, memories, stories, and beliefs. It is not a thing possessed only by the elite—normal and easy interaction between two people is impossible without some shared culture. With a person of my own culture, I know what greetings and compliments are appropriate, what sensitive topics should be avoided, what requests are acceptable, what words and actions are offensive. When I encounter an alien, on the other hand, I become apprehensive; I no longer know the rules of the game. This apprehension doesn't mean that I hate the alien, even unconsciously. Common culture simply makes possible a level of comfort which is not possible in its absence. The discomfort of not knowing what to expect from others is so intolerable that a common culture will form automatically if a people live together long enough. This benevolent process can be thwarted in only two ways. The first is a continual movement of population, so that people never settle long enough to form communities. The second is a coercive act of the government to prevent the formation of an established culture, generally in the name of "multiculturalism" or "making outsiders feel welcome". (The only way for the outsider to feel as welcome as everyone else is to make everyone else feel as alienated as the outsider.) Unfortunately, both of these things are prevalent in today's world.

Common culture also indicates shared loyalties and beliefs. If I say in the company of other Americans that the USA is a great country and that she has been abundantly blessed by God, I can expect most of them to approve both the beliefs and the sentiments. If I say this around European atheists, the statements would be contentious, even dubious, and I would be expected to defend them. Now, it is good for beliefs and customs to be sometimes subjected to criticism, but it is unhealthy for them to be criticized all the time. A belief must have some respite from attack for internal development, just as a religion should cultivate not only apologetics (its response to attack) but also theology, in which a community of believers takes the truths of their faith for granted and considers their implications. A belief must also have some respite to be lived: the Mass is no place to debate the Real Presence, and a 4th of July celebration is no place to debate America's alleged wickedness. Even liberals grant this point when they insist that minorities be given an affirming, supportive atmosphere. Majorities need this too.

Another great benefit of people living in a community with shared beliefs is the pressure to conform. Concern for status is a universal human trait; it can either be given a productive function in a community's moral standards, or it will manifest itself in unproductive ways such as the pursuit of wealth and in conspicuous consumption. Men are often better restrained from wickedness by fear of lost reputation than by fear of the police. Also, communal censure can proscribe acts—such as public rudeness, gossiping, insulting the dead, or flirting with married women—that disrupt the community but which it would be unwise to actually outlaw.

In order to function, a culture must establish itself over some region. If only a few separated people follow a custom, this is not culture but personal eccentricity. To function as culture, a custom or belief must be sufficiently widespread to be taken for granted. A few oddballs won't hurt anything, but once a fifth or so of the population repudiates a custom, it can no longer function as cultural. When a culture establishes itself over the lives of a people, this will naturally be reflected in their laws. The best way to ensure cultural health and diversity is to promote local government. Allow each region, in some cases even each neighborhood, to establish its own laws regulating education, holidays, pornography, and blasphemy. These will naturally reflect and protect the culture of the locals. Since the established culture is local, those who don't like living in it don't have to move far to find more agreeable company. Members of incompatible cultures will naturally separate over a few generations. Call this "segregation" if you like, but it's the only way to have multiple healthy cultures in the world.

Wedge minorities

Being cosmopolitans, liberals hate culture and seek out ways to attack it. This is usually done with the use of wedge minorities. The wedge minority can be any outsider to the established culture, so the liberal can attack this culture on the grounds that it "excludes" the minority. Blacks, Mexicans, Muslims, homosexuals, and Jews are the most notable wedge minorities today. Where no usable wedge minority exists, liberals will attempt to import one by promoting immigration. This strategy leads the liberals to an apparent inconsistency: in order to serve its purpose, the minority must maintain its cohesion, so it must be allowed to keep its own beliefs and customs, the very things the liberals are working to eradicate in the majority. Thus, blacks are allowed to be loyal to each other and to celebrate their heritage, but whites can have no ethnic loyalty and must despise their ancestors. In the end, though, liberals will the destruction of all cultures. Minorities will only be allowed to keep their cultures so long as this serves the larger goal by undermining the majority culture. In the short term, being a wedge minority brings undeniable privileges. In the long term, blacks, Mexicans, and Muslims should remember that the friend of the conqueror is only the last to be conquered.

Human Sacrifice and the Eucharist

According to the Law almost everything is purified by blood, and without the shedding of blood there is no forgiveness.

–Hebrews 9:22

What is it that constitutes the essence of religious worship? It is sacrifice.

--Chateaubriand

Sacrifice: the purpose of religion

The point of religion is not to make men moral or to make society just, not to foster community or even to win eternal life. The point of religion is to glorify God. The religious man knows that he has duties to God. First, he owes God gratitude for creating him. Second, he reveres God because this is the just response to God's intrinsic goodness—to His ontological grandeur as the perfect and unlimited being and to His moral beauty as seen in His generosity and mercy (and, Christians would add, as being Himself a community of love). Of course, the religious man doesn't just experience God as a good Thing to be approved; he experiences God as holy. Those things which are consecrated to Him are sacred things, and profane things seem impure in His holy presence.

How does man do his duty to God? One way is to care for His creatures, most especially by showing love and justice to other people; a kindness done for them is done also for their Creator. However, this is not the only, or even always the primary way that a man discharges his duty to God. A man's purpose is not fulfilled by his service to finite goods. True, a man can occupy his whole life in service of his family or his country, or to advance knowledge or social causes, but the horizon of his mind is larger than these things. In understanding the world, his mind ascends from effect to cause, not resting until it reaches the First Cause, the Necessary Being. In justifying moral duties, the mind ascends from means to ends, from relative goods to absolute Good, from delegated authority to its ultimate Source. This infinite horizon of the mind causes men to desire a direct a relationship with God, something in addition to the implicit contacts with Him given by relationships to His creatures. The religious man craves God's presence. He desires sacred spaces ("holy ground") so that he can physically face God. He wishes to make offerings to God, both to express his devotion and to draw closer to the Divinity. The offering of goods establishes a new bond with the Creator, and those things which are offered to God thereby become sacred objects, that is, conduits which mediate the divine presence. The sacrifices a man offers represent himself—they express his desire to offer himself to God and thereby to become holy, to be a thing consecrated to God.

Objections to sacrifice

Liberalism in religion can be defined as hostility to the idea of trying to please God with ritual and sacrifice, and indeed hostility to the idea of dividing the world into the sacred and the profane. The liberal regards such ideas as degrading, as superstitious, as reflecting a debased idea of God and an unjust contempt for His creation. The liberal's objections are serious, and should be considered in turn.

First, it is said that prayer and sacrifice are distractions from our duties to our fellow man. God, being omnipotent, has no need of our gifts, while the needs of the poor are great and urgent. This is the old "you shouldn't have beautiful churches when people are hungry" argument. And since the poor will be with us always, a society could never invest any resources in religion, art, or pure science if this argument is valid. Fortunately, it is not, but it is worth considering because it highlights the fundamental difference between the liberal-communist ideal of justice—"to each according to his need"—and the conservative-Aristotelian ideal—"to each his due." We make offerings to God not because He needs them, but because He deserves them. If I fail to offer God the first fruits of my labor, I am not responding to things according to their true value; I am, in a sense, not living in the real world. Of course, we may occasionally postpone our direct service to God when emergency strikes and the needs of our fellow men are pressing, but the mere fact of poverty and want cannot negate our religious duties. Indeed, I suspect that most of the offense against church "wealth" comes from middle-class intellectuals rather than the truly poor. After all, our cathedrals are more truly at the service of the poor (for they too wish to worship God) than are our universities or our art museums.

But surely, it is next claimed, if we must offer something to God, it would be better to offer our service to our fellow man. If God is as generous as we say, wouldn't he be more pleased by justice and charity to others than by ritual and sacrifice? Two things should be said to this. First, it presents a false "either-or" choice. According to most religions, love of neighbor and ritual sanctification are complementary and mutually-reinforcing. Second, it would not be fitting for God to declare that the only worship He wants is good behavior towards other people. An offering to God is meaningless if it consists of nothing but things we should be doing in any case for other reasons. The religious drive is to unmediated self-offering to God, and if the Lord failed to provide some way of making such offerings, He would be frustrating the noblest aspiration He placed in us.

Finally, it could be said that all this talk of "offering" things to God is meaningless in any case. Everything already belongs to God. Therefore, we should regard everything as equally "sacred"; to do so would surely augment our respect for other people and the natural environment. This objection does contain a truth: all things do belong to God, and all things do bear some likeness to their Creator and deserve our respect for carrying this likeness. However, though all things belong to God, not all things belong only to God. Food, technology, and good government exist ultimately to glorify God, but they glorify Him through their service to us. Sacred things are those things set aside only for God, to be used by us only in our worship of Him. A thing may be good without being sacred.

These are the liberal's objections. The religious man, who wants to offer prayer and sacrifice, has questions of his own. What shall I offer to God, and how should I offer it? It must be a sacrifice worthy of the All-Holy One, and it must be so connected to me as to make the offering to be a gift of my very self. And who am I that I should dare to offer myself to God? I am a "sinful man", a "man of unclean lips", one unworthy even to enter into the divine presence. Pious men of every religion have always felt their inadequacy for such an exalted task. God Himself must make His own worship possible. "God Himself will provide the victim for the holocaust" (Gen 22:8), Abraham told his son, speaking a deeper truth than he knew. In every religion, men believe that their cult was established by God Himself; they know their offerings please the Lord because He told them they would. To address man's unworthiness, a second act is added to the ritual: the purification rite. The worshiper's sins are washed away and he is made pure. Sacrifice and purification can happen in either order or simultaneously. A priest may ritually wash himself before offering sacrifice, or an animal may be sacrificed and its blood—which is now sacred, having become a thing of God—used to consecrate and purify the people or their temple.

Abraham and Isaac

Abraham's sacrifice of his son Isaac is a perfect instance of a sacrificial act. It clearly shows the basic truth that all sacrifice is ultimately human sacrifice. The ram that Abraham ultimately slaughters is offered "in place of his son" (Gen 22:13). Killing an animal would be meaningless without this identification. Liberals are typically scandalized by this story; it seems wrong to them that Abraham should be blessed because he was willing to commit murder. Yet the Jews have treasured this story for millennia. Why? Is it because it proves Abraham's devotion to God? This is certainly true, and the Bible itself draws attention to it, but there is more than this. When Abraham offered his son to God, binding him upon an altar with the intention of slaughtering him, Isaac became God's property, a sacred thing, a thing "set aside" for God. That God decided to leave Isaac alive does not change his consecration, and the people of Israel, who are the seed of Isaac, are also a thing set aside for God. So this episode is one of the many acts in the Old Testament in which the covenant between God and "His people" is affirmed and renewed. Only as a people set aside for God can Israel be a light to the nations, because a thing offered to God becomes a conduit to God. In this way also, Isaac is the prefigure of Christ—also sacrificed by his Father— who, as the supreme sacrifice to God, becomes the supreme conduit to the Father, the ultimate "sacred thing" which removes sin and renews communion with God.

The symbolism of blood

A religious ritual is a symbolic act, and as such it makes use of preexisting symbolic meanings. Sometimes these meanings are fixed by the culture, as when I offer God what my culture recognizes as a salute, or when I place a cultural symbol of value (i.e. money) in the collection basket. The most powerful rituals, however, make use of natural symbolic meanings. For example, sexual intercourse naturally denotes union, and some peoples (such as the Babylonians) have tried to effect symbolic union with God through temple prostitution. In fact, this is an abuse of the sex act, whose meaning is too fixed to procreation and family life to be legitimately "stretched" in this way. However, we should acknowledge that a real religious impulse, and not mere lust, is at the foundation of this practice. What we need is a natural symbol that, like sex, signifies love and union and, again like sex, is asymmetric between the participants, but which, unlike sex, signifies a one-way donation of one's life. This is the symbolism of blood.

Across the world, widely disparate peoples have chosen as their offering to God the flesh and blood of animals, and occasionally even of humans. Why has this seemed a fitting sacrifice to so many cultures at so many times? It can only be because of the natural symbolism of blood. "Since the life of a living body is in its blood, I have made you put it on the altar, so that atonement may thereby be made for your own lives, because it is the blood, as the seat of life, that makes atonement" (Lev 17:11). Blood is the life force; to offer blood is to offer life, and a union of blood is a merger of lives. The blood and flesh of the sacrificial victim become channels of divine Life. Blood purifies the Temple on the Day of Atonement (Lev 16:15-19). Blood protects and purifies the house during Passover (Ex 12:7). Moses sprinkled the people with blood to establish the covenant (Ex. 24:6-8).

The Christian sacrifice

It is sometimes thought that, as a civilization progresses and gains a more "spiritual" understanding of God, sacrificial offerings should become a less important part of religious life until religion itself is more or less reduced to poetic exhortations to philanthropy. This is not inevitably the case. The period 0-1000AD was marked in Europe by the replacement of paganism by the most intensely sacrificial of all religions, namely Christianity. Christianity is the most sacrificial religion? That may not be obvious, especially to the post-Vatican II crowd, but let's think about it.

People of all religions believe that the offering of oneself to God—in prayer, sacrifice, asceticism, charity, or martyrdom—is the noblest of human acts. According to the doctrine of the Trinity, offering of self to God is also a divine activity. God offers Himself to God: the Father in "begetting" gives the Son His full divinity, and the Son [the "lamb of God" (John 1:29)] offers His life back to the Father through perfect obedience (c.f. John 5:30, Luke 22:42). Thus, the Christian believes that self-offering to God does more than establish a relationship with the Creator. It can "atone" in a more perfect sense by allowing one to share in God's own inner life. Glorifying God and being united with him are not only related (as in paganism); they are essentially the same thing. When God's grace allows us to participate in the sacrificial act which defines God the Son, we become ourselves "sons" of God the Father. Thus, for Christians, the benefit of Christ's sacrificial death is not that we are able to get out of paying the debt of our sins, but that we are made able to do so. St. Paul insists that the baptized share in Christ's death and in His resurrection (Col 2:12). On its own, Christ's life and death would be enough to redeem humanity in a corporate sense: even if every other human being were in league with the devil, Christ would "tip the scale" so that mankind's overall response to God would be one of obedience. On its own, Christ's sacrifice is the perfect expression of God's nature, "translated" into the condition of fallen humanity for us to see, understand, and relate to. None of this, however, will save the individual soul if it does not appropriate Christ and share in His work. This is done through faith and the sacraments, most especially the Eucharist. In the Blessed Sacrament, the sacrifice on the Cross is sacramentally re-presented, so that the Church may join herself to Christ's offering. By the natural symbolism of blood, the presentation of Christ's flesh and blood means a sacrifice to God. By the natural symbolism of food, to consume the host means to join oneself to the offering. By natural symbolism and divine efficacy, the Sacrament makes a statement to God. It means something like the following: "By taking the body of the Savior, I join myself to Him, and I join myself to His sacrifice. As He eternally offers Himself to You, heavenly Father, so now He offers me as well, since I am taken up into Him. Everything I have and everything I am is Yours." Of course, a given Christian who takes Communion may or may not be thinking these things, but they are what his actions mean regardless.

That's what is meant by natural or objective symbolism, such as Christians believe that acts like sex and the Eucharist possess. Given the weight of meaning Christians attach to the Blessed Sacrament, it is not surprising that its reception is treated with such seriousness. Those engaging in grave sin are told they must not participate in it, since for such people the above prayer would be a lie.

I conclude with a quote from St. Augustine of Hippo, that great exemplar of religious conservatism, which perfectly expresses what I, in my more cumbersome way, have tried to express in this essay on the nature of sacrifice.

> *Thus a true sacrifice is every work which is done that we may be united to God in holy fellowship, and which has a reference to that supreme good and end in which alone we can be truly blessed...For, though made or offered by man, sacrifice is a divine thing, as those who called it "sacrifice" meant to indicate. Thus man himself, consecrated in the name of God, and vowed to God, is a sacrifice in so far as he dies to the world that he may live to God...in order that, being inflamed by the fire of His love, [his soul] may receive of His beauty and become pleasing to Him, losing the shape of earthly desire, and being remolded in the image of permanent loveliness...it follows that the whole redeemed city, that is to say, the congregation or community of the saints, is offered to God as our sacrifice through the great High Priest, who offered Himself to God in His passion for us, that we might be members of this glorious head, according to the form of a servant... This is the sacrifice of Christians: we, being many, are one body in Christ. And this also is the sacrifice which the Church continually celebrates in the sacrament of the altar, known to the faithful, in which she teaches that she herself is offered in the offering she makes to God.*

> *–The City of God, X*

In Defense of Monarchy

The principle of authority

The distinguishing characteristic of primitive peoples, according to Emile Durkheim, is the strength and rigidity of the conscience collective, the moral consensus of the community. This collective consciousness is above and distinct from the consciousness of each individual member of the community, and it possesses an authoritative character by its connection to the social order. The primitive man experiences the will of society as the will of a higher being, who he imagines to be God. Justice in such societies is retributive; it expresses the community's outrage over the violation of its norms. For an atheist liberal, Professor Durkheim was quite perceptive.

It is quite true that the purpose of the state—any state, not just a primitive one—is to embody the conscience collective. This is only to repeat Cicero's observation that a republic is distinguished from lesser forms of association by possessing a shared conception of justice. A strong conscience collective can obviously be a powerful force for encouraging just behavior and discouraging unjust behavior. However, the purpose of collective morality is not just to promote individual morality: public laws and standards have a positive moral value in themselves. For example, suppose there were two cities in which the citizens were so peaceful that no murders ever took place in either one. Now suppose that murder is prohibited by law in one polity but not the other. The society which prohibits murder would be morally superior to the society which doesn't. In both cities, each individual respects his neighbor's right to live, but only one citizenry collectively recognizes these rights. In the other city, each individual may be morally upstanding, but their society is still morally deficient. The opposite situation is more common: laws may have positive moral value even when they can't be effectively enforced.

The function of government is to symbolize justice—to represent the community's moral consensus to itself—and to execute justice by punishing the wicked. Of these two functions, it is government's symbolic role which is the more important. It is the ability to symbolize justice that gives the state its authority over its subjects. This is the meaning of the scholastic doctrine that government derives its authority from being "established". The very fact that, through whatever series of historical accidents, a people has come to see a governing body as the representative of justice suffices to give that body real moral authority. The source of the state's authority is in the minds of its subjects. It is, however, in their intellects, not in their wills. The state's authority has nothing to do with anybody's consent; a man might wish he didn't have to obey his government while still recognizing its legitimacy. Moreover, we should not think that a people first exists and then decides on a principle of legitimacy (a constitution). It is such a principle which makes a people to be one people and not a mere aggregate. So, for example, there is a French people, but there is no united "Caucasian people" or "people of western Illinois". Caucasians are found among many people, and western Illinoisans recognize no authority which is not also recognized by eastern Illinoisans. Also, it's not true that Americans created their principle of legitimacy at the Constitutional Convention. The procedural rules which we call the U.S. "Constitution" draw their authority from America's prior sense of legitimacy. The "Constitution" had to be ratified by the thirteen states, whose authority was taken as given, and the delegates of the Convention never imagined questioning that the United States comprised these and (at the time) only these states.

The branches of government

By symbolizing justice, the state is also a symbol of God (as Durkheim realized in his way). In particular, it represents God's role as the just Judge. A healthy state is structured to make this symbolization as clear as possible. Thus, there are three branches of government, corresponding to the triad of memory, intellect, and will in Augustine and Bonaventure's psychological model of the Trinity. Note that this triad does not correspond to Montesquieu's better-known division of the state into legislature, executive, and judiciary. Monarchy cannot be properly understood using this latter scheme.

The first branch of government is the traditional or repository branch, corresponding to government's role as the memory or self-consciousness of the nation. Included in this branch are the king, the hereditary nobility, and the ministers of the established church. The repository reminds citizens that they are members of a nation which endures through time, that they have a collective past and a collective future. As the representative of the past, the repository upholds inherited traditions, the will of the dead, against the transient will of the living. It also upholds the nation's inherited commitments and obligations: treaties, debts, etc. It is responsible in a particular way for honoring the dead and promoting whatever basic historical narratives the nation uses to understand itself. Finally, the repository is the defender of the nation's most basic principles, including its constitution (which, as Aristotle pointed out, guarantees the continuity of the state) and its religion. Since the repository represents the past against the present, its officeholders (the nobles) are ideally chosen by their connection to the past, i.e. by hereditary succession. By choosing them in this way, the king and nobility are given a strong incentive to fulfill their duty of defending tradition, since this is the only basis of their own authority.

The second branch is the legislature, the creator of laws. The third branch is the executive or ministry, which applies the laws to specific cases and enforces them. Each of these branches operates on a more specific level than the branches above it. The repository (analog of the memory) expounds general historical commitments. The legislature (analog of the intellect) translates these into abstract laws. The executive (analog of the will) in its judicial aspect determines how the laws apply to specific cases, while the executive in its civil service aspect is authorized to make technical decisions regarding how the legislature's desires can be fulfilled most expediently. The executive includes most of the employees of the state: judges, policemen, soldiers, teachers, and bureaucrats. Since their jobs require special expertise, it is reasonable that they should be chosen by merit. That is, executive functionaries should be hired or appointed; they should not be elected to their posts or inherit them. The legislature includes the national parliament, state or district legislatures, and city councils. Lawmakers are usually elected; choosing them in a way different from that used by the repository and executive branch ensures that the legislature will have an independent character. (The separation of the legislative and executive guarantees the rule of law.) The state will thus have a mixture of monarchical, aristocratic (meritocratic), and democratic elements, as recommended by Cicero and Thomas Aquinas.

The role of the monarch was misunderstood by some eighteenth and nineteenth century observers of imperfectly functioning monarchies. Thus, Montesquieu identified the English monarch with the executive, and Bonald more or less identified the French monarch with the legislature. The former's confusion was carried over into the constitution of the United States, with the president being given some of the features of a monarch and some of the features of a prime minister. In fact, the branch of America's federal government which most closely resembles the repository branch is the Supreme Court. Not all philosophers mistook the true division of the branches of government. Hegel, in his *Philosophy of Right*, provides a rationalization of the modern state which is very similar to the description I've given above. Unfortunately, the true genius of Hegel's political thought is often obscured by the Marxist lens through which he is generally read.

Other advantages of monarchy

From the previous chapter, one easily sees the primary shortcoming of democracy: it allows no real repository organ in the state. God and ancestors are completely disenfranchised, and the desires of the current generation are entirely unchecked. As Charles Maurras wisely put it, "democracy is forgetting."

Many are the blessings of living under a hereditary monarch, but a few deserve special mention. First, heredity monarchy is the only form of government which assumes a real equality of all human beings. Both technocracy and democracy are designed to fill positions with the "best" men. In a technocratic regime, positions are filled by the man who's aptitude and qualifications most impress his fellow experts. In an election, each candidate tries to convince the populace that he is superior to his rivals. Actually, of course, winning an election only proves that a person is a good campaigner, which has nothing to do with being a good leader. For the position of monarch, however, we do not choose the most experienced man, the most intelligent man, the bravest man, or the most popular man. We reject the association of government office and personal greatness. The greatest man in the kingdom may well be a garbage collector or kindergarten teacher; the honor we give the king derives entirely from his role, because of what he represents. Unlike an expert or a democratic politician, the king knows that as a man he is no better than those born into less illustrious roles. This is one reason to expect humility to be more common among kings than among experts and politicians. Also not to be ignored are the advantages of being ruled by a man who has not actively sought power for himself, but who has inherited it as a duty. In democracies and meritocracies, power can only be acquired through grueling competition, so that those who win power in such societies are most often power-mad megalomaniacs.

By his hereditary status, the king is uniquely independent of popular and expert opinion. Already when our republic was young, Tocqueville observed that politicians flatter the people with greater obsequiousness than was seen at Louis XIV's court, and the passage of years has made them yet more shameless. How often do we hear that "the American people deserve better" or that "the American people are the greatest on Earth" or other such inanities? What if what the American people actually deserve is to be rebuked for our decadence, greed, criminality, cowardice, impiety, and selfishness? Who would ever tell us? Certainly a politician facing reelection would never speak this way. Yet to criticize faults is a basic function of authority, one that belongs naturally to the king in his fatherly role.

Finally, there is the fact that the monarch is a person to whom we relate personally, while the legislative and executive are and must be impersonal—as impersonal as the law, as faceless as bureaucracy. Thus the king is uniquely suited to certain personal tasks. One such task is the issuing of pardons to convicted criminals. Forgiveness is an act that can only be directed from one person to another. If instead the executive operated a "Bureau of Mercy" it would need an impersonal rule: commute these punishments for these acts in these circumstances. But this would be no different than just making a law against assigning such punishments; it would be, not mercy, but a dilution of justice. Justice demands that the act be condemned and a proportionate penalty assigned, but the king can pardon the man, although only on a case-by-case, that is only on a personal, basis.

In Defense of the Patriarchal Family

It should be obvious that nothing, absolutely nothing, is more important to a society than the structure and authority of the family. Around half of people are young or old dependents at any given time, and all people are dependents for some part of their lives. In every society that has yet existed, the family is the institution by which the half that is able to work cares for the other half (after and before being cared for in turn). This transfer of wealth and service far exceeds the redistributive actions of even communist governments. In the family we encounter human dependency at its most naked, and from these dependencies arise our most solemn duties and our largest (indeed, unpayable) debts. What could be more important to men's self-understanding? So it is for good reason that no institution is more important to a conservative than the authoritative domestic society, the patriarchal family. Also, no institution faces such merciless attack from clear-headed leftists.

The maternal and paternal roles

When it comes to the family, the facts are well known. Humans reproduce sexually. Unlike many other animals, our young are born completely helpless and take more than a decade to reach maturity. They require an enormous investment of time and effort from their parents if they are to survive long enough to reproduce themselves. Because it is only the woman who can be pregnant, give birth, and nurse, she is naturally more involved in child care, at least during the early years. For his progeny to survive, the man has had to assume those tasks which the woman can't do while caring for a child—acquiring food and repelling attacks. Men and women have acquired (by natural selection) special physical, mental, and psychological features to assist them in their specific tasks.

Patriarchy is the idea which assigns moral significance to these facts. The good toward which the patriarchal family is ordered is procreation. Its basic principle is the embrace of dependency. The child depends on his parents, and the parents depend on each other. These experiences of dependency, both of having others depend on us (and the responsibilities this creates) and of depending on others (and the humility this engenders), are regarded as positive goods. The more deeply each member relies on the other, the more the family can be said to thrive. Thus the family is not merely an illiberal institution; it is positively anti-liberal. Nothing is more opposed to its ethos than independence, in either the sense of autonomy or of self-sufficiency.

However, we have not completely specified the family just by identifying dependency as its principle. After all, dependence on other people is an inescapable fact of human existence. One can imagine an alternative to the family, in which children are raised by child-care experts employed by a large government bureaucracy. The children would still be dependent, but it would be an organization rather than particular people who would be ultimately responsible for their welfare. Of course, particular people (teachers, nurses, etc) would be assigned to care for the children in various ways, but this would be delegated responsibility; these technicians could be replaced by others at the bureaucracy's discretion. Parental dependency is personal dependency: it is the mother and father who are fully responsible for the child, and this responsibility is not delegated to them by the state, society at large, or any other organization. Similarly, the duties of a child to his parents belong to the child as an individual.

Dependency has two poles. One being may depend on another for its internal self-development and the flourishing of its intrinsic nature. This is the nurturing or maternal pole. However, because all animals live in potentially hostile environments, there is another pole. One being may depend on another to protect it from the hostile outside, to prepare it to survive in the hostile outside, or to extract resources from the outside world for use in the home. This is the protector-provider or paternal pole. Together, the two poles form a home, a safe and nurturing place, with the mother as the home's heart and the father at the interface between the home and the outside world.

According to the patriarchal idea, the roles of mother and father are distinct and irreplaceable. The claim is not "a child needs two parents"; the claim is "a child needs his mother and his father". Neither a single parent nor two caregivers of the same sex can adequately substitute for a natural family. Furthermore, the two roles cannot be combined in one person. Nor can they be divided equally by two people, with each parent playing mother half of the time and father the other half. Being a mother or father is not a job, not a role one steps into and out of. It is a vocation by which one understands oneself and orders one's life, and it is the most fundamental level on which one relates to other members of the family. No child thinks, "On formal occasions, X has to play the role of being my father, but underneath it all, he's just my friend X." The deepest level is always, "He is my father." Fatherhood is not a mask that we can go beneath. For the father himself, his vocation is the most fundamental part of his personality. For the child, any other relationship would be less significant.

The need for distinct roles is particularly evident for the father's protector role. One cannot be a protector unless someone else allows herself to be protected. A useful contrast would be to a company of soldiers. There is a sense, of course, in which soldiers protect one another. One man standing the night watch is protecting his sleeping companions until he is relieved and protected in turn. However, because the roles are continually switched, they cannot be the basic way that the soldiers understand their relations with each other. In fact, we would not want one soldier to feel protective of another the way a husband should feel for his wife and children. A good husband would never allow his wife to take a turn on the front line. A chivalrous man will insist on protecting any woman or child, and since chivalry is a good thing, we should not undermine it by having women in the military or police.

The distinction of roles is also important for their ability to represent authority to the child. The mother is the practical and compassionate face of authority. As the nurturer, she commands what is good for us and forbids what is bad for us or for other members of the family. There is another, no less valid, face of authority. This is the face of objective law: laws of God, laws of nature, laws of custom, laws of the state. Basing themselves on the absolute claims of morality, these laws are implacable in their demands and indifferent to our desires or the desires of those close to us. As the interface with the outside world, the father is the natural representative of this authority. As the representative of objective law, he is the one who is compelled at times to stand as an outside judge of his own children. To fail to do so would stunt their moral development. However, as a representative of the "outside", the father lacks some of the empathic closeness to his children that the mother enjoys. The mother, in turn, must use the face of objective judgment much less often to avoid compromising her indispensible nurturing role. To put it another way, although a child should always know that his parents' love is unconditional, it is good that there is one parent whose respect he feels he must earn. A boy is propelled toward independence partly by this desire to be seen as a man in his father's eyes. It is important that the father give this respect, but, for it to be real, he can't give it indiscriminately. We see some recognition of this duality of sex roles in the world's mythologies: it is usually the sky/father god who is lord of law and justice, while the nurturing earth/mother goddess is far less morally vindictive.

Obviously, it is neither possible nor desirable for the roles of mother and father to have no overlap. The overlap is considerable. Of course fathers feed their children and mothers disciple them. Of course a mother must defend her children from outside attack if the father is absent and none of the sons is of age. However, the roles must remain basically distinct. It is not a question of whether, for example, a woman can do the things a father does. "Mother" and "father" are not jobs. They're not what you do; they're what you are. A woman can't be a father. "Father" is a way of understanding one's duties and one's place—it is incompatible with (although complementary to) the idea of "mother".

Masculine and feminine virtues

To be a man means to be a father, at least potentially. That is, it means that one is "father material." Similarly, to be a woman means to be a potential mother. Motherhood and fatherhood are the ideas which allow us to make sense of our sexual natures. Why do women have breasts? To nurse their children. Why are they on average far more empathic and linguistically adept than men? So that they can raise and educate their children. Why are men on average much stronger and more aggressive than women? So that they can protect their families. The patriarchal ideas make biological facts meaningful. Note that statements about sexual natures are essential rather than empirical: to say that physical strength is a masculine quality is not the same as to say that men are stronger on average than women. A certain woman may be stronger than many men, but this would only be an accidental quality for her sex; she wouldn't understand her strength in terms of a gender-specific calling to service, the way a man would. Accordingly, there can also be statistical differences between men and women which are not essential differences. For example, men seem to like steak more than women, but since this fact has no relevance to his paternal duties, it is meaningless. A man who lacks the strength to defend his family is lacking in masculine perfection, but there's nothing wrong with a male vegetarian.

In societies which accept the patriarchal ideas, "man" and "woman" are not just biological givens; they are ideals toward which one must strive. To say that someone embodies the ideal is a great compliment. ("What a woman!" "Now there's a real man!") Masculinity and femininity each have their characteristic virtues. The manly virtue is called "chivalry". It is the virtue of one who has internalized the ethos of the protector. Courage in danger, prowess in battle, mercy to the vanquished, courtesy toward women, gentleness towards children, piety towards elders—these are the qualities of the chivalrous man. Feminists often attack chivalry because it legitimates male aggression. However, male aggression is a biological fact which will be with us whether we legitimate it or not, unless one plans to turn men into docile weaklings using conditioning and drugs (a path that parents and teachers seem regrettably eager to pursue). The ideal of chivalry ennobles this biological given by allowing men to understand it in terms of a moral duty. In fact, there is no way to explain feminist's horror of domestic violence without invoking chivalry. If men have no special duties to women, then why is it any worse for a man to beat up a woman than for him to beat up a weaker man?

Chivalry is closely connected to courage, but courage itself is both a masculine and a feminine virtue. The female virtue of femininity is a special kind of courage: the courage of allowing oneself to become vulnerable. By the woman's characteristic empathy, she opens herself to others' pain. In marriage, she sacrifices some of her own defenses so that her husband can assume his role. In pregnancy and childbirth, she offers her own body for her child, an offering which has cost many women their lives.

Of course, each nature has its characteristic deformations, but it is always a gross error to identify a thing with its deformation. Machismo is a deformation of chivalry for men who have forgotten that their prowess is to be put in the service of the weak. The bully's manliness is imperfect. Similarly, one should never identify femininity with girlish vanity and frivolousness. Masculinity and femininity are essentially relational virtues. They inform all of our closest relationships, which are always relationships of dependence. It is only for very superficial relationships that I can say that the relationship would be no different if my partner were a man rather than a woman, or vice versa. This is why the drive to eliminate masculine and feminine personalities must be resisted. An androgynous person would lack both the male and female capacity for intimacy. A man who sacrifices masculine virtue does not thereby acquire feminine virtue. Nor does a woman gain masculine virtue by losing her femininity. An effeminate man is not maternal, and a tomboyish woman is not paternal.

The family as a society

The family is meant to be a nexus of dependency. It can only serve this function if it is sufficiently reliable that the family members can count on its services. Therefore, the duties of each member must be absolute and indissolvable. If divorce were allowed under any circumstances, the family would no longer by essentially a society of total self-offering and dependency. As a practical matter, each member would have to hedge his or her bets given the possible defection of other members. Indeed, the possibility of divorce is often invoked to discourage husbands and wives from becoming "too dependent" on each other. As intelligent beings, the anticipated future has a present reality in our minds. This is why it makes no sense to say, for example, "I am totally yours, but only for today," or "only as long as we continue to get along," or "only as long as you do your part." A total commitment is bound to extend itself through the whole field of one's consciousness, including the future in all its contingencies. The marriage commitment can demand tremendous sacrifices, but that is why it is so greatly honored. We honor spouses for the same reason we honor soldiers—because of the magnitude of their commitments. If soldiers were allowed to desert in times of danger, what would there be about them to admire? Similarly, as divorce becomes more common, marriage necessarily falls into contempt.

In order to function as a unit, the family must have a center of authority. At first appearance, it would seem that the mother is the natural center of authority. Her primary job is nurture, while the father's primary job is defense, and it is obvious that defense exists for the purpose of nurture, and not vice versa. Since ends should always dictate means, one would conclude that the wife should command the husband. However, all known societies have reached the opposite conclusion, that the husband should rule. The reason lies in the ways that mother and father symbolize authority. The father has a particular duty to represent the objective, transcendent moral law, and the authority of this law overrides every other consideration, even the good of each family member or of all put together. Therefore, the father holds ultimate authority.

Finally, the family can only be a nexus of authority if the members do, in fact, rely on it. Now, it is appropriate and just for the wider society to assist families that, due to extreme poverty or misfortune, cannot provide for their members. However, government agencies must never interfere in the family to such a degree (e.g. to preempt mistakes on the part of the parents, to compensate for their defects, etc.) that the dependence of family members on each other is reduced to a formality, while the real dependence is on the bureaucratic organs of the state. Nor should the state intrude in education or discipline in any way that would compromise the father's authority.

There is a more insidious threat to family independence which comes from industrial capitalism and commercialism. To alienate family functions to the marketplace is an even worse error than to alienate them to the state (which can at least symbolize authority in some way). As late as half a century ago, household production by the housewife contributed nearly as much to the wealth of the typical American family as did the husband's income. The family was significantly self-supporting and independent. A century before that, most families were totally independent on subsistence farms. Today, American families depend on factories in China for everything they consume. Even their children are raised by television and day care. Employers no longer need to pay a family wage now that women have been "liberated" from the home—much better to hire both husband and wife and pay each half as much! Ennobling dependence on loved ones has been replaced by servile dependence on corporations and the state.

Chastity

Let us now consider the act so associated with the marriage bond that it is called the "conjugal act" or the "marriage debt." Here we must confront the modern tendency to reduce all of nature—in this case one's body and that of one's partner—to raw material to be manipulated to serve one's will. Modern men believe that everyone is free to assign his or her own meaning to the sexual act, so they make of it a meaningless recreation, a means to "empowerment", or a sign of uncommitted affection. However, human sexual nature is not a collection of facts that have no meaning until we freely assign them one. Sexual intercourse has a natural teleology; it is ordered to procreation. This natural end provides a context which itself assigns a meaning to the sexual act. This meaning is "natural" in the sense that it "presents itself" to the mind of a sufficiently intelligent participant without requiring any decision on his or her part. If I make love to a woman, it means "I choose you to be the mother of my children." This, and only this, is directly and naturally signified by intercourse. However, for an intelligent being, able to consider the future, it has profound implications. Children require a family, so the sexual act implies an irrevocable commitment; it initiates a new society consisting of the spouses and their prospective children. In the conjugal act, the spouses pledge their allegiance to this society—this also is virtually contained in the act's one natural meaning. It is a grave mistake to think that the conjugal act has two independent natural meanings: a "procreative" and a "unitive" meaning, so that one can frustrate the first while still affirming the second. Sex has one meaning, and that is procreation which implies unity. Without its procreative telos, sex could only signify love by convention, and conventional signification is a much weaker thing than natural signification. In any case, the natural context is inescapable. If one wickedly frustrates the sexual act through contraception or sodomy, one does not simply take the natural meaning of sex "off the table"; one actively rejects it. Unnatural sex acts themselves carry a natural meaning, namely the rejection of what would be positively affirmed by natural sex. "I reject you as the mother of my children." To add a conventional meaning of "I love you", but the action itself speaks against it.

Sexual morality is more than just avoiding evils like birth control and fornication. There is also the positive virtue of chastity. To be chaste is to be alive to a whole world of value and beauty in the relations between the sexes. In a way, it resembles the aesthetic sensibility which allows one to appreciate art, and a man without this sensibility should rightly be an object of pity, because his cynicism has made him blind to a thing of great beauty. Thus, it is not quite accurate to say that conservatives want to teach teenagers abstinence. A married woman who refuses to sleep with her husband out of mere squeamishness would hardly meet with our approval. What we want to teach is chastity; we want our children to hear the body's own language and to see their bodies as more than just raw material. We would even say that there is value in this appreciation even for those who, out of weakness, surrender to lust at some point in life. A man who fornicates and then feels guilty for desecrating a holy thing is living on a far higher plane of spiritual existence than a man who fornicates without guilt and without thought except for how to gratify his lust in the future.

Chaste man and woman will feel awe that their bodies are capable of expressing in the body's own language the momentous pledge of lifelong fidelity in the marital bond, and they will approach this act with due reverence. Above all, they will recoil from approaching it in the infernal spirit of calculation which seeks to use the act for pleasure, power, or any other private end. Here we see starkly the existential choice between liberal and conservative. Either our acts are meaningless so we are free to do as we will, or our acts do have meanings which must guide us.

Filial Piety

Piety is the reverence due to one's mother and father, and it is every bit as essential to family life as chastity. Filial piety demands several things. Most basically, it demands that one care for the welfare of one's parents, to defend them from criticism and care for them in old age. Still, piety demands more. One must obey one's parents (unless this violates the natural law). Even as an adult, one should defer to them when possible.

Still, piety demands more. One must honor one's parents. One must never speak disparagingly or even lightly of them. Indeed, one must cast away even irreverent thoughts about them. In ordering one's own life, one must consider how one's actions reflect on one's parents, and one must strive to be worthy of them. Only thusly can one repay the debt to those who gave one life.

Brotherhood

The relationship between siblings reveals another beautiful dimension of personal dependency. It is often invoked by various partisans of impersonal dependency such as republicans advocating a "brotherhood" of citizens and advocates of world government, who believe their proposed tyranny would embody a "brotherhood" of all mankind. In fact, these calls for collective fraternity misunderstand the nature of literal brotherhood, which is always a bond between two individuals. Among brothers and sisters, the moral and authoritative element which dominates the parent-child relationships is subdued or absent. The "face" of dependency which predominates is the mutual reliance of comrades; they share common a common loyalty to their parents and the family, and each knows that he can rely on the others in times of need. This is still a form of personal, not corporate, responsibility. If my brother is in trouble, I personally have a duty to help. There is no collective body called "the brotherhood", consisting of all siblings, who have this duty, so that I would be acting only as an agent of this body. Whether or not all the brothers cooperate, the duty to help our brother falls on each of us as individuals. The only corporate bodies which contain the brothers qua brothers are the nuclear and extended families, and these only act collectively through the authority of the patriarch.

All that was said above is also true of the relationship between sisters and between brother and sister. For brother-sister relationships, the ordering of the sexes becomes relevant, most notably through the incest prohibition. This rule is designed to protect the intimacy between siblings, not to hinder it. Once it is established that sexual relations are out of the question, family members can be much freer about physical contact. This is also the reason for the incest prohibition between parents and children: it seems to me that a world where a father couldn't embrace his daughter or pat her cheek without her taking it as a sexual overture would be a nightmare.

We can see then why all the talk about brotherhoods of citizens or humanity is so misguided. The idea appealed first to the French revolutionaries primarily because of their hatred of authority; they imagined creating a nation that would be like a family without parents. But there is no such thing—as we noted above, a corporation of "brothers" is an entirely different thing from real brotherhood. It is also an entirely different thing from a real state, in which the moral-authoritarian element always dominates. The image of extended brotherhood is also used by those, like the nationalists and one-worlders, whose main desire is to discourage loyalties to groups smaller than their preferred unit, be it the nation or world government. In this case, the insistence that all citizens or all men are brothers is being used to illegitimately apply the incest prohibition against the formation of smaller units.

Patriarchy and the Christian revelation

It might seem that Christianity undermines patriarchy: didn't Christ say that we must be prepared to abandon mother and father for Him, and that we should not even call anyone but God "father"? In fact, for two millennia patriarchal authority has had no stauncher ally than the Catholic Church. Christians as well as Jews are commanded to "honor thy father and mother". Christ Himself restored marriage to its pristine dignity by forbidding divorce, and Saint Paul used marriage as an analogy for the relationship between Christ and the Church. From apostolic times, the ministers of the Church have been called "father", and her leaders have long been called "patriarch" or "pope", words which mean "father". The patriarchal bond holds the most exalted place in Christian doctrine, because it is the relation which defines the first procession of the Trinity, the begetting of the Son by the Father. Christ can thus be seen as a perfect example of filial obedience and devotion. In the order of nature, God our Creator can rightly be thought of as mother and father, for He is both imminent and transcendent. The Christian, however, believes that his relationship with God transcends the Creator-creature relation. Through God's grace, the believer is united to Christ and adopted as a son of the Father. The Christian calls God "father" but not "mother" because he is addressing the Father not just as a creature but as a participant in God's Trinitarian inner life, using a voice "borrowed" from Jesus Christ.

From the Trinitarian perspective, it is true that our Father in heaven is the only true father, and that all other fatherhood can only be a reflection of Him. However, earthly fatherhood must be a real reflection of Divine fatherhood, if Trinitarian language is to be meaningful. The father lost his internal pagan dignity, but he gained a dignity "borrowed" from God as a special image of the Father. In addition, the Church has yoked the paternal relationship to her own service, allowing some men to exercise their paternal vocation in a spiritual way. We call the man who re-presents Christ's sacrifice on the altar "father" because he relates to us paternally. His parishioners are his children —he is allowed no other. A woman could do the things a priest does (excepting the sacraments), but a woman could not be a priest, because a woman cannot be a father. Like all fatherhood, priesthood is a vocation, not a job.

In Defense of Religion

Why do we regard certain things as "sacred"? Why should anyone believe in God? Where does such an idea even come from? Why do religious believers always bring God into discussions about right and wrong? Is it credible that God would send revelations to just a few people and force the rest of us to take their word for it? I examine all of these questions in the essay below. It's a bit of a monster (19 pages), but these are big questions, so we shouldn't expect single-sentence or even single-paragraph resolutions to them. They also happen to be the most important questions, so I think readers will find them well worth thinking through.

This essay is dedicated to my brother, who inspired me to start it.

I. Why the sacred cannot be explained away

This essay as a whole will concern the chief claim of all the world's religions: the existence of a divine order. Today, it seems that one must actually be willing to offer a defense, not only for accepting religious claims, but even for being willing to give them serious consideration. After all, it is said, hasn't science (meaning psychology, anthropology, or evolutionary biology) already explained why people have religions? Since these explanations are entirely materialistic, doesn't this prove that all religions—since they claim to relate to the supernatural—are false? Why even bother with the philosophical arguments for and against theism?

False explanations of religion

You'll notice that I referred to scientific "explanations" not "explanation", a first indication that the skeptics' house isn't entirely in order. The explanations are many and unrelated. Let us consider a few. First, it is claimed that religion is based on infantile wish-fulfillment fantasies. People who can't cope with the responsibilities of adulthood imagine that they are protected by some benevolent supernatural power. People who can't face death imagine that they will survive in some sort of afterlife. Second, it is said that religion is a personification of social forces. Because primitive people can't refer to abstract concepts like "community", they attribute the pressures applied to them by their communities to immaterial gods. They are so impressed by parental or tribal authority that they attribute divinity to ancestors and kings. Third, it is said that religion is a primitive form of science. Ignorant savages try to explain things like the weather or the growth of their crops by invoking the agency of imagined gods.

They personify forces and aspects of nature, and even their own inner impulses, by identifying them as gods. So, for example, there is the god of the sea, the god of love, the god of death, etc. Fourth, it is said that religion is a scam perpetrated by the clergy. By persuading the people that the clergy can influence the gods, the shaman and priest have arranged to live off of others without having to work.

There are other theories, but I think this is a representative sample. The first thing to ask is how these explanations fare as purely scientific theories. Do they correctly predict the features of most religions, or at least of most religions among primitive people? The answer is no, not even remotely. When we look at primitive religions, the gods are more often capricious than benevolent. Nor is the promise of a pleasant afterlife a major part of most primitive religions. The Old Testament hardly mentions life after death. The original goal of Buddhism was to avoid an afterlife. When peoples later do develop an idea of life after death, it is often at first imagined to be an unpleasant and shadowy existence like that of Sheol or the Plains of Asphodel. Later, when the idea of justice is added to the idea of an afterlife, it is hell that receives far more attention than heaven. Nor do religious people have any trouble distinguishing between the laws of the community and the laws of God, as examples like Antigone and Thomas More make clear. In fact, most religions do draw a connection between the authority and the gods. However, it is not the psychological pressure that the community is able to exert on individuals that is considered divine, but the aspect of moral legitimacy—the fact that one is morally obliged to obey one's father or king whether one feels like it or not. Moral duty is an entirely different thing from psychological pressure. (Imagine one loyalist standing alone against a gang of mutineers.) The former is a spiritual thing, so it is no scandal that religion should be associated with it. The theory that religion is primitive science also fares poorly when confronted with actual religious experience. As just mentioned, one aspect of all religions is that they expound moral duties and prohibitions. They declare not only the existence of the gods, but also our duties towards them. Now, science itself can never lead to moral imperatives; science limits itself to empirical description. This in itself proves that religion is addressing more than scientific issues. Also, one often sees religious people, both primitive and modern, ascribing the same effect to both a natural and a supernatural cause. Consider a family that offers thanks to God for the food that they have just bought and prepared themselves. Obviously, the family is attributing causality on different levels to themselves and to God. Finally, if religion were a clerical scam, we would expect to find primitive religions to be the most clerically organized, but in fact the opposite is true. Also, the life of the shaman is often hardly enviable.

All of these explanations have several features in common. First, they are only plausible if we assume that primitive peoples are unbelievably stupid. However, anthropologists have been studying primitive peoples for a century and have found them to be as intelligent as any other people. Second, when confronted with evidence that conflicts with their theories, the debunkers will blame the evidence rather than modify their theories. For example, the fact that religious people don't treat their beliefs like scientific hypotheses is said to prove that they are too stupid to do scientific thinking properly rather than that they're doing something other than science. But this way of proceeding is not proper scientific procedure. If the evidence doesn't support the theory, it is the theory and not the observed phenomenon that is at fault.

More seriously, none of the proposed explanations of religion can possibly succeed, because all of them ignore essential attributes of all religions. Each begins by mentally replacing religion with something simpler and more amenable to materialistic explanation, say servile fear or a tendency to believe comforting lies. They then proceed to concoct an evolutionary explanation for this thing and then claim that they have explained religion. Of course, this is only valid if religion really is reducible to one of these other things, or perhaps some combination of them. But we know that it isn't. Anyone who has experienced fear of nature, respect for authority, and religious reverence knows that these are qualitatively different intentional responses of the soul. Each has its own distinct nature; each responds to a different aspect of being. You can imagine increasing the fear directed at an object to as intense a level as you like, but it would still be only fear—it never transforms itself into respect or awe, because these are different things. Nor can one explain a qualitatively distinct response as a mere combination of other emotions, because this couldn't explain the unity of the thing. For example, materialists will often make claims such as that love is really a combination of sexual desire and possessiveness. Anyone who has been in love knows that this is simply false, and false as a matter of definition, because it ignores love's qualitatively distinct features. You can't combine purely selfish responses (like lust and possessiveness) and end up with an altruistic response (like love).

Chesterton puts this very nicely:

> *"It is commonly affirmed, again, that religion grew [from a combination of] first, the fear of the chief of the tribe...second, the phenomena of dreams, and third, the sacrificial associations of the harvest and the resurrection symbolized in the growing corn. I may remark in passing that it seems to me very doubtful psychology to refer one living and single spirit to three dead and disconnected causes... Suppose Mr. Wells, in one of his fascinating novels of the future, were to tell us that there would arise among men a new and yet nameless passion, of which men will dream as they dream of first love, for which they will die as they die for a flag and a fatherland. I think we should be a little puzzled if he told us that this singular sentiment*

would be a combination of the habit of smoking Woodbines, the increase of the income tax, and the pleasure of the motorist in exceeding the speed limit. We could not easily imagine this, because we could not imagine any connection between the three or any common feeling that could include them all. Nor could anyone imagine any connection between corn and dreams and an old chief with a spear, unless there was already a common feeling to include them all. But if there was such a common feeling it could only be the religious feeling; and these things could not be the beginnings of a religious feeling that existed already. I think anybody's common sense will tell him that it is far more likely that this sort of mystical sentiment did exist already; and that in the light of it dreams and kings and corn-fields could appear mystical then, as they can appear mystical now. For the plain truth is that all this is a trick of making things seem distant and dehumanized, merely by pretending not to understand things that we do understand...Who does not find dreams mysterious, and feel that they lie on the dark borderland of being? Who does not feel the death and resurrection of the growing things of the earth as something near to the secret of the universe? Who does not understand that there must always be the savour of something sacred about the authority and the solidarity that is the soul of the tribe?"

The true nature of religion

To understand religion, we must consider it in its essence. What, then, is religion essentially? I think a suitable definition would be this: religion is man's response to the sacred. This definition has two key words—"response" and "sacred". When I say that religion is a response, this means that religious acts are intentional acts; they are always directed at something, and, I would include, are directed at something outside of oneself. In this way, religion is like sight or smell, like love or hatred. Religion is not a thing like fatigue—which need be directed at nothing in particular, nor is it a thing like self-confidence—which is directed at oneself. The other key word is "sacred". What religion responds to is a quality called "the sacred" or "the holy." When a person responds religiously to tribal authority, to the immensity of a storm, or to the cycles of death and rebirth in nature, it is to the aspect of holiness in these things that the religious person responds. All of these aspects of life—and many more—are indeed connected to religion, not because they "cause" it, but because these things reflect or participate in the sacred. Although it manifests itself in many ways, the sacred is a single, distinct dimension of being. This unity of object gives religion its coherence. The religious man knows that there is a logic connecting the concepts of God, purity, sacrifice, and priesthood. It is therefore foolish to look for separate evolutionary causes for the various aspects of religion, when we know that they are intelligibly connected. Given the basic facts of men's apprehension of the sacred and their capacity for abstract reasoning, we can count on them to have been drawn into the logic of the thing. We have no need for further hypotheses.

II. The meaning of the sacred

Modern man has a terribly impoverished sense of the sacred, but most of us have experienced a hint of it at some point in our lives. It may happen in a church or other holy ground, at a funeral or other solemn event, at the sight of something immense like a mountain or something beautiful like music. Whatever the occasion, we felt ourselves to be in the presence of a mysterious Something. This "something" I will call "the sacred" or "the holy", because we have not yet established what it is. Historically, men experienced this awesome presence before they developed the concepts to explain it. Before we can decide whether religion is true, we must first know what it claims and how it views the world. That is the goal of this chapter.

The sacred as precious

Even today, men use the word "sacred", as when one says that nature, human life, or marriage is "sacred". What do such claims mean? Most obviously, they are assertions of objective value. If a thing is sacred, we certainly shouldn't wantonly destroy it. What's more, we shouldn't treat it as a mere means to our own ends; a sacred thing demands to be respected for its own intrinsic goodness. Even this recognition, however, only begins to capture the value response demanded by something sacred. The sacred demands not only respect, but also reverence. It makes claims not only on our words and actions, but also on our thoughts and feelings. In this, the sacred is like other objects we rightly revere, such as our parents and our country, although even reverence is a weaker value response than the esteem we give to a thing we regard as holy.

When I am in the presence of the sacred, I feel that it demands my entire attention. Any turning away toward other things—what I cannot help but call "lesser things"— would be grossly inappropriate. The sacred impresses me with its supreme *purity*, a word that those who have never experienced the sacred can't hope to understand. With the idea of the sacred comes the idea of the profane, of those things in which the sacred is absent or veiled. Profane things are not worthy of being in holy places. To rightly remain in the sacred presence, a thing must be consecrated, that is, the sacred must assimilate the thing to itself. The worshiper knows himself to be naturally profane, and he will only dare to approach the holy presence after separating himself from the rest of the profane world through ascetic practices and only with the aid of rituals that effect his own consecration. What is true of the worshiper is more emphatically true of the priest—he undergoes a more elaborate ritual consecration and makes a more extreme renunciation of the profane world.

The irreligious often have trouble understanding the idea of profanity. To be profane does not mean to be bad; it's no more an insult than not being royalty is an insult. In fact, many profane things are recognized by the religious person as good in themselves. Whereas bad things should not exist anywhere, profane things have their rightful place, but that place is outside the temple. For example, talking and joking among friends is itself a great blessing, but it is not compatible with the solemnity of worship. (Thus, the post-Vatican II effort to make Mass more "friendly" by encouraging parishioners to shake hands and chat reflects a gross lack of understanding of religious worship, as does the unfortunate habit priests have developed of telling jokes during the homily. The Mass is not meant to be fun or friendly—these things are good but profane. The Mass is meant to be a religious sacrifice.) Thus, the religious person recognizes more levels of value than the secular person. While the latter organizes the world into evil, neutral, and good, the former recognizes evil, neutral-profane, good-profane, and holy/sacred.

The religious man builds his world around his idea of the sacred. As Mircea Eliade pointed out, this is true even in a purely spatial sense: the holy ground provides a "center of the world", a fixed point with which to orient oneself, and around which everything else is ordered. At the heart of the home and the city was once a sacred place, an inner sanctuary. The home is where the sacred fire is kept, where the hearth gods dwell, where ancestors are worshiped. Even today, millions of worshipers face the holy city, Jerusalem or Mecca, to worship as a way of facing God. A religious people also put the sacred at the center of their social world. They are driven to consecrate and ritualize all that is most important to them: political authority, marriage, childbirth, coming of age, and death. This provides a holy ground to these things, a religious assurance that they belong above the level of mere instrumentality.

The sacred as awesome

This begins to touch on other aspects of the sacred, because this word means more than just "supremely valuable". A thing may be valuable but fragile, like civil peace. A thing may be valuable but unnecessary, like an appreciation for art—a good thing, but a person who lacks it should not feel that his life has been superficial or incomplete. The sacred is not like this. It is central not only socially but ontologically. A man who encountered the sacred is convinced that he has touched the mysterious center of things. It's not just another aspect of reality that he's encountered; it is the most fundamental aspect, the most real. Whatever sacred beings he believes in, he knows that their being is the truth that lies beneath the surface of everyday life. Therefore, he can't help but see the life of the irreligious man as radically incomplete and superficial. Here, he thinks, is someone who lives only on the surface of things, who has never sensed their depth.

The sacred is indeed mysterious—how could the ultimate reality be anything else? Men have always sensed that something about the universe exceeds the grasp of their minds. The sacred is said to be immense, awesome, all-powerful. To describe the force of its presence, those who experience it use images of fire, of mountains, of storm and thunder. However, we must understand that sacred power has a distinctive character, just as sacred goodness does. Most especially, we must realize that these are not separate qualities, but two aspects of holiness. It is not like the case of a king who is both just and powerful, but the two qualities are independent and could exist in separation. The power of the gods is at once physical and moral. It is more like the case of an immensely strong personality, in whose presence men fear their own personalities would be overwhelmed and overwritten, a personality that speaks with such authority that one almost expects the stones and the trees to obey it. This is the sort of force that the sacred has, not only to destroy me, but also to transform me. A fearful thing, indeed! A unique power gives rise to a unique dread, but also a unique hope. Here we should also remember that "awesome" does not mean "strong enough to kill me", although no religious man doubts that the gods could do that. We also describe a brilliant sunset or a vast canyon as awesome. The sacred captivates my soul by its immensity, which is not just formless bigness, but overwhelming beauty. Such is the divine majesty, and we can see how baseless is the atheist claim that religious people only worship their gods because they fear them.

The sacred as principle

Since the gods are, in some ways, beyond our understanding, one might expect them to be a disorderly influence in the world whose actions would always be associated with the irregular or the inexplicable. In fact, religious peoples have generally had the opposite belief. Namely, they hold that the divine is the source of the order in the universe. From the earliest times, man has been impressed by this order: season follows season, the stars follow precisely the same courses each year, and each animal reproduces its own kind. Surely, he thinks, the God who is the ultimate reality must be the author of this order. The cosmic order itself comes to be seen as a manifestation of the divine presence, i.e. it comes to be seen as a sacred order. By its very existence, it reveals the rationality of God. This intuition continued in man until at least the nineteenth century. For example, when Maupertuis and Euler discovered the principle of least action, they were convinced that something so simple and beautiful must be the work of God Himself. It is a strange claim made by atheists that the reason primitive man was religious was that he didn't know the world is governed by regular laws. In fact, it was the existence of regular laws that struck him as the most obvious manifestation of divine forces.

The religious view of cosmic order includes more than what we would now call the laws of physics and biology. The basic laws of morality, the natural law, were also thought to be part of the same order. To commit murder or adultery was to put oneself in antagonism with the order of the universe, to become "unnatural". Such sins offend and enrage the gods, all religious men agreed. So it must be, for just as the motion of the stars reveals one aspect of God's rationality, so the natural moral law reveals the moral aspect of His rationality—His supreme justice. In fact, once the cosmic order has "tipped us off" to this aspect of the divine nature, we realize that it is a necessary part of the sacred. A god who did not love order and hate sin would not be God.

The sacred as source

Since nothing has existence apart from its essential order, to bestow order is at the same time to give existence. This is another universally-agreed quality of the sacred presence, that it is uniquely creative. Religious man always finds his god at the source or origin of things. The images of creation and ordering are found in every religion: God separates the sky from the earth, the water from the land, and thus fashions our world. He is both the center, the heart, of the world of beings and also the source of their being. Here is another aspect of man's attraction to the divine: he wishes to return to his source, to recover the original purity of his existence. In Eliade's words, religious man has "nostalgia for origins" which is "nostalgia for being". Communion with the sacred offers him a chance for "rebirth", a chance to be "made new". An echo of this religious desire is seen in a modern man's pining for lost innocence. This desire is not, as those who would dismiss it say, a wish to lose the wisdom and experience one has gained through life. Nor is it merely the moral desire to stop sinning; a guiltless man can have the same yearning. It is a fundamentally religious desire to be back at the heart of things. A man gripped by it feels that his life is being dissipated in unimportant, superficial things, and he longs to recollect himself to the important and the real.

Beginnings are sacred—creation is when God touches the world. This is why the bond between parents and children partakes of the sacred in every culture. Because the divine creative force acted through my parents to create me, I owe a special religious duty to them. My parents are a personal religious icon, an image of God, for me. We should not be surprised to find that ancestor worship is one of the oldest and most common religious forms. The parental image carries over to a people's highest gods, whom they call "father" or "mother". The holiness of creation also acts in the other direction. I myself have heard mothers speak of a religious awe inspired by their newborns. Here one intuits with particular clarity the connection between newness/purity and the sacred. Not surprising is the special horror with which religious people regard parricide as well as (in those cultures where the humanity of the child is fully recognized) abortion and infanticide. These crimes are not just murder, but also desecration.

We needn't consider so exalted a thing as the creation of a human being to ignite the religious imagination. Anthropologists as far back as Frazer have noted the deep link between mythology and agriculture among primitive peoples. A divine power controls the growth of their crops, primitive farmers are convinced, and so farming is a religious practice. Properly understood, this is by no means a stupid or "superstitious" belief. Nor are such sentiments limited to primitive religions. It is by no arbitrary choice that Christian churches face east. The sun rises in the east; the eastern horizon is where the day begins, and hence where God—the source of all that is new—"touches" the earth.

How can this sacred presence be the source of every being? Why does it alone possess the power of creation and renewal? It can only be because the Holy One possesses being in its full plenitude. It possesses every perfection and every power necessarily and to a super-eminent degree. Such has been the conviction of theologians and mystics the world over. We exist by participating in God; He is where the stream of being finds its source.

This is religion. It is a set of experiences and a way of viewing the world. Seen in its true nature, we see how ignorant are those who dismiss it as foolish, or childish, or craven. Religion addresses man's highest intellectual, moral, and imaginative faculties. It does, certainly, assert a number of truth claims. Religion asserts that there exists a sacred Being, or a sacred aspect of all things, that is supremely good, powerful, majestic, beautiful, rational, and just. This sacred Being is the source of all other aspects of being, and It has no source outside Itself. The just and fitting response to this Being is worship. No matter how noble and beautiful religion is, for it to be valid, these claims must be true.

III. Puzzling aspects of existence

The existence and nature of God are philosophical problems, and it is to these that we now turn. To address these problems effectively, it will be necessary to first take what might seem like a detour to build up the needed metaphysical concepts. We will start by analyzing what it means for something to exist. This turns out to be less straightforward than one might think.

Positive existence vs. mere instantiation

Let's start with a statement, an intuition we all share. We all know that light is something, but darkness is just the absence of light, not a thing in itself. Of course, if one wanted to, one could say that light is the absence of darkness—sometimes it's even convenient to describe a light pattern in terms of shadows rather than light rays. Still, the ontological truth is that it's light that exists. Does darkness exist? It depends on what we mean by "exists". One meaning of "darkness exists" would be "somewhere, something is dark". In this sense, darkness certainly does, or at least can, exist. This meaning is the only one recognized by most analytic philosophers, but notice that it fails to capture the difference that we intuit between the way light exists and the way dark exists. By this first definition, it's entirely the same. So let's introduce a second definition: to exist means to be a positive presence, to be a "something there" rather than an absence or a relation. By this second definition, darkness doesn't exist. Let's consider a second example. You are out on a walk, and you see a wall with a hole in it. Does the hole exist? By the first definition, yes; "the hole exists" just means "the wall has a hole in it". By the second definition, no; the hole is an absence, not a presence. (By contrast, the air in the hole exists in the second sense.) Below, I will use the terms "presence", "actuality", and "positive existence" as synonyms for the second definition of "exists".

There are things that can be true only of things with positive existence—these are the prerogatives of actuality. One of these is the ability to be a cause, to share its presence with other things and act on them. True, we sometimes explain some effect in terms of an absence, e.g. we might blame our city being sacked on the aforementioned hole in the wall. But what we obviously mean is just that if the rest of the wall would have been present, the city wouldn't have been sacked. We don't really attribute a positive force to something without positive existence. Another prerogative of actuality we might call intelligibility or unity. Presence is never just presence in general; it's always presence of some particular kind of thing—some nature, some pattern, some qualities. What is present in the wall? One type of solid. What is absent in the hole? An infinite number of kinds of things.

Material, vital, and rational existence

Let's expand on this latter point. We can identify several layers of presence, sometimes all in a single thing. The most obvious level is material presence: a thing has mass, energy, electric charge, etc. Matter has a certain degree of intelligibility represented by the laws of physics. Living organisms possess another degree of presence (in addition, of course, to the material degree). In an organism, we find real, intrinsic teleology: the heart not only has a size and mass; we can also identify its function, how it keeps the organism going. This is a qualitatively unique feature of life. One could, of course, start identifying purposes to the parts of an atom or a star, but those purposes would either be arbitrary, or they would be defined by reference to something else (e.g. usefulness to us). For a living being, on the other hand, the function is forced on us. With it comes an objective meaning of health versus sickness or injury. It's meaningless to say that a rock is healthy, but it's exactly and scientifically meaningful to say that a dog is sick. Notice that the vitality of an organism is not a material distinct from the matter that makes up the organism. Nor is the telos of an organ a force acting on it the way pressure and gravity do. If these things were physical materials and forces, we would not be dealing with a different level of being. Indeed, if one were only interested in material level, one could consider an organism as a collection of molecules in equilibrium; in studying the motion of each molecule, one would never be forced to consider the function of each organ or the unity of the organism. This would, of course, be to miss the forest from the trees, to disregard a higher unity and intelligibility. Mental existence is a third level of being. With conscious subjects, we have another level of intelligibility above the material and the vital. There are more questions we can meaningfully ask and answer. For a material being, we can ask what caused it to do something. For a rational subject, we can ask what reason he had for doing something. Again, this does not mean a different kind of "stuff"—there's no "soul-stuff"—but it does mean a different kind of presence: conscious, rational, intentional presence. This is reflected in conventional speech, when we say that an inattentive person is "not with us" or "not all there".

There is, of course, a major objection to all this. The materialist will insist that the first level of being, the material, is all that really exists. An organism or a person, he will say, is a collection of molecules; all vital or conscious activity can be reduced to the motion of these molecules. Therefore, a living or conscious being has no more "presence" than that of the atoms in its body. Against this, I will first say that I (a person) am obviously not identical with the molecules in my body. The material in my body has changed throughout my life while I have remained identifiably the same person. Furthermore, when I die, I will cease to exist (at least in my body), although the material of my body will still be there. The more sophisticated materialist will admit that there's more to me than my molecules—there's also their arrangement and the pattern they execute. If he admits this, he has largely granted my point. He may say that the material is somehow more fundamental than its arrangement, but it's not clear how this would be maintained. The arrangement can't exist without the material, true, but material can't exist without being in some kind of arrangement either. One might say that molecules are understandable on their own apart from any arrangement, and so this makes them logically prior to their arrangement. However, biological and mental activity are also comprehensible on their own apart from the matter that instantiates them. One doesn't need to know elementary particle physics to understand what knees are for or to understand the connection between love and jealousy. In fact, it's no help whatsoever, because living beings and persons could just as well have been made of radically different types of particles, if such had existed, so long as they gave rise to suitably similar materials at the macroscopic level. This brings us to the most damning criticism of materialism: material causality cannot explain biological and mental activity because it can't even address them. Function, reason, and intentionality are simply not material categories, so a material theory can't even address them without importing ideas from outside.

For mental life, the arguments are particularly strong. Philosophers have long pointed out that qualia—what it's like to experience particular mental states—is something that can't be described in material terms, almost by definition. Imagine trying to describe the colors red and blue to a man who's been blind from birth. He could know the wavelength of light for every color. He could know atom-for-atom what the state of the brain is for someone who's seeing each color. None of this would get him any closer to knowing what red and blue actually look like. "What red looks like" is a meaningful question, but it's not a material question; therefore materialism is wrong. One might say the same thing regarding hypothetical personal-identity paradoxes. If I downloaded my brain state into a computer, would the computer program really be conscious, and would it really be me?

A different, but related, line of criticism comes from some idealists, who also deny us warrant to speak of living or conscious beings. Here, the argument is that we divide the world into separate "things" or "beings" because it's the only way to fit them into the categories of our thought, or, at least, of our language. All of our knowledge of the world is about distinct subjects because that's all our language (in which sentences are arranged as subject-verb-object) allows us to talk about. It says nothing about the world as it is "in itself". Here the asserted fact is simply not true—we don't regard each thing as a unitary subject. I have no word for my-cat-and-my-smoke-detector, and I certainly don't apply the category of substance to this combination. I do apply the category to my cat and my smoke detector separately. I don't apply it to the right half of my smoke detector. Why do I apply it sometimes but not other times? Apparently, some collections of atoms are more "subjectifiable" than others. That is, "substance" applies to them "in themselves" because they have a real principle of unity.

Inadequate theories of existence

Let's return to existence. We had little trouble above identifying cases of positive existence, but what criterion did we use to do that? What is it that things with positive existence have in common? The two simplest theories will turn out to be flawed. The first would be to say that things that exist have many properties and many actions, and that one of these acts/properties is existence. Existence means the same thing for all existents—it's a sort of base line property; what makes things different and unique is the additional act of being a particular kind of thing on top of existing. This theory is wrong. I don't have an act of existing and an act of being a man on top of it—the two are not separate even notionally. For me, to be is to be a man. As I said above, presence is always presence of something. To be a life form means to live. To be a conscious subject means to be aware. When I exist and a rock exists, we're not doing the same thing by existing.

Again, what do things with positive existence have in common? A second theory would be to say that, since existence doesn't mean exactly (univocally) the same thing in different subjects, it means something analogous. By "analogous" I mean the sort of analogies you identified on college entrance exams: "air is to bird as water is to fish", etc. A technical name for this is "analogy of proportionality". Perhaps we could say that human existence is to human nature as rock existence is to rock nature. Unlike the first theory, this one isn't plainly wrong. In fact it is true as far as it goes, but it is incomplete. The reason it's incomplete is that it doesn't allow comparisons across species, but sometimes this can be done. Imagine you were an omnipotent being, and you saw a rock, and you decided to add consciousness to it, as Aphrodite did to Galatea. Rocks are by their nature non-sentient, so this would change our rock into something else, something more on the level of a human being. Now, if being were only proportionately analogous, we could not speak of an addition or subtraction of presence, merely of presence of a different type. However, in this example, it is quite clear that we have a greater and deeper presence after the metamorphosis than before. Something is missing in our description of existence. To sum up, the first theory exaggerates the commonality of the act of existence between different species, while the second theory exaggerates its difference.

IV. Unqualified being

The idea of Unqualified Being

The above thought experiment about adding consciousness to a rock brought out a new aspect of positive existence: it admits of gradations. This is quite different from the first definition of existence (x exists = x is instantiated), which is an on-off affair. Of course, it is true that a thing either has some presence or none at all, but one thing may be present more deeply or extensively than another thing. A rock's presence is limited; it lacks the vital and mental degrees of presence. Furthermore, its presence is limited in space and time, and even in those regions of space that it does occupy, at each point only a part of the rock is present, rather than the whole thing. One might say that the existence of the rock is qualified; we say "it is present", then we add "but..." followed by a list of qualifications—"here" but not "there", "in this way" but not "in that way". This might seem an excessively negative, glass-half-empty way of looking at things. Why not express this as "and" instead of "but": "the rock is present, and it is here"? The reason is that "x and y" is only correct if y is not already contained in x, but "presence" already implicitly contains "presence here". It's not another concept. If I were to say "x is present, period", i.e. without qualification, the natural way to understand this is that x is present everywhere. Mental actuality provides another good example. Wisdom is an aspect of mental actuality, and one that admits of gradations. However, when I say that a person has a high degree of wisdom, I don't add another quality to that of wisdom; there is something odd in saying "he is wise, and to a high degree." On the other hand, we can say that a man is wise in some areas but foolish in others. His wisdom is qualified; he is wise, but with "buts" attached. If I say, "he is wise, period", this would imply the fullness of wisdom.

So actuality admits of degrees, and the highest degree seems to be the simplest one, the one in terms of which the others are understood. This suggests a third way of understanding actuality: in terms of a perfect case that all positively existing beings resemble except as they are limited in various ways. Existence would then be analogous, but by participation (i.e. by common reference to a single exemplary case) rather than proportionality. Do we ever assert connections like this in daily life? Here's an example. Suppose we read in the newspapers about three imperfect states. One is a gangster state where rulers wield power for selfish ends; a second has just rulers but ones who lack the coercive power to enforce their decrees; a third is ruled by libertarians, whose mad theories lead them to neglect the economy, the environment, and public morals. What do these three have in common? They are all imperfect states. The state itself is a simple idea: the nexus of authority that imposes justice and protects the common life. There are many ways of falling short of this one idea, though. Still, the three states fall into a single class by their reference to a common standard.

Could there be such a thing as pure existence, existence without qualification? Surely such an idea is crazy—there are an infinite number of ways of existing, and many of them contradict each other. A thing can't be both red and blue; it can't be both a bird and a fish. Whatever it is, it must miss out on the perfections of the things it isn't. Remember, though, that we mean unlimited existence of the second (presence) kind, not the first (instantiation). Each of the above things possesses a positive element and a negative element. Only the positive element is the actuality part. Red is light at one wavelength; blue is light at another. There's no reason why one can't have light at both wavelengths; it's only the definition of each color that excludes this, i.e. the definition contains this negative element. Similarly, if a fish is an animal that swims but doesn't fly, and a bird one that flies but doesn't swim, then there's no reason one couldn't have a being with the positive elements of both, an animal that both flies and swims. It's only the negative elements in the definition of "fish" and "bird" that would prevent us from calling this being a fish or a bird. It's not that fish and birds have something that the unqualified existent lacks. So existence without qualification would be some combination of light at all frequencies and a flying-swimming animal? No, because the terms "light", "flying", "swimming", and "animal" themselves contain negative elements as well as positive ones. Our work is just begun if we want to extract the purely positive. Thus, it is not obviously crazy to assert the idea of unqualified presence, although I certainly haven't yet proven that there are no hidden contradictions. Still, it seems that between one kind of being and another, it's the negative element in their definitions, rather than their positive actuality, that clash and can't combine.

Omnipresence

Let us assume that unqualified existence is conceivable; what would its properties be? The most obvious form of limitation is limitation in space; a material object is present in some places but not others. Unqualified being can't be like that, so it must be everywhere and pervade the whole universe. However, it wouldn't do this in the way of an infinitely large object, such as a gas of infinite extents. Such a gas would be divided into parcels, and only one parcel would be present at each point in space. Therefore, only a small part of the total object (gas) would be present to each point, so its existence everywhere would be limited. The unqualified being would have to be totally present everywhere, a property called omnipresence. Being totally present everywhere, it could not be spatially divided into parts; we should in fact say that an unlimited being is immaterial. This doesn't mean that it lacks any of the actuality of material beings (the way a ghost lacks a body), but that it lacks all of the limitations inherent in material existence. Assuming we can grant some ontological status to the past and the future, this same line of reasoning will apply to time as well as space, so that an unqualified being should be atemporal and eternal as well as immaterial and omnipresent.

The principle that divisibility into parts betokens limitation doesn't just apply to spatial and temporal divisibility; it is quite general. When a being's existence comprises several unrelated acts, this means that some acts are not present to others; the being is not fully integrated. For example, for human beings, the vital and mental processes are not fully integrated. I can't consciously control my heartbeat, and my heartbeat doesn't enter into my awareness. Parts of me are limited in their presence even to other parts of me. The unqualified being must be fully integrated, so that it either consists of only one utterly simple act, or all its acts are so interconnected and interpenetrating that they are like one act. The unqualified being supremely fulfills one of the prerogatives of actuality identified in the last chapter: unity.

Omnipotence

The other prerogative of actuality we identified was causality. The ability to exert causality we may call power, so an unlimited being must be supremely powerful, i.e. omnipotent. What would omnipotence be like? Our physical intuition, that power consists in the ability to apply force on other things, gives a very impoverished intuition of power at its utmost limit. Just as omnipresence is qualitatively different from being infinitely big, omnipotence is qualitatively different from being able to apply infinite forces. At its heart, causality means sharing actuality; its positive (in the ontological, not just moral, sense) aspect is the ability to create. The ability to destroy has more to do with the limited ability of other beings to receive actuality than it does with the intrinsic power of the destroyer. The fact that I can make fire with my lighter is a real power; the fact that I can burn paper with this fire is just a statement on the weakness of paper. More real power means more real ability to create. We finite creatures are very limited in our creative ability—even those things we call our creations derive only a small part of their actuality from us. When a sculptor creates a bronze statue, he doesn't create the bronze; nor does he keep it in existence. All he does is impose a shape. An omnipotent being could generate all of the being of its creations; it would have no need of outside help from raw materials. This would be creation *ex nihilo*, a thing beyond our experience, but a necessary power for an unlimited being.

Omniscience

What about the mental dimension of awareness? In the last chapter, I argued that consciousness is a real and irreducible level of existence. Therefore, an unlimited being must have it, and to an unlimited degree. What would this entail? Mental presence is called awareness, and the distinct property of awareness is that it is intentional, i.e. it's awareness of something. Unqualified awareness would include awareness of everything —it would mean knowing everything, i.e. omniscience. Omniscience includes knowing all the true facts about the universe, including the past and future. However, it means much more than this. An omniscient being also has the fullness of what we call understanding and appreciation. It would have a perfect aesthetic and moral sense. It would be absurd to think that you could observe a work of art or a heroic act and appreciate something in such things that an unqualified being wouldn't also notice. That would mean you having an awareness that it lacks, so that its awareness wouldn't be unlimited. Also, an omniscient being would fully appreciate the value of individuals —it could see that unique beauty in each person as much as (in fact more than) that person's own mother. This kind of appreciation is something that we finite beings only really have for those we know and love deeply. So omniscience, unqualified awareness, includes complete knowledge, the fullness of wisdom, and the fullness of the appreciative aspect of love toward itself and every other being.

Our purpose, you'll recall, is to see if the idea of unqualified existence is coherent. Our method for attempting to show that it is coherent is to derive a fairly complete set of properties such a being should have and to show that they are mutually consistent. If they are inconsistent, then the idea of unqualified being is meaningless. We have found that unqualified actuality in the material, vital, and mental orders would entail omnipresence, omnipotence, and omniscience. Are these properties consistent with each other, or do they clash? Clearly, they are mutually consistent. One doesn't need to have any weakness to have all knowledge, etc. In fact, the different aspects of actuality actually seem to lose some of their distinctions in this limit. The material and vital aspects of presence basically collapse into the mental aspect for an immaterial being. Omnipotence and omniscience together constitute omnipresence, because they mean that a being's knowledge and power are everywhere. When an omnipotent being creates something ex nihilo, it must have complete knowledge of its creature, because the creature has absolutely nothing in it that the creator didn't put there. Since, as it will turn out, all finite beings are creations of an unqualified being, this being must be omniscient simply by knowing itself and its own creative decisions.

Perhaps unexpectedly, the third explanation of existence succeeds. The common element of everything that exists is that all things participate in unqualified being; they are all differently truncated versions of this being. Another surprise is to notice that, although "unqualified being" is such a counterintuitive—even esoteric—idea, every great civilization has known of it; they all call this being things we may translate as "God". So far, we have only shown that the idea of God is coherent, not that He actually exists. In the example of the three imperfect states, which we said were related by reference to a common standard, there's no reason to think this standard must actually be instantiated somewhere. Its existence might be purely Platonic. "Big deal," an atheist might be tempted to say. "Who cares if the idea of God is coherent? The idea of Santa Claus is coherent too, but it's still silly for people to believe in him." True, but we have shown more than that the idea of God is coherent; we've shown that this idea is the hidden basis of the most profound truths about the cosmos: what distinguishes presence from absence, and what makes all of the beings in the universe a single family. One may disbelieve in God if one wishes, but it shows a gross lack of understanding to compare this belief to belief in the Great Pumpkin or flying spaghetti monsters. God isn't just an idea; He's the core idea. If He doesn't exist, the universe is a rather absurd place for pointing to Him.

V. Individuality and existence of God and creatures

There can only be one God

There's a serious objection that could be made against the idea of unqualified being. In the last chapter, when we talked about limits or qualifications to existence, they seemed to serve an entirely negative function—they keep a being from being everywhere, from knowing everything, or from having any of God's other perfections. However, in actual, concrete finite beings, limits don't seem to be entirely negative. In every finite being, one can identify an active element and a passive element. The active element is the element of positive existence, the quality we've described above. The passive element is the subject that receives this actuality, that in which the element of actuality is instantiated. The passive element (sometimes called "potency", but I will continue to use the term "subject") limits the act to itself, but in doings so it also individualizes the act. It makes the finite being to be a concrete individual. Consider a human being, like myself. My passive elements are quite important to my existence. My human nature is a sort of subject of my act of existence; this nature limits my existence, and in doing so makes it to be existence of a particular kind. Human nature is itself a form, a pattern, which can only have concrete existence if it's instantiated in a subject, namely the matter in my body. My life pattern is limited to my matter; the passive element provided by my matter creates a "gap" between human nature in general and my concrete life form, so that I never exemplify the full possibilities of human nature. On the other hand, without my matter, the subject, my human nature would just be an abstraction with no concrete existence. The passive, limiting element is necessary to make me a real individual.

Now if individuality is necessary to be a real, concrete being, and a limiting, passive element is needed to make a thing individual, than it would seem that God can't really exist. We've been too greedy with the demand for unlimited actuality, and we've ended up with something that can't be anything but an abstraction. Remember, though, our method for establishing divine attributes. For each quality in finite beings, we separate the positive and the negative elements, and attribute only the former to God. The first necessary condition for the coherence of God is that the two elements can logically be separated. The second is that purely positive elements don't clash. Can we perform this separation operation for this case? The two functions of the passive element in finite beings are individuation and limitation. The first, which denotes concrete rather than abstract existence, is positive, so we must attribute it to God. The second function is negative, and so does not belong to God. Thus God must be individual without having a passive element; there is no subject logically distinct from God's unqualified actuality that receives and limits this actuality. Unqualified being is individual on its own. An immediate consequence is that there can only be one God. This is a remarkable conclusion. It's not just that two Gods couldn't coexist because the universe isn't big enough for two omnipotent beings; it's that the divine nature itself specifies one individual. It's as if you set out to describe human nature in general, and your description ended up singling out your friend Bill who lives next door as the Unique Man. In God, there is no distinction between act and subject, between nature and individual.

Here's a simpler way to see that there could only be one God. Suppose there were three possible Gods; call them "Zeus", "Apollo", and "Demeter". What could make them different? It would have to be something positive—differing personality traits for each God—or something negative—limitation into different subjects, e.g. Zeus is made out of this matter here, while Apollo is made out of that matter there. It can't be something positive, because each unqualified being would have to have every positive quality. It can't be something negative either, since unqualified beings can't have limitations. Therefore, there can be nothing to distinguish between two or more Gods.

There must be one God

It turns out that the number of finite beings is actually more problematic than the number of Gods. Finite beings have a passive element, so the same pattern can be instantiated multiple times. Why, then, should there be any particular number of any given type of being? Why are there six billion humans but zero unicorns? For that matter, how do I know an infinite number of unicorns won't pop into existence in five minutes and fill up the whole universe? Unlike God, finite beings seem to be dangerously underdetermined.

As a matter of fact, we must be pretty sure that an infinite number of unicorns aren't going to pop into existence. If things like that could happen, the universe would be completely unintelligible. It would not evolve according to regular laws, as it seems to. How do we explain this? First, let me note two explanations that won't do. First, we can't explain why things don't pop into existence by invoking a law of physics: conservation of mass or energy, symmetries in a Lagrangian, a divergence-free stress-energy tensor, etc. These are just mathematical restatements of the fact that things don't just pop into existence. Second, we can't get away with saying that things can pop into existence, but that they probability for its occurrence is low (like quantum tunneling across a high energy barrier), so that it happens sufficiently rarely that it is unnoticed. Suppose this were true, and a certain non-existent object had a certain low probability of popping into existence. I could always imagine another object, no more nonexistent than the first, with all of the same properties but a very high probability of popping. All nonexistent beings are equally nonexistent, so this second kind of object is as valid as the first. If we say that the probability of popping is set by some other object that actually does exist, than that object would be the cause of the other thing's coming into being. We would have a case of one being acting to cause another, something that doesn't raise any problems for the intelligibility of the universe. It seems that this type of coming into existence, that of being caused by something that existed already, is the only way that finite beings can come to exist.

One might object that things popping into existence uncaused must be possible, because physicists sometimes assert that such things happen: virtual particle-antiparticle pairs pop into and out of existence out of nothing, and the universe itself is said to have popped into existence during the big bang. No doubt physicists do make such claims in popular expositions of their work, but it's a very sloppy description of the actual theories. I once attended a colloquium at which a string theorist boasted that it had been proven that the universe came into existence out of nothing, but that "nothing" has a structure which they're still working out. Now, of course, if something has a structure, one with causal effects on the actual universe, it's most certainly not "nothing". Similarly, the picture of particles popping into existence uncaused is not a tenable interpretation of quantum field theory. First of all, it's not just anything, but standard-model particles in particular combinations that are said to populate the vacuum. If this really were uncaused creation, any particle one could imagine might pop into existence, the popping wouldn't satisfy any conservation laws (like charge or lepton number), and so forth. Of course, this doesn't happen. What does happen is limited by the standard-model Lagrangian. Why? It must be because this Lagrangian reflects the nature of something—a field, a collection of fields, or a medium of which the known particles are oscillations—that actually exists prior to the particle creation and, being its cause, fixes what can even temporarily come into being. Avoiding the metaphysical impossibility of uncaused creation is the very condition for having a sensible interpretation of these or any other physical theories. (A good deal more might be said about the pitfalls to be avoided in going from mathematics to ontology in contemporary physics, such as the unwarranted assumption that terms in a series expansion—which is all Feynman diagrams really are—represent actual events. However, what I've said already should convince the reader that modern high-energy physics does nothing to alter the basic problem of finite existence.)

So, finite beings have a passive element which adds an element of indeterminacy to them. Some of their qualities, including their fact of existing itself, are not self-determined but have to be set from outside. Now, how can it be that my existence is determined by something outside myself? Surely, it's because this "something" is giving me my existence—otherwise it couldn't be the determining factor. To insure the intelligibility of the universe, we assert that *limited being is received being*. God is the only being who could be entirely self-determined. He alone has no element of indeterminacy that has to be fixed from outside.

Could it be that God doesn't exist, and finite beings are all that there is? Can a collection of entities, each of which receives its existence from outside itself, exist without a self-sufficient being (God) to cause them to exist? There are only two ways one might try to set up such a system. First, we could imagine a cycle. A receives being from B, who receives it from C, who receives it from A (schematically: A-> B->C->A). Could this happen? No. If it could, A+B+C systems could randomly pop into existence. A receiving being B is very different from A depending on B or B being be a necessary condition for A. Being dependent and being a necessary condition can be mutual; giving and receiving being cannot be, because a received being has nothing that its cause doesn't give it. Therefore, this cycle demands that A get its actuality ultimately from itself, which we've already said can't happen for a finite being. Nor would it help to have A receive being from both B and C, or any other combination of dependencies. The second possibility would be to extend the series out to infinity: A->B->C->D->E->... Could this work? No. An infinite series of possible beings is not one step closer to existence without an actual being to actualize the whole series. The above would allow infinitely large systems to pop into existence, which is hardly an improvement. Therefore, a collection of beings with received existence cannot exist unless God creates it. Since finite beings do exist, God necessarily exists also.

The existence of a creator God vindicates a large part of most religions. God is the sacred something that religious people worship. He is indeed as awesome and powerful as one could imagine, infinitely more so, in fact. He is truly the source of all being, the source of the order of the cosmos, and the ultimate truth about the world.

VI. Value, morality, and God

The idea of God allows us to make sense of otherwise puzzling aspects of positive existence, particularly the fact that it seems to be neither univocal nor straightforwardly analogous. God performs the same function in the realm of practical reason, where the relevant quality is not being, but value or goodness. We can ask of value the same thing we asked of actuality: what do valuable things have in common? What makes something good? Of course, I should point out at once that by "goodness" and "value", I mean the value something has in itself, *not* the value something might have for us as a means to some other goal. Things valuable in themselves may also be valuable for us, but the sign of intrinsic value is that we feel obliged to recognize the goodness of something whether or not it is of any use to us.

Being has at least three levels—material, vital, and mental—and value also has these levels. At the material level, we have aesthetic value or beauty. For living beings, there is the value of organisms achieving their own telos, i.e. health and vitality. Mental existence has a different kind of teleology, and thus a different kind of goodness, because mental life is directed towards other beings, not to some purely immanent kind of completion. Goodness for conscious beings means giving everything its due. The most important virtues are the moral virtues that allow us to respond adequately to the value of other beings. Just as in the case of actuality, univocal and proportionately analogical theories of goodness fail to explain the thing. A good dog, a good novel, and a good neighbor don't have a quality, the same for all of them, that makes them good. Understanding "good" in an analogical sense is better; we could say that to be good means to fulfill one's nature, whatever it is. A good dog is one that fully executes canine nature, rather than imperfectly instantiating canine nature due to sickness, injury, isolation from the pack, or whatever. Similarly, to be a good bridge, a good argument, or a good eye means having the relation of full execution to bridge, argument, or eye nature. This is true as far as it goes, but value seems to have an element that cuts across natures. It's better to be a good dog than a bad dog, and better to be a good human than a bad human, but it's also better to be a human than to be a dog. We have no trouble making the latter comparison of value even though there's no common nature to use as a reference. If goodness were just proportionately analogous, all we could say about a dog that transformed into a human is that it got better by the standard of human nature but worse by the standard of dog nature.

So we need a third theory. Inspired by its success in studying being, the religious mind naturally tries analogy by participation—we postulate a mode of being that would be unqualified goodness, and say that other things are good by participating in this type of goodness but to a limited extent. Not surprisingly, unqualified being and unqualified goodness turn out to be the same thing, namely God. This is because value is always associated with some form of actuality, while vice is always associated with the absence of something that should be present: an incomplete execution of some nature, a failure of self-control, or a failure to fully recognize the value of something or someone.

Thus things are ultimately good by reference to God. This does not mean that they are valuable only because God arbitrarily chooses to value them (although since He is unqualified goodness, we can be sure that He fully values all that is valuable). It means that they are valuable insofar as they reflect His nature, insofar as they are "close" to Him. On the one hand, the religious man values all good things for God's sake; on the other hand, it is his knowledge of God that prompts him to see the intrinsic goodness of all God's creatures. An injustice against any creature is a mistreatment of a divine manifestation and hence an offense against God. Furthermore, since all beings are linked by drawing their existence and goodness from a single Source, a sin against one being can be seen as a sin against them all. From this intuition comes the conviction that a single sin can separate a man from nature, society, and God. The intuition that all sin offends God also gives believers a stronger motive to avoid "victimless" crimes like non-malicious lies, use of pornography, masturbation, or disrespect toward the dead. An atheist may realize the immorality of these things, but he would not have the same incentive to avoid them, because, after all, he wouldn't see how they harm anyone. The believer's love for God gives urgency to all aspects of morality.

In Chapter II, we introduced the idea of the holy—holy things attain a higher level of value by the fact that they are uniquely close to God and because they have the power to show forth His presence. This idea of sacredness is the main thing that distinguishes religious from secular morality. Where the two clash, it's always because religious men and women identify something as sacred, and their secular colleagues can make no sense of this. One way to test the plausibility of theism versus atheism is to compare the moral intuitions fostered by each and ask which seems more adequate and wiser.

First, religious reason and secular reason differ in how they explain the special value of human beings, i.e. what reason is given for the "dignity of man". From the religious point of view, this is simple: the greatness of man is that he is ordered directly to God, and his fulfillment is to know and love God. Lesser beings can be fulfilled by finite goods. An animal with food, warmth, mates, and children is completely satisfied; if it knows how to procure these things, it will have no further curiosity about the world. Human beings have a higher calling. Our minds are open to all of existence, even those parts—like distant galaxies—that don't affect us. Our intellects search for the reason behind everything. Morally, we feel obliged to respect all true values; we would acknowledge the rights of extraterrestrials if we ever found them. We might violate those rights, but then we would be sinning, and we would know it. Now, if an animal got nutrition from anything with some certain chemical, we would say that that chemical itself was a part of, or a prerequisite to, that animal's flourishing. Since humans recognize goodness in all its forms, the goodness we are ordered to isn't just some aspect of goodness, but goodness itself, i.e. unqualified goodness which is God.

The atheist also recognizes this radical openness of human beings. However, he can only state it negatively. He sees that no finite good exhausts man's capacity for allegiance, but he knows of no other kind of good. Therefore, he expresses the intuition by saying that man's dignity is that he has no fulfillment. He has no fixed nature to fulfill. Through his own will, he creates his own self, his own values, and his own meanings. His dignity lies in his indeterminacy and freedom. Justice between persons is reduced to giving equal weight to each person's will. There is something to the atheist's idea of human dignity, but it is insufficient—it reduces a human being to his capacity for free choice, while taking away the idea of objective value that makes our choices meaningful. The religious man knows the intuition that the atheist is getting at, and with the language of God, the religious man can express it more adequately.

Second, religion deepens a person's idea of authority. For the religious man, all legitimate authority is delegated from God. When a man obeys his ruler, he is really obeying God. Without a divine commission, what right would any man have to rule over any other? To express it concisely, authority is sacred. It doesn't matter whether the authority is monarchical, aristocratic, or democratic; however the ruler or rulers are chosen, their authority comes from God. Whatever the majority thinks, these rulers are bound by the laws of the One who grants them their legitimacy. The atheist, of course, rejects the idea that government is in any way sacred, but in doing so, he finds it impossible to maintain the idea of authority at all. He invents devices like the "social contract", which justify government by invoking the implicit consent of the governed or appealing to their enlightened self-interest. In either case, the reality of authority is lost. Saying a people should obey because they have (implicitly) decided to obey is not a reason. Saying they should obey because it's in their interest is a reason, but a practical rather than a moral one. It doesn't capture the distinct nature of authority, which is a kind of moral obligation.

Third, religions assert that sexual intercourse belongs to God in a special way. This is the act whereby new humans are made; it is a portal through which the divine creative power replenishes the human world. Religious men and women feel a particular awe for everything touching on the sex act. It is a sacred thing, and religious sexual morality is largely an expression of the religious imperative to keep the sacred unpolluted by the profane. The simultaneous religious and sexual overtones are perfectly captured in the virtue called *purity*. The pure man and woman see the sexual realm as belonging to God in a direct way. They do not presume to enter this realm without the divine permission of a wedding ceremony. Once married, they refuse to instrumentalize the act by frustrating its natural end—it is not for us mortals to pick out bits and pieces of a sacred act to suit our fancies. Of course, nothing infuriates the atheist more than this idea of sex, which he doesn't understand at all. Sex is not sacred, he says, and thinking that it is just makes people miserable by keeping them from harmless satisfactions. However, in "liberating" sex, the atheist inevitably trivializes it. Why limit oneself to one partner? Why think the act creates any kind of bond, any more than having someone scratch your back creates a bond? Why not engage in the act in public for the whole profane world to see? Surely there is more to sex than the atheist allows.

These are the main differences between the religious and the atheist moral visions. In each case, the religious vision seems to more fully capture our moral intuitions about the world. The atheist vision, by contrast, seems gravely inadequate. I would not say that this is a proof that the former is true, and the latter is false, but it is important collaborating evidence.

VII. The reasonableness of revelation

Of course, no one believes in religion in general; nearly everyone who believes in God believes in some particular religion—Christianity, Islam, etc. These religions contain the elements described in earlier chapters: a sense of the sacred, God, and His connection to morality. They contain another element, though, and this is the assertion that a revelation has taken place. Each religion that is more than a school of speculation affirms that, at some particular times and places and to certain particular people, God has communicated information about Himself and instructions to His worshipers. The rest of the followers of the religion get these messages not directly from God, but from other believers, who in turn got them from other believers, and so on until we get back to the people who directly received the revelation. The original revelation is generally given to very few people, often just one, and usually in isolated places like a cave or a mountain, where there is a dearth of witnesses.

I think it's fair to say that revelation is the thing about religion that strikes atheists as being the most absurd. Even if the above chapters were to convince them that there is good reason to believe in God, surely it is too much to believe that the Creator of the universe would arrange his relations with mankind in this way. Of course, one cannot deny that God could supernaturally communicate with particular people, just as the revelation stories say—He is omnipotent, after all. Nor I think does it make sense to say that God would have no motive for communicating with His creatures. Man, as we have shown, is ordered to God, so there would be nothing more beneficial to us than for God to help us to know Him and to establish a regular relationship with us. No, what makes the whole thing seem implausible is that it seems like an omnipotent Being could have gotten His messages across in a more certain and forceful way. Why act through messengers at all? We can understand why a professor with a class of hundreds would have most of his teaching done through teaching assistants—there's just too many students for one man to give them all any kind of attention. But that's because the professor is a limited being. God is not limited; He could give everyone a revelation if He wanted to. If He wanted to, He could have equipped every human being with a sort of spiritual antenna and then blared out His messages at all times and places, so that everyone would get them loud and clear. He could have done it, but He didn't. Why?

Let's rephrase the question. Is there any reason, other than lack of ability to do otherwise, that a teacher would instruct some students and then have those students instruct other students, rather than having them all get it directly from the teacher? I can think of one reason. It may be that the teacher's intention is not just to share knowledge, but also to form a connection of his students with each other. If all the students were to sit passively and listen to the teacher, each of them might as well be alone with the teacher. The presence of other students contributes nothing. (Any teachers reading this will know that it actually detracts something, because students are more reluctant to ask questions in large groups, and teachers are unable to interact with individual students to see how well they're following the material.) On the other hand, if I have to learn something from another student, then I must rely on that student, and he has an obligation to me. If I know that I'll have to pass down the knowledge in turn, then I'll be learning not just for myself, but for the students that I'll have to instruct later.

Of course, we can't prove that God has done or will do one thing or the other; He can do whatever He wants. However, it's not unreasonable that He might want His revelation to both connect humans with Himself and connect humans with each other. He might want His revelation to become a tradition. "Tradition" literally means something handed down. A tradition can be a belief or a practice, but what separates it from other beliefs or practices is that it creates a bond between the people who share it. For example, walking upright is a practice, but it's not a tradition. If I see a total stranger walking upright, I don't think to myself, "Here is another of my people, who shares my customs and history!" It doesn't mean anything that a man walks upright, because that's the only sensible way for a biped-structured animal like man to walk. Two men may both walk the same way and have no cultural affinity whatsoever. To be a tradition, therefore, a thing must not be necessary. To be meaningful as a tradition, it can't be something that everyone just logically must believe or do. So if God wanted to establish a tradition, He couldn't just blare out His message always and everywhere. If He did, belief would create no bond among the faithful, everyone would have God's revelation with no dependence on anyone else, because not believing would be as crazy as walking on all fours. Actual religions are traditions; they bind the faithful currently living to each other, and they bind them to the dead and the unborn. Revelation is a trust received with gratitude ultimately from God, but directly through our ancestors. The story of revelation coming to Ireland involves both Christ and Saint Patrick, and the more the Irish revere Christ, the more grateful they will be to Patrick. Through tradition, God doesn't usurp the honor given to our ancestors, but rather cements it by making our ancestors His own messengers. Nor does the believer think revelation is given to him solely for his own use and his own salvation. Like all traditions, it is a trust, and each link in the chain has a sacred duty to pass down what they have received. Each generation knows that if they apostasize, they will break the chain and condemn not only themselves, but future generations as well.

None of this, of course, establishes which if any of the world's religious traditions is founded on a genuine revelation. To determine that, one would have to examine the historical evidence of each revelation to see how strong it is, and one would have to examine the content of each revelation to see how compelling it is and whether it is consistent with all we know from other sources. However, it is certainly plausible that one revelation is genuine (or more, if they don't conflict with each other). My recommendations are as follows: First, truth must always be the ultimate issue, not whether a religion is popular, whether its adherents are morally or intellectually exemplary, or whether it is regarded as "progressive". Second, where truth is doubtful, be not quick to abandon the faith of your fathers and the bond to home and kin you'll find in it.

In Defense of Tradition

It would seem that conservatism is internally incoherent. Most conservatives acknowledge two sources of authority: natural law and tradition. Both are essential if the conservative is to fulfill his role as defender of particular cultures without falling into complete cultural relativism. However, there is a priori no reason to think that these two authorities will always be consistent. Nor is this point academic—liberals never tire of pointing out many allegedly wicked customs of past ages: enslavement of enemies, infant exposure, temple prostitution, gladiatorial combat, polygamy, foot-binding, etc.

How not to defend tradition

There are two common defenses of the authority of tradition. The first argument was used by Burke and developed by Friedrich Hayek. It claims that societies have, over time, passed through a process of natural selection, and the folk ways people have ended up with are those that proved successful. Society is so complex that we may not be able to understand the function a given tradition serves, but to assume that it has no function and that institutions can be redesigned at will defies evolutionary logic. The second argument also goes back to Burke and has been advanced most recently by Roger Scruton. Prejudices and superstitions are, it concedes, irrational, but the irrational emotions they cultivate serve rationally identifiable purposes, such as solidifying group loyalty. However, the emotional manipulation can only be accomplished if its ultimate end is hidden by a veil of tradition from its participants.

There is danger in relying on these sorts of defenses. They both associate tradition with ignorance, because if people had a perfect understanding of society tradition would be either unnecessary (in the first defense) or ineffective (in the second). Such defenses of tradition might cease to apply as society's self-knowledge improves. The standard arguments are forced to invoke ignorance because they implicitly concede that tradition must ultimately justify itself by utilitarian liberal standards to be justified at all. If we drop this requirement, we can defend our cherished customs straightaway.

The meaning of tradition

In fact, most arguments for and against tradition are irrelevant because they have nothing to do with the things actually defended as traditions. Both the criticisms and the defenses imagine that a tradition is any custom which has lasted a long time and whose existence is not obviously justified on utilitarian grounds. However, nobody feels an obligation to uphold every kind of old custom. Only a special subset of a people's customs should be called traditions in the strict sense which I will use. *By this special sense of tradition, I mean a custom which 1) makes a moral claim and 2) establishes a bond among those who observe it by 3) allowing the members of the community to collectively recognize some objective good in a culturally particularized way.* The good apprehended and secured through the tradition is known perfectly well by its participants. They are also entirely aware that the tradition is not universal. The very fact that a tradition is only followed by one group allows it to serve as a group marker and to intensify the bond between members. Its efficacy in no way depends on ignorance, irrationality, or obfuscation. It is the insider-participant, not the outsider-anthropologist, point of view which discloses the tradition's essential meaning, as we shall see from looking at some of the most important examples.

Codes of behavior

First, there are traditional rules of behavior. For example, all cultures have codes of modesty which require that some parts of the body by covered in public and that the conjugal act by protected by some veil of privacy. Its meaning is to recognize the dignity of persons as separate centers of subjectivity. Through modesty, we acknowledge that each person is a "secret world" unto himself and that he can reveal himself through his body in a unique way in the marital act. Ironically, it is the very fact of concealment which trains us to recognize this dimension of depth in each person. Clothes remind my eyes how little of a person I can really see. The sharing of subjectivity by the participants is of the essence of sex, so the outsider's viewpoint is inherently degrading and must be excluded. Thus we exclude outside viewers.

Cultures also have established standards of courtesy which recognizes persons as dignified by an accepted place in society. Addressing people by titles ("miss", "doctor", "sir", etc) obviously fulfills this role. So do expressions like "hello" or "excuse me" which convey no information except "I recognize you." As Montesquieu noted, each people also has its own conception of freedom, the dignity we accord persons as beings with free will addressed by the moral law. This culturally conditioned freedom can be quite different from liberal autonomy. For example, a soldier is a free man rather than a slave—even if he was conscripted, even though his life is minutely regulated, even though he may be ordered to risk his life. What makes him free is, ironically, his duty to obey. To command someone over whom one has recognized authority is to appeal to him as a moral agent. An animal could only be conditioned, and a slave could only be threatened. The distinctive mark of freedom is also seen in the treatment of criminals. A free society does not excuse or condition them; it punishes them. Punishment appeals to a belief in free will and a common standard of justice.

Each of the above behavior codes varies from culture to culture. In some aboriginal cultures women bare their breasts, while in some Arab cultures women cover their faces. This doesn't scandalize the traditionalist, any more than one would worry that different languages have different words for the same thing. The thing itself is always the same, but to communicate effectively a community must agree on a word. The same is true of traditional codes: they articulate objective moral truths. Every woman really is a sacred mystery. Modesty doesn't condition me to believe arbitrary nonsense; it trains me to recognize something real. Still, I can only respond to these realities through the rules of a particular culture. Without these rules, words like "dignity", "respect", and "honor" are practically meaningless. Within a culture, one can know exactly what they demand. And within that culture the demands of tradition carry the full force of the natural law. It really is wicked for a woman to publicly show her knees or her breasts in one part of the world even though it is unproblematic in other lands.

Rituals

A second class of traditions involves rituals—funerals and weddings being common examples. It is becoming more and more common for a person to modify the traditional forms in order to express the idiosyncrasies of his personality, such as when couples write their own wedding vows. The conservative can only lament this trend of "personalizing" ceremonies, because the significance of ritual formulae comes not only from the words themselves, but also from the very fact that they are the words used by our ancestors and descendents across time and by our contemporaries across space. To step into a ritual role is indeed to step outside of one's personality, but this de-personalization makes possible a truly authentic response to the event being commemorated.

How can this be? A man tends to form an idea of his personality which resembles a fictional character defined by a few traits: "I'm too shy to do that." "I wouldn't say something so solemn. I'm just a regular chap." "I'm the sort of person who always does this." This self-image hides a man's full freedom from himself, and the call to "be yourself" often encourages a person to go more deeply into this inauthentic state which Sartre called "bad faith." When I participate in a ritual, I step out of the illusion of personality and become everyman. The words I say are not conditioned by "the sort of thing I would say" but come solely from the thing being confronted: the reality of marriage, the reality of death. I realize that what I am experiencing is not just an event in my own life, but that I am participating in something universal. As, let us imagine, I speak the sacred words and offers sacrifice at my father's grave, I remember how he once did the same for his father, and I think of how someday my son will do the same for me. Time collapses; all ages and all generations which performed the ritual seem present to me. Rituals take place in what Mircea Eliade called "sacred time"—by re-enacting the archetypical action of the gods (e.g. the marriage of the first god and goddess) the gods' original action in the mythical beginning is made present again, and its divine power is shared with the participants. Thus, by ritually stepping outside myself, I can better see both its aspect as a permanent feature of the human condition and the link it gives me with past and future generations. Again, these insights should not be considered illusory just because they rely on tradition. There is no hidden function which is the "real" reason for the ritual. Nor is it problematic that different cultures have different ways of establishing marriages or honoring the dead.

Conclusion

I conclude that the objections against tradition fail. A tradition proper is a particularized embodiment of the natural law, and cannot contradict this law without negating its own nature as a tradition. Historical examples of bad "traditions" usually refer to bad customs which were not understood to be morally obligatory the way a tradition is. For example, it was never considered morally obligatory to keep slaves or be a slave or to have more than one wife. Note that moral progress has always involved a tightening of moral strictures, never a loosening. Current liberal efforts to loosen traditional morality are thus not analogous to past instances of moral progress. A tradition may indeed be corrupted if people lose sight of the good it serves to reveal; then reform and renewal are called for. However, we must not abandon tradition itself, lest we lose access to the goods which can be apprehended in no other way.